A STUDENT'S GUIDE TO
Mass Communication Law

A STUDENT'S GUIDE TO

Mass Communication Law

Amber Nieto

and

John F. Schmitt

ROWMAN & LITTLEFIELD PUBLISHERS, INC.
Lanham • Boulder • New York • Toronto • Oxford

ROWMAN & LITTLEFIELD PUBLISHERS, INC.

Published in the United States of America
by Rowman & Littlefield Publishers, Inc.
A wholly owned subsidiary of The Rowman & Littlefield Publishing Group, Inc.
4501 Forbes Boulevard, Suite 200, Lanham, MD 20706
www.rowmanlittlefield.com

P.O. Box 317, Oxford OX2 9RU, UK

British Library Cataloguing in Publication Information Available

Library of Congress Cataloging-in-Publication Data

Nieto, Amber, 1980–
    A student's guide to mass communication law / Amber Nieto and John F. Schmitt.
        p. cm.
    Includes bibliographical references.
    ISBN 0-7425-3841-9 (pbk. : alk. paper)
    1. Mass media—Law and legislation—United States. I. Schmitt, John F., 1950–
II. Title.
    KF2750.Z9.N54 2005
    343.7309'9—dc22   2004021017

Printed in the United States of America

The paper used in this publication meets the minimum requirements of American
National Standard for Information Sciences—Permanence of Paper for Printed
Library Materials, ANSI/NISO Z39.48-1992.

This book is dedicated to the "grand dames" of my family,
Amelia "Molly" Schmitt and Mary H. Linder.

—*John*

I wish to dedicate this book to Brian, Kaitlyn, Emma, Mom, Dad,
Lindsay, Joel, Jacob, and my grandparents. With their love and
encouragement all things are possible. Also, to Anna, Krisie, and Melanie,
my closest friends who have always been my cheering section.

—*Amber*

Contents

Contents

Preface

ohn Schmitt: This book came about as a result of the hard work of a very fine student and the urging of a very fine professor (that's me) for that student to strive to do her very best.

During the summer of 2002, I was teaching Mass Communication Law and Ethics at what is now Texas State University, San Marcos. I approached the lectern from the back of the class every day, but on one particular day I was rather shocked to see a student looking over an organized, outlined set of notes for the class.

Thinking there might be some Internet skullduggery at work, I asked her where she got the notes. She told me that she typed them every night after class, using her written notes from the day's lecture as her guide. The law class meets five days per week in the summer. Then I looked around her and saw that all the students sitting around her also had the notes. When asked, they all swore by them as a valuable study tool.

The student who did that amazing work—and who got an A in the course—was Amber Nieto. To date, she has sold hundreds of sets of her notes to the students who have followed her at Texas State.

Amber Nieto: This project was born from a set of notes I compiled to aid me in a media law class I was taking while attending Southwest Texas State University (now formally called Texas State University, San Marcos).

At the time I never would have dreamt that these notes would turn into such an amazing opportunity. As anyone who knows me can tell you, I am a person who is never happy with less than an A. At the beginning of the first class, Professor Schmitt told us that his would not be one of those "sleep through" classes. He pointed out that not only was the material itself difficult but that we were either brave or gluttons for punishment to willingly take the class during the summer session.

I wanted to prove to him and myself that I was one of the brave ones. So, I made myself a promise to spend at least four hours after every class rereading my chapters and cleaning up my lecture notes. I ended up rewriting more than I planned. I found that completely outlining each chapter helped me to better understand the material and the lectures. And what I came to realize was that although the course material was difficult, it was not impossible when everything was right in front of me in an organized format. After spending more than one hundred hours working on the notes, I did get that A; but more important, Professor Schmitt saw the potential for the notes to be something more. He saw the potential for them to be a valuable learning tool for anyone who takes media law, or mass communications law, as it is known on some campuses.

With his enormous help and encouragement, we have been able to turn these student notes into a well-developed supplemental guide to media law.

Nieto and Schmitt: We would like to point out that these notes are meant to serve as a supplement to, not a replacement for, your normal textbook. We have tried to put them in a format that will allow you to work with any number of law texts.

First, as you will see, we worked with *Major Principles of Media Law,* by Wayne Overbeck. Two years ago, a group of our top students was given the opportunity to choose from among five or six texts, and they unanimously chose Overbeck's. The book still gets overwhelming approval in semester-end student evaluations.

Second, we relied to a lesser degree on the text *Media Law,* by Ralph Holsinger and Jon Paul Dilts. Jon Dilts is a friend of Professor Schmitt's, and they converse from time to time about textbook content. In fact, Schmitt was listed in the acknowledgments of the fourth edition of Dilt's text.

The other texts referred to or relied on, in no specific order, were

- *The Law of Public Communication,* by Kent Middleton, William Lee, Bill Chamberlin;
- *Mass Media Law,* by Don Pember and Clay Calvert;
- *The First Amendment and the Fourth Estate,* by Barton Carter, Marc Franklin, and Jay Wright;
- *Communication Law in America,* by Paul Siegel;

- *Fundamentals of Mass Communication*, by Donald Gillmor, Jerome A. Barron, Todd F. Simon, and Herbert Terry;
- *Communications Law: Liberties, Restraints, and the Modern Media*, by John Zelezny; and
- *Mass Media Law*, by Marc Franklin, David Anderson, and Fred Cate.

Finally, we urge students to remember two things:

1. Your teacher is *always* right, regardless of what is said in these notes; and
2. Your teacher's chosen textbook is *always* right, regardless of what you read here.

With those things in mind, study hard and good luck, *buena suerte*, and *bonne chance*.

Sources of the Law

I T IS IMPOSSIBLE TO begin the study of America's media law without knowing the system through which that law works. This chapter will tell you where our law comes from and where you can go to find it. For anyone involved in the fields of mass communication, this is important knowledge, and these are important skills.

What's Important Here?

Words that appear in the text as simply boldfaced, **like this**, are important, and you should know their meanings. Words that are boldfaced and italicized, ***like this***, are very important and likely to be the subject of text or examination questions.

Unless otherwise noted, Supreme Court refers to the U.S. Supreme Court; Constitution refers to the U.S. Constitution; and president refers to the U.S. president.

Sources of the Law

	1. *Constitution*	
Judicial	**Executive**	2. **Legislative acts/ statutes**

5. *Common law*
   —Court reporting
   —Law courts
6. *Courts of equity*
7. *Judicial interpretation*

3. *Administrative bodies*
4. *Executive orders*

1. ***Constitution***—basic law; creates the judicial, legislative, and executive. We usually think that all laws come out of legislature, but the laws they make are based on the Constitution.
2. ***Legislative***—creates laws and acts; also creates administrative bodies.
   a. The administrative bodies they create put together their own legislation and regulations and enforce them, but are governed under the executive branch.

EXAMPLE: Homeland Security
a. Congress will create department under executive branch and will empower department to make certain administrative regulations and rules because Congress cannot be precise enough.
b. They will cover such things as airport regulations.

---

3. ***Administrative bodies***—any administrative body created by Congress cannot go beyond the powers granted to it by the statute that created it.
4. Executive orders.
5. ***Common law***—started in Old England.
   a. King used to hear disputes, but this became too big of a job, so they created the **law courts**. (We still use these cases if there is no precedent in U.S. law.)
   b. King appointed **circuit judges**, and they would ride to places to hear trials. When they would come together in London, they compared notes and came up with uniform decisions. Thus, common law **court reporting** was born. Reported cases/decisions and then bound them.

   > EXAMPLE OF NO. 4:
   > In 1948, Harry Truman, as commander in chief, desegregates military forces.

   c. Also had **circuit lawyers** who followed the courts (Abe Lincoln).

> EXAMPLE: In a case involving carnal relations with a chicken, defendant challenged bestiality statute on the basis of biblical definition of a "beast." State found a similar case in English common law identifying a duck as a beast.

    d. Use common law to try to find **precedent**—use of old law/decision to uphold an outcome of a new one . . . doctrine of ***stare decisis***.

        An example of a case being overruled by a later Supreme Court is *Brown v. Board of Education* (1954) in which the court overruled *Plessey v. Ferguson* (1896).

        case on point—means the precedent directly relates to the same question of law.

        As case loads and challenges grew, law courts created a new branch:

6. ***Courts of equity***—provide extraordinary remedies.
    a. Most common—divorce, adoption.
      i. Provide injunctions, restraining orders.
      ii. Deals with civil law.
      iii. Jurors are usually not seated in cases of equity.

Civil law
    a. Anything not criminal.
    b. Only outcome is financial damages.
    c. Money is not collected by state but by plaintiff.
    d. Plaintiff can be anyone including natural person, corporation, partnership.

Criminal law
    a. Breaking some rule of society.
    b. Plaintiff is always the state.
    c. Only two outcomes:
      i. Fines assessed and collected by the state.
      ii. Incarceration.

> EXAMPLE: A stream runs between two properties. One person diverts the stream, so you get no water. You file for a **temporary restraining order (TRO)** to make him share the water.

    caption—title of the case.
Injunction system—
    a. TRO is filed when complaint is filed.
    b. Usually expires in 10 days.

   c. Then must have a preliminary hearing.

   d. Then a more permanent **restraining order (RO)**.

   e. Final hearing issues a permanent injunction.

7. Judicial interpretation—wholly American.

   a. Congress enacts clear or unclear statute.

   b. Statutes not cleared up by administrative bodies.

   c. Court must then determine the meaning, often by referring to the *Congressional Record* or even a dictionary. See "Words & Phrases" books.

NOTE: Louisiana is the only state that does not use the common law system. Its law is based upon the French court system and the Napoleonic code. Also, most textbooks cite six sources of the law, omitting the seventh. The authors of this book recognize a separate body of law, as seen in "Words & Phrases." Follow your teacher's instruction.

Law Suit Progression

Federal Court System

Supreme Court

|

Writ of certiorari

or

Hearing en banc

|

Circuit Court of Appeals

|

Motion for New Trial / Notice of Appeal

|

District Court

1. **U.S. District Courts**

   a. Trials take place here.

   b. Hears criminal/civil cases affected by federal law or diversity of citizenship.

   c. Only place where facts of the case are at issue.

   d. Only place in federal system where there is a jury and witnesses.

2. **U.S. Circuit Courts of Appeals**

   a. Has three judge panels assigned to hear cases.

   b. The United States has a total of 13 courts of appeals, and 11 are divided into regions.

There are also the U.S. Court of Appeals for the Federal Circuit (patents, customs, etc.) and the U.S. Court of Appeals for the D.C. Circuit.
   c. From this point, the only question is whether the correct law was applied in the case.
3. **Means of getting to Supreme Court**
   a. Hearing *en banc* can avoid the court or offer a less-expensive alternative
      i. Not required to get to the Supreme Court.
      ii. It is when all judges in a circuit hear the case.
      iii. Their decision becomes law for only that circuit.
      iv. EXAMPLE: Sixth circuit in Cincinnati heard a case *en banc* about Kentucky State University administration seizing yearbooks to protect administrators. The circuit court looked at the earlier decisions on this sort of case and said the action was unconstitutional. *Kincaid v. Gibson*, 236 F.3d 342 (2001).
   b. Writ of certiorari
      i. You must petition the Supreme Court to issue this for you. This is required to have your case heard by the Supreme Court.
      ii. It is an order sent to the clerk of the appeals court by the Supreme Court saying that the Supreme Court needs the case file to hear the case.
   c. Original jurisdiction
      i. Very few cases, like those involving ambassadors and fights between states, may go to Supreme Court before any other. See *Indiana v. Kentucky*, 136 U.S. 479 (1890).

writ—an old-fashioned word for an order from the court.

Typical title page (caption) of a court case: **Law action**

State
Name of the court

Plaintiff name
v.   **Case (cause) no.**
Defendant

NOTE: In your notes, save on writing by using π for *plaintiff* and Δ for *defendant*. Also note that unlike boxers, lawyers and courts use only the letter *v.* to represent *versus*. Boxers use *vs*.

Complaint for Damages

Plaintiff   party that filed complaint for damages.

Defendant   one who answers to complaint.

Typical title page (caption) of a court case: **Equity**

State
Name of the court

Petitioner

Case (cause) no.

Respondent

Petition for Temporary Restraining Order

> NOTE: Called *petitioner* because the person is asking (or "petitioning") the court to award extraordinary remedies. Called *respondent* because responding to petition.

et al.—"and others"

Sample case for "et al.":

Supreme Court of the United States
No. 98-1682
United States et al.
v.
Playboy Entertainment Group, Inc.

Court Progression

1. State courts (see figure 1.1, right column)
   a. They are called many names: superior courts, district courts, family, or probate, and so on.
   b. This is where the trials are, so they are trial courts.
   c. A person can appeal to the appellate court if there is a problem with how the law was applied by the state court.
   d. They can then appeal to the state supreme court if the appellate court's ruling is not satisfactory.

e. Texas has
   i. Texas Supreme Court—hears civil cases.
   ii. Texas Court of Criminal Appeals—hears all others.

| EXAMPLE: recent executions. |

U.S. Supreme Court banned the execution on the mentally infirm. Stated that a judge may not give someone the death penalty. A federal question might deal with constitutional issues—for example, sodomy law, *Lawrence v. Texas* (2003).

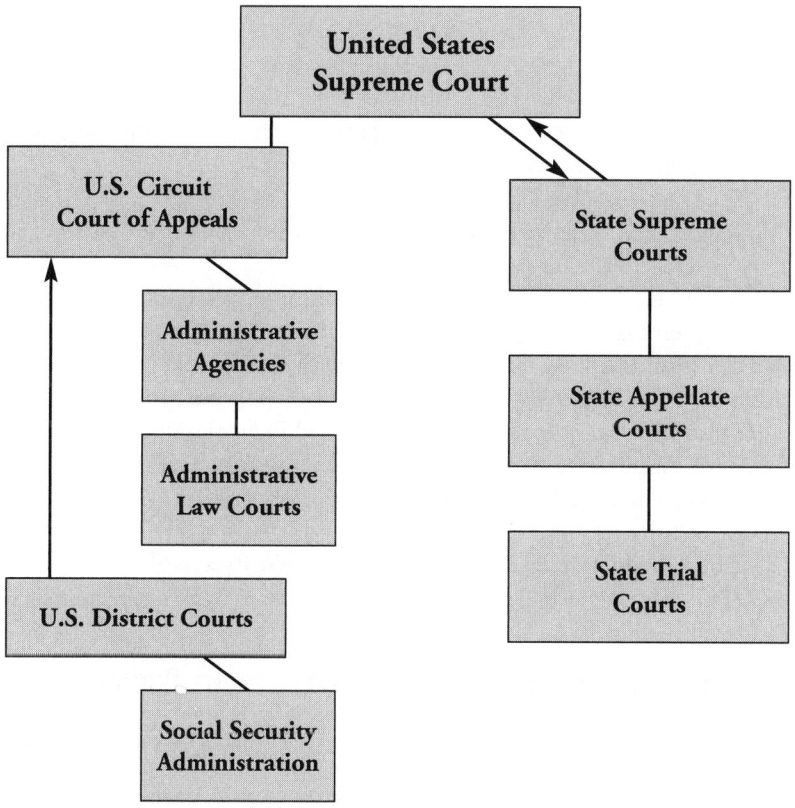

FIGURE 1.1 Trials begin in the "lower courts" and always "go up" or are "taken up" by one of the parties to a "higher level" of the court system. This chart provides insight into how the administrative agencies and their law courts fit into the system. Most administrative appeals go to the U.S. Court of Appeals, except for things such as Social Security disability claims. Those appeals, numbering many thousands, would clog the appellate system. Note also that the U.S. Supreme Court can refer a case back to a state supreme court for definitions of state law. Illustration by John F. Schmitt.

> NOTE: When you "go up" or "take a case up" on appeal, you are the *appellant*. The opposing party becomes the *appellee*. This goes back and forth through the process. For example, when you go to the state supreme court, the appealing party then becomes the appellant (in most states), and the other, the appellee. The best way to get to the U.S. Supreme Court is to show that two different circuit courts came to different decisions on the same law. To get from the state supreme court to the U.S. Supreme Court your case must present a *federal question*.

2. Federal courts (see figure 1.1, left column)—can look at the constitutionality of state law and have authority over state cases if there is:
   a. Diversity of citizenship—when the parties are from two different states.
      i. Everyone involved must be from different states.
      ii. Has to involve $75,000+.
      iii. If the U.S. Supreme Court has a question about the state law, it refers to the state supreme court.
      iv. When the state supreme court offers its interpretation of the statute, then the U.S. Supreme Court will render its decision in federal cases.
   b. Constitutional questions that conflict with state statute (vice versa).
3. Administrative agencies—have something of a trial capacity. Appeals from administrative law judges' decisions are argued in front of the commission or board. Agency also has attorneys to defend government's position. Appeals generally go to U.S. Circuit Court of Appeals.
4. Social Security Administration
   a. Offers disability compensation and social security appeals.
   b. Appeals from this body go to the district courts because of the numbers.

Looking at the Source of Government Power

jurisdiction—Government is allowed to regulate commerce between the states.

1. Jurisdictional power is dependant on what power is given to the federal government by the Constitution and what is reserved to the states (10th Amendment).
2. The Constitution allows the government to regulate patents and copyrights, govern military courts, determine statutory violations, and issue money.
3. Power of the federal government preempts state action: *preemptive jurisdiction*.
4. All municipalities are creations of the state legislatures.

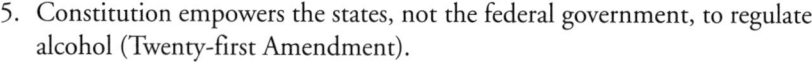

5. Constitution empowers the states, not the federal government, to regulate alcohol (Twenty-first Amendment).
6. In May 2004, the Ninth Circuit Court of Appeals ruled that the federal government did not have the power to challenge the state of Oregon's "assisted suicide" law, which allows doctors to aid terminally ill patients in arranging for their own deaths.

> NOTE: Nebraska is only state with unicameral legislature.

The court said that state governments are the primary regulators of professional medical conduct.

Trial Procedure—Example Case

1. **Torts**—legal (civil) wrongs.
   a. Most common is negligence (auto accident, product liability, malpractice).
   b. *Negligence*—common law term.
   c. Elements of a tort:
      i. Legal *duty* to act in a certain fashion (judge's question of law).
      ii. Must be a *breach* of the duty (question of fact, determined by jury).
      iii. Must be resulting *damages* (question of fact = damage; consequence of the breach = resulting) determined by jury.
      iv. Breach must be the *cause* of the damages.
   d. Damages defined:
      i. *Compensatory/actual*—those that are provable out-of-pocket expenses.
      ii. Also called "specific" damages.
   e. Other damages—general, pain and suffering.
      i. Those set out by statutes.
      ii. Conversion/theft—cover value of what is taken plus attorney fees.
      iii. **treble**—three times the actual damage (bad check cases).
      iv. **liquidated**—agreed damages if promises in a contract are not kept.
      v. Punitive damages meant *to punish* actions already taken and *to deter* others from doing the same. Supreme Court said in 2003 that punitive damages should generally not exceed nine times the actual damages suffered by the plaintiff.
2. Sample lawsuit.
   a. File *complaint* and serve papers.
   b. Defendant files an *answer*.
      i. If the defendant or the plaintiff want a jury, must file request then or within 10 days of answer.
      ii. Usually has a limit of about 30 days to file the answer.

c. Can file a ***motion to dismiss*** in rare cases (based on only the argument that if everything the plaintiff says is true, they are still not entitled to money).

> NOTE: Common reason for this is statute of limitations (in torts it is 2 years in many states; with land, maybe 20 years because it usually involves written contracts).

d. ***Discovery***—allows you to find out what the other person's case is; promotes settlement.
  i. ***interrogatories***—written questions to be answered under oath.
  ii. ***request for production***—request for documents to parties or nonparties.
  iii. ***depositions***—face-to-face meetings under oath.
  iv. ***subpoenas***—order to appear for questioning or something.
  v. ***subpoenas duces tecum***—order to show up "and bring documents with you."

> NOTE: States never appeal criminal cases because of double jeopardy rule of the Fifth Amendment.

> NOTE: Some states also call all damages (except punitive) "compensatory" or "general."

e. Trial.
  i. Begin process of jury selection from the "***jury pool***."
  ii. ***voir dire***—"to see, to say"; ask questions, see what they say and their reactions.
  iii. ***preliminary jury instructions***—usually instructions about behavior during trial.
  iv. ***opening statements***—unimpassioned statement by lawyer about what they expect the evidence to be.
  v. Presentation of evidence.
    (1) This is done through witnesses or documents.
    (2) Plaintiff goes first because they have the ***burden of proof***—means they must prove their case ***beyond a reasonable doubt*** in criminal cases.
    (3) Must prove case by a ***preponderance of the evidence*** in civil cases—tips the scale of justice (50.1 percent of the case).
    (4) Must prove case by presenting clear and convincing evidence that the law is needed (in constitutional cases). Example: kid porn—animated cannot be made illegal; no child involved.

(5) If additional evidence is presented by defendant in its case, the plaintiff has right to respond.

(6) Witnesses are questioned in order as same as plaintiff/defendant.

  vi. Order of witness questioning:

(1) *direct examination*—talks to own witness.

(2) *cross examination*—other party talks to witness.

(3) *redirect examination*—comes back and talks to own witness.

(4) *recross examination*—other party asks questions again.

  vii. *closing arguments*—emotional rendition of the evidence.

  viii. *final instructions*—judge gives information and laws concerning the case to the jury.

  ix. *deliberation*—jury talks over case.

(1) *verdicts*—jury renders verdict.

(2) *judgments/decisions/orders*—courts enter the result.

  f. Appeal process.

    i. Move up all transcriptions, documents, evidence.

    ii. Questions if the judge gives right jury instructions, questions on admissible evidence, objections, and so on.

Short Glossary

affidavit   sworn statement in writing.

affirmed   agreeing with judgment of trial.

concurring opinion   when judge goes along with outcome of ruling but for different reasons.

dissenting opinion   the statement of the justice who is against the ruling.

majority opinion   when the ruling of appeals courts writes down the winner's opinion.

motion for new trial   if either party disagrees with verdict; also called motion to correct errors. Motion for new trial is first step for appeal. You must cite particular argument or error.

motion to quash   motion to keep out case, subpoena, or evidence ("motion to kill").

remand the case   sends it back to the court.

reversed   disagreeing with trial judgment and issues a new trial.

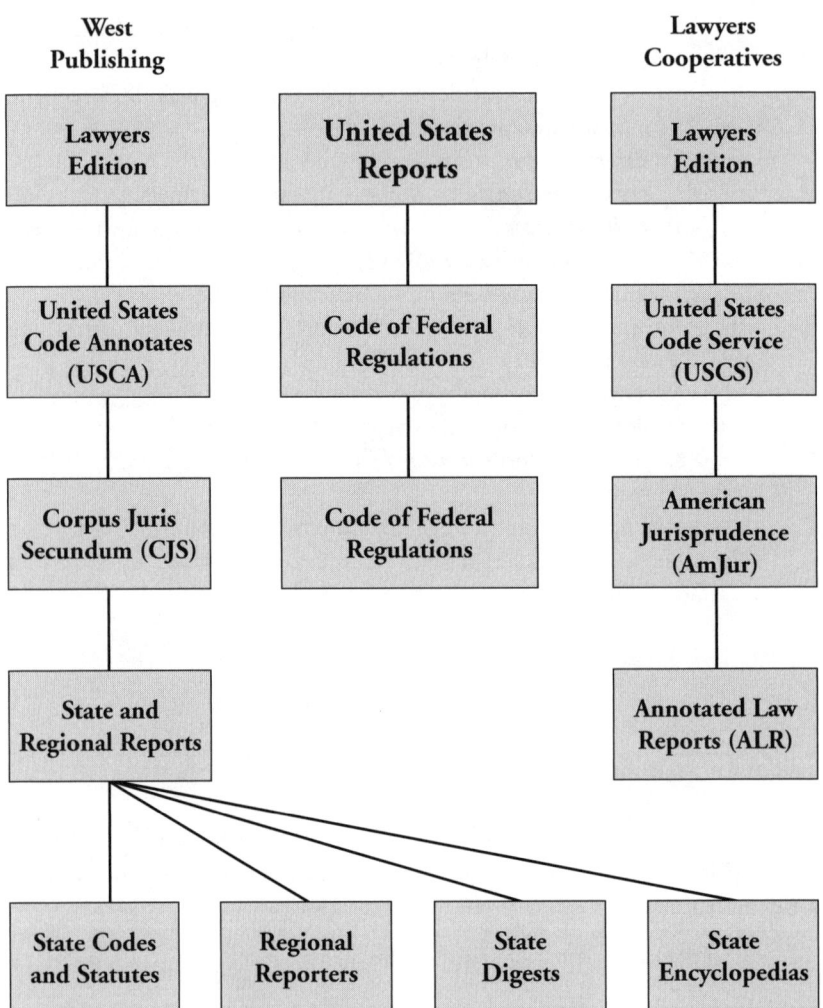

FIGURE 1.2 The bulk of major legal reporting is provided by the three publishers identified here. West's "key numbering system" allows for the easy interchange between federal and state law and between the law of the various states. Illustration by John F. Schmitt.

Researching American Law

Major Publishers of Court Decisions

1. Largest publishers (see figure 1.2):
   a. U.S. Government (U.S.)—U.S. Court Reports

      b. Supreme Court Reports (S.Ct.)—West Publishing Company

      c. Lawyer's Edition (L.Ed.)—Lawyer's Cooperative

2. Differences between the publishers:

      a. Indexing systems are different.

      b. Introductions to cases are different.

      c. The government's (U.S. Reports) synopsis is the only one you can site in an argument.

      d. West's "key numbering system"—only West Publishing has this.

      e. Breaks down every area into the smallest part.

3. L.Ed. will break down a single case if they think that it is important.

4. Reporters can tell you where case is from—for example, any case in the court of appeals will be in the West "Federal" reporters.

      a. 307 F.2nd 1048—Federal Circuit Court opinions only

      b. 401 Fed.Supp. 1112—Federal District Court ruling

      c. 47 CFR 101.(B)—Code of Federal Regulations (Administration Agencies)

      d. U.S., S.Ct., L.Ed.—Supreme Court decisions are found with these. In very old cases, the reporter of the Supreme Court was someone with an individual contract to report the cases. When you see a very old case, use vol. name page/2 Wheat 322.

           Full citation form: *Jones v. Wilson,* 365 U.S. 1291, 117 S.Ct. 865, 12 L.Ed. 4th, 188 (1998).

Origin of American Free Speech and Free Press

SOMETIMES WE AMERICANS assume that free speech is just some-thing that was always here, like the wind and the sky. But history teaches us that our freedoms started as seeds in the minds of great men that grew to be ideas for which countless men and women would fight and die. Our record has not always been clean in these regards, but we move forward with words attributed to Voltaire as our guide: "I may not agree with what you say, but I will defend to the death your right to say it."

Evolution of Expressive Freedom: England to Adams

1. Censorship, for American purposes, began in England with the "divine right of kings." It was often considered treason to say disparaging things about the king, true or not.
   a. Censorship also came in the form of a licensing system on printers.
   b. This system did not grant licenses to people with unacceptable views. It also allowed for precensorship of material by the government.
2. Political thinkers who advocated freedom of expression.

a. **John Milton** wrote an argument against governmental censorship titled *Areopagitica* in 1644. The work focused on two main ideas:

    i. self-righting process—the theory that true ideas would succeed over false ones making censorship unnecessary.

    ii. *marketplace of ideas*—the idea that freedom of expression should be open to everyone except those who wished to express ideas that he believed to be false. Milton also did not feel this right should be granted for "popery" (support of the Roman Catholic Church).

b. **Roger Williams**, leading settler of Rhode Island, wrote an argument for freedom of expression titled *Bloudy Tenent of Persecution for Cause of Conscience*. It advocated the freedom of expression to Catholics, Jews, and Muslims (something Milton did not do).

c. The **Levellers** were a Puritan group in England who felt freedom of expression was necessary for the pursuit of religious freedom and limited government.

d. **John Locke** is most noted for his development of the *social contract theory*, which basically expressed the belief that the government was to serve the people, which is directly contrary to the idea of the divine right of kings. The power to govern is given to the government by the people with the understanding that the government will protect the natural rights of the people. Included in these natural rights are the right to life, liberty, and property ownership.[1]

3. While licensing was abolished in 1694, the use of *seditious libel* remained an effective way of dealing with those who tried to publish unacceptable views, especially those that criticized the government or government officials, as being "false, scandalous and malicious."[2]

a. The courts used the maxim "the greater the truth, the greater the libel,"[3] which simply meant that the truth was not a defense against libel, and the more harmful the statement, the greater "damage" seen by the government.

b. In 1792 Parliament passed the **Fox Libel Act**, which made it the responsibility of a jury, not a judge, to decide if a statement made was libelous. This act made it harder to prosecute for libel since it was more likely that a jury would sympathize with the defendant.[4]

c. In 1843 Parliament passed **Lord Campbell's Act**, which finally made truth available as a defense against charges of libel. A number of states in America also changed their state laws and constitutions (see Indiana and Texas) at about this time to allow for truth as a defense.

4. Example of an American seditious libel case—The Zenger trial:

a. John Peter Zenger, printer of the *New York Weekly Journal*, was accused of seditious libel because he printed material in opposition to Governor

William Cosby. Andrew Hamilton, Philadelphia lawyer, successfully defended Zenger, not by changing the law, but by convincing the jury members to disregard the judge's instruction that truth was not a defense to a charge of seditious libel.

5. **America defeated Britain in 1781.**
   a. Thirteen colonies formed the Articles of the Confederation; did not work because of people's fear of central government.
      i. As a result, the Constitution was drafted.
      ii. James Madison was the author of many of the Federalist Papers, which were pro-Constitution.
   b. While all the states ratified the Constitution, many citizens demanded a ***Bill of Rights (BOR)*** listing the limits of central government power.
      i. In the beginning the BOR applied only to the federal government.
      ii. John Adams, a Federalist (the only organized political party), becomes president, 1796.
      iii. He led the fight for the ***Alien and Sedition Acts in 1798*** to stifle opposition to his plans for a possible French war.
      iv. The acts had a time limit and expired in 1801.
   c. There were 25 arrests and 15 indictments under the law; all targets were anti-Federalists.

NOTE: Thomas Jefferson was the leading fighter in an emerging opposition party, later known as the Democratic-Republican Party. He was elected president in 1800 and pardoned all of those convicted under the acts. In modern times, he and President Andrew Jackson are seen as the founding figures of the Democratic Party.

United States of America: Heritage of Free Speech or Legacy of Censorship?

1. ***absolutists***—those who believe that "Congress shall make no law" to abridge freedom of press/speech.
2. ***Professor Zechariah Chafee***
   a. Harvard—1941 book *Free Speech in the United States.*
   b. When dealing with the First Amendment, there will always be a balancing act between the priorities of government (national security) and the individual rights of citizens, and speech should be limited only in cases where public safety would be impaired and only where "words will give rise to unlawful acts."

3. *Alexander Meiklejohn*
   a. Incitement does not occur unless an illegal act is performed and the prior words can be directly connected to the illegal act.[5]
   b. Constitution protects all words but some more than others. Political speech and other matters of social importance, including the arts, philosophy, science, and so forth, are entitled to full protection. Other matters, such as advertising and personal communications, get less.
   c. This is called the "weighting of words."

> EXAMPLE: Discussions concerning government theory and practices carry more weight than an Internet joke or a love letter.

Early Court Cases Establish Roles of Federal, State Governments

1. *Marbury v. Madison* (1803)
   Secretary of State Madison did not give official appointment documents to Marbury, a last-minute appointment by John Adams. With this case, the Supreme Court took upon itself the right to declare statutes "null and void." (Constitution never explicitly gave the court this power.)

   > NOTE: Court reporters' names were in the middle for early U.S. Supreme Court (e.g., 1 Cranch 137).

2. *United States v. Hudson & Goodwin* (1812)
   Gave the precedent that the federal court cannot interfere with state common law. Is there such a thing as federal common law? No.
3. *McCulloch v. Maryland* (1819)
   Defined that states may not tax a federal government agency.

Slavery, Free Speech, and Free Press

1. **John Quincy Adams**—Sixth president of the United States went to Washington to fight against these rules. Was the first nonfounding father

> NOTE: All of these were testing the power of the states vis-à-vis the power of the central federal government. With these new looks at the law, the question of slavery came into play.

~

> HISTORICAL NOTE: Built into the original Constitution was the "3/5 compromise." The states used this as a means to reinforce slavery. So if anyone spoke out against slavery, especially in the South, it was grounds for seditious libel prosecution.
>
> Slave states enacted their own laws about speaking against slavery on the basis of this.
>
> As another result, gag laws were also enacted in the House of Representatives to prevent any of the congressmen from speaking ill about slavery.

president and the only president to return to office after leaving the White House.

2. **Abraham Lincoln**—Unlike modern presidents in time of war, Lincoln did not want any authority over freedom of speech during the *Civil War (CW)*. Did not have anything like the Alien and Sedition Acts, as Adams did.

> MOVIE NOTE: The film *Amistad* deals in part with Adams's antislavery efforts.

There was widespread repression of freedom of press in the Confederacy; some incidents were in the North, where newspapers were closed by the military or were denied access to telegraph lines.

End of CW brought about the 14th Amendment.

3. **John Stuart Mill**—wrote *On Liberty* in 1859 before CW.

He stated that an attempt to shut down free press deprives people of something important, even if it is the voice of a one-person minority or even if the suppressed opinion is wrong.

Rise of American Capitalism and the "Invasion" from Eastern and Southern Europe

1. State charges of sedition were a way of stopping free expression and opinion—also called seditious libel, criminal sedition, criminal syndicalism, anarchy, and criminal anarchy. Often used against labor union organizing drives.

2. Immigration into the United States changed from early British, French, and Dutch to Germans and Irish in the 1850s and to the East European "Bohunks" and the Italians, Greeks, Central Asians, and Jews in the late 1800s, early 1900s. The rapidly expanding American capitalist machine

needed labor in great quantities, and the villages of Europe were sometimes leafleted with flyers describing the United States as having "streets paved with gold." In reality, incoming workers often worked 70-hour weeks for $10 to $12, forcing them to live in slums and crowded tenements.

3. This brought about a lot of turmoil and organizing efforts by the American Federation of Labor, the American Communist Party, and the Industrial Workers of the World (IWW), known by many as "The Wobblies." Theirs was the broadest plan, seeking to organize all workers in the world into one giant union.

4. Violence was common in the organizing efforts. Many were killed. Some of the unions were radical, based in part upon the theories of Karl Marx and Frederick Engels that had been circulating in Europe since the 1840s.

1914: World War I, "The War to End All Wars"

World War I—called "the great Capitalist War," 1914–1918. Openly opposed by IWW, Socialist Party, and the Communist Party as a war fought by working people against working people, all for the benefit of the rich.

> MOVIE NOTE: *Reds, Doctor Zhivago, Nicholas and Alexandra* for background.

1917—United States enters the war on the side of England, France, and Russia against Germany, Austria-Hungary, and the Ottoman Empire. At this time there were also Socialist and the Bolshevik (Communist) Revolutions in Russia. This caused a lot of worry in the United States because of the number of immigrants (Slavs) we had from Russia. We were fighting against the Germans and Austria, and we did not want immigrants from those countries in the United States to revolt against our government. We were also afraid of the Socialists, Communists (left wings), and Germans who were in the country. Thirty percent of the U.S. population in 1914 was foreign-born.

1. The 1917–1918 congressional acts
    a. The Espionage Act was passed in 1917, and the Sedition Act followed in 1918.
    b. Under the acts 2,000 were arrested, 1,000 were convicted, and 245 deported to the new "Soviet Union."
2. The federal cases
    a. *Schenck v. United States* (1919)
        i. Secretary-general of the Socialist Party.
        ii. Convicted of circulating leaflets denouncing draft to recruits.
        iii. Convicted under Espionage Act.

HISTORICAL NOTE: John Reed, an American journalist and the only American to be buried in the Kremlin, wrote *Ten Days that Shook the World*, the detailed story of the Bolshevik takeover of Russia. Also, U.S. troops were later sent to Russia to try and overthrow the government after the Bolshevik Revolution. The Communists were called Reds, those in favor of the monarchy were Whites, and liberals were later labeled Pink, not quite Red and not quite White.

    (1) Tried to defend by using the 1st Amendment, but Supreme Court decided the amendment was not absolute.

    (2) Justice Oliver Wendell Holmes (not the *Green Acres* character) wrote the majority opinion about "clear and present danger." He was in favor of the conviction because he said free speech was not absolute. Shouting "fire" in a crowded theater was not protected.

    (3) Before this there was only "bad tendency test."

  b. *Debs v. United States* (1919)

    i. Debs was the widely known head of the Socialist Party.

    ii. Convicted under the acts because he defended antidraft activists.

    iii. He was convicted and put in prison. While he was in prison, he was nominated for president and received one million votes in the 1920 election.

  c. *Abrams v. United States* (1919)

    i. Convicted of dispersing antiwar leaflets and criticizing President Wilson for sending troops to Russia.

    ii. In this case Holmes swaps sides about his thoughts on free expression. He is joined by an old friend who was placed on the court, Justice Louis Brandeis, the first Jewish Supreme Court justice.

    iii. Their minority opinion said there must be "present danger of *immediate evil*" before opinion may be limited by law. This later became a majority opinion.

HISTORICAL NOTE: The home of Eugene V. Debs has been faithfully preserved and may be seen on the campus of Indiana State University in Terre Haute, Indiana. Brandeis University, founded in Boston in 1948, is named after Justice Brandeis.

> MOVIE NOTE: The romanticized biography of Holmes can be seen in *That Magnificent Yankee.*

3. State law cases.
   a. *Gitlow v. New York* (1925)
      i. Wrote the *Left Wing Manifesto* and newspaper *The Revolutionary Age.*
      ii. Gitlow lost his appeal but was able to use the Fourteenth Amendment to apply the First Amendment to the states, and states could no longer interfere with the federal rights of the citizens. (Rest of BOR applied over the years.)
   b. *Whitney v. California* (1927)
      i. Convicted of violating a law that forbade belonging to a group advocating forcible change even though she was against those beliefs of the organization.
      ii. Member of the Communist Labor Party.
      iii. Brandeis wrote a concurring opinion saying speech could amount to a "clear and present danger" only if it were "so imminent that it may befall before there is opportunity for full discussion."
   c. *Fiske v. Kansas* (1927)
      i. Convicted of being member of the Wobblies because of the calls for overthrow of the capitalist system contained in the preamble to the Constitution.
      ii. Court ruled that was not sufficient evidence to convict.

1930s and 1940s: Depression and War

August 1939: Stalin in Soviet Union and Hitler's Germany united through treaty. September 1, 1939, Germans, Russians invade Poland. England, France declare war. Now our enemies were the Communists, Fascists (Italy), and Nazis. Pro-German American groups called **bunds**—which had been active in the United States in the 1930s—were big sources of concern for the country because many advocated Hitler's "master race" philosophy.

   With the new war in Europe and Japanese activity in Asia came new efforts to limit freedom of speech in the name of "national security." Thousands of Japanese American citizens placed in "camps."
1. **Smith Act**, or the Alien Registration Act of 1940.
   a. Made it a crime to advocate the violent overthrow of the government or to belong to a group that advocated same.

b. Applied in war and peace time.

c. Government did not have to have proof the things they advocated would be acted out.

2. With the end of the war in 1945, we enter into the *McCarthy Era*.

a. McCarthy Era started in 1950—also called the "Second Red Scare." Senator Joseph McCarthy from Wisconsin charged that there were many Communists working in the U.S. government, especially in the State Department.

b. Americans had become very concerned because Soviet army did not pull back from Eastern Europe but instead built an "Iron Curtain," according to Sir Winston Churchill.

c. Worries became full blown in 1949 when the Communist revolution took place and all of China became Communist.

d. In the United States, McCarthy blamed the fall of China on some U.S. politicians because, he said, there were many Communist employees or Communist sympathizers working in Congress and the administration who helped to bring about the Chinese revolution.

e. Most of the targeted politicians were Democrats (ploy to unseat the Democratic president Harry Truman).

f. While McCarthy uprooted the Senate, the House Un-American Activities Committee controlled the "Red baiting" in the House of Representatives.

g. Nixon was a senator who was called a Red baiter. He ran against Democrat Helen Gahagan Douglas and used the Red Scare as a way to make her lose (called her "the pink lady").

h. McCarthy's undoing came when he challenged Eisenhower and claimed that "Ike" allowed the Communists to work in the Pentagon. For this and other abuses, McCarthy was censored by the Senate.

3. *Dennis v. United States* (1951)

a. Takes place in the prime of the McCarthy Era.

b. He is convicted of sedition under the Smith Act after a nine-month trial, and the Supreme Court upholds the conviction.

c. Just Harry Vinson adopts the viewpoint of appellate judge Learned Hand, says the courts must "weigh the gravity of the evil against the probability of it happening," and finds that the overthrow of the gov-

---

MOVIE NOTES: Jim Carrey's movie *The Majestic* and the Woody Allen movie *The Front* both deal with the blacklisting that took place during the McCarthy Era.

> NOTE: Recent LBJ biography says that he used Red baiting to smear a fellow Texan who worked for Truman and helped regulate the oil industry.

ernment is such a grave threat, that there needs to be little probability of it happening for the speech advocating revolution to be unlawful.

1953: Earl Warren and "The Warren Court"

Warren was a former conservative Republican California governor appointed chief justice of the Supreme Court by President Eisenhower. He arguably became the most liberal chief justice in American history. Eisenhower is once supposed to have said, "Earl Warren was the biggest mistake I ever made."

1. *Yates v. United States* (1957)
   a. Supreme Court overturned conviction of 14 people who belonged to the Communist Labor Party.
   b. The Court's new view that there must be actual proof that there is imminent danger of overthrow of the government.
   c. Must prove that there was a concrete action.
   d. It was the last case to be tried under the Smith Act because the government had the burden of proving action beyond mere advocacy. Simply advocating overthrowing the government is not enough to convict. There had to be action.
2. Other matters "shake the known world":
   a. 1954: *Brown v. Board of Education* overturns segregation practices.
   b. 1956: Montgomery, Alabama, bus boycott makes Rosa Parks and Martin Luther King Jr. national figures.
   c. Elvis Presley and "rock and roll" take off in America.
   d. 1957: Russians launch Sputnik satellite.
   e. Cardinal Roncalli elected Pope John XXIII.
   f. Desegregation of schools and public facilities through the United States lead to ongoing racial turmoil.

1960s: "The Torch Is Passed to a New Generation"

1. The "youth culture" develops a full head of steam.
   a. 1960: John Kennedy (young, liberal, Catholic) elected president.
   b. 1962: Catholic church changes its doctrine to be more liberal (Second Vatican Council).

    c. August 1963: March on Washington; "I Have a Dream" speech.

    d. November 22, 1963: Lee Harvey Oswald kills Kennedy. Kennedy "canonized" in the minds of the American people.

    e. Johnson administration comes into effect, continues civil rights and voting rights work.

    f. February 1964: The Beatles arrive in America.

These matters cause a disruption of the staid conservative era of the Eisenhower years (Television: *Ozzie & Harriett, Leave It to Beaver*).

2. Vietnam

    a. United States went into Vietnam out of fear of monolithic Communism (belief that all Communists are bad and always act the same).

    b. Also wanted Communists out of Vietnam because of belief in ***domino theory***: If Vietnam fell, so would Laos, Thailand, Cambodia, and so on.

    c. We had problems from the start because we were fighting against Ho Chi Minh (Vietnam's George Washington). Even though he was Communist, most of the country liked him for fighting against the French and Japanese to estabish a Vietnamese homeland.

3. Gulf of Tonkin "incident"

    a. United States claimed that Vietnamese gunboats attacked U.S. destroyers off North Vietnamese coast.

    b. The story was used to pass Gulf of Tonkin resolution, which allowed the government to send as many troops as needed to support the weak South Vietnamese government. At the time we had 15,000 U.S. advisors to teach South Vietnamese how to fight.

    c. Johnson had said he was not going to send U.S. troops "to do the job Vietnamese boys should be doing." Johnson used this stance to put down his opponent by running a television ad about a little girl in a flower field who gets blown away by a nuclear bomb (opponent Barry Goldwater wanted to use nuclear war to end the Vietnam conflict).

    d. Johnson ended up sending a maximum of 450,000–500,000 troops to Vietnam with the help of the military draft.

4. 1968: Mass demonstrations advocating the end of the war.

    a. Democratic convention in Chicago led to rioting.

    b. Nixon won election because of his "secret plan" to end the war. He also won in 1972 using the phrase "Peace is just around the corner."

    c. While this is going on, there is still an active civil rights movement going on because a disproportionate number of blacks were going to Vietnam (Black Panthers and other groups become more aggressive).

5. 1970: Nixon escalated the war when he bombed Cambodia and Laos (neutral areas). As a result, they turn against the United States.

    a. We did this because they were harboring North Vietnamese and help-
ing to supply the guerrillas (Vietcong), and they allowed the North
Vietnamese to use the Ho Chi Minh trail that passed through the
countries.

    b. Kent State University, 1970: National Guard opens fire on college
demonstrations and kills four students. Happened after Nixon's bombing.

6. *Brandenburg v. Ohio* (1969; Klansman free speech)

    a. Arrested for speaking at rally: called for "revengence."

    b. He wins in Supreme Court because First amendment gives him the
right to call for action so long as "the speech is not directed to inciting
or producing imminent lawless action."

7. *Cohen v. California* (1971)

    a. Cohen wore a jacket at a court trial for antiwar protesters. Arrested
because of the statement on the jacket ("Fuck the draft").

    b. Supreme Court said he could not be arrested because it violated his free
speech rights, despite the unpleasant nature of the word, because "one
man's vulgarity is another's lyric."

8. *Texas v. Johnson* (1989)

    a. Defendant convicted in state court for desecrating U.S. flag at Republican
National Convention.

    b. Supreme Court said flag burning is a protected form of symbolic speech,
especially when it occurs in a clearly political context. A later federal statute
was also knocked down by the court (*United States v. Eichman*, 1990).

Interpreting the Constitution

You can be an **absolutist** or someone who tries to do a **balancing test** or **preferred position**.

Preferred position = Meikeljohnian theory—for example, we will give individual words more weight than the government will, although still balancing.
Highest protection of words comes with those that deal with public policy.

Also, bear in mind the following case: *United States v. Congress of Industrial
Organizations* (1948; the latter known as the Congress of Industrial Organizations,
now a partner of the American Federation of Labor, or the AFL-CIO).

compelling state interest   when the government has to deal with a problem
that is of such overwhelming importance that it must act, even when its proposed rule hinders First Amendment rights (child pornography).

presumptions   idea that we are going to change presumption from "when
a (state) statute is enacted, it is considered valid until a challenger proves

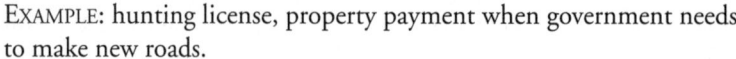

> EXAMPLE: hunting license, property payment when government needs to make new roads.

otherwise." Now, where the act appears on its face to be a restriction on First Amendment freedoms, we will presume it to be invalid until the state can prove otherwise.

rational relationship   there must be a rational relationship between a proposed law and the government's objective (what it wants to do versus the means by which it wants to do it).

Modern Problems

The Patriot Act and other rules and regulations passed since September 11, 2001, have had the tendency to limit rights of free expression and other civil liberties. Journalism coverage in Iraq and Afghanistan has been limited by the Pentagon, and international journalists have even been killed by U.S. military personnel. More than one claim has been made that our soldiers have even targeted journalists.

Citizens of the Unites States, Afghanistan, Pakistan, and other countries have been held *incognito* and *incommunicado* in prisons, and rights to civilian trials have been limited or denied, although Supreme Court decisions in June and July 2004 may have opened the U.S. court system to many of these detainees.

These threats, and the threat of more actions to come, have made many Americans greatly uneasy about the Patriot Act and the proposed Patriot Act II.

Notes

1. Wayne Overbeck, *Major Principles of Media Law* (Belmont, Calif.: Thomson-Wadsworth, 2004), 37.

2. Kent R. Middleton, William E. Lee, and Bill F. Chamberlin, *The Law of Public Communication* (Boston: Allyn & Bacon, 2004), 119.

3. Overbeck, *Major Principles of Media Law*, 38.

4. Donald M. Gillmor, Jerome A. Barron, Todd F. Simon, and Herbert A. Terry, *Fundamentals of Mass Communication Law* (St. Paul, Minn.: West Publishing, 1996), 5–6.

5. Overbeck, *Major Principles of Media Law*, 45.

Censorship or "Prior Restraint"

AMERICANS DO NOT accept the legitimacy of any government or any plan that suggests that news or other information should be censored before the people have a right to see or hear it. Instead, we prefer a system of subsequent punishment; that is, we think people should be allowed to print the ideas they believe, absent serious conflicts with our national security, and then be made to pay for it if they have defamed someone, invaded someone's privacy, or interfered with intellectual property rights.

1. Usually called *prior restraint* of communications by government.
2. United States has traditionally favored *subsequent punishment*: allows you to publish without censoring, but the consequences afterward are yours alone and allowable by law.

> EXAMPLE: the target filing a lawsuit afterward (libel) or the government doing so (issues of national security).

3. Prior restraint is much more of a threat to civil liberties than subsequent punishment is.
   a. Ways in which government tries to enact prior restraint:
      i. Censor news media to prevent the dissemination of information that they see as a threat to national security.
      ii. Restrict the rights of unpopular groups to demonstrate or distribute literature in public places.
      iii. Forbidding "hate speech" on the basis or ethnicity, religion, gender, sexual orientation.
      iv. Discriminatory taxation of mass media.
      v. Government censorship of controversial films.
      vi. Attempts to regulate stock market newsletters.
      vii. Forbidding media to print confidential info—that is, names of juvenile offenders.
   b. *self-censorship*—when publishers or writers censor themselves by calming down their advocating an issue, to avoid offending a government or someone else.

EXAMPLE: In the Republic of Moldova inauguration, where two papers opposed to the new government were not allowed to participate, other publishers calmed their criticism of the government so that they were not shut out of future proceedings.

Censorship of Publications

1. *Near v. Minnesota* (1931)
   a. Minnesota state nuisance law used to stop the publication of the *Saturday Press* because it had published several articles critical of government officials.
   b. Supreme Court overturned the trial verdict and said that paper could not be punished for its action (5–4 decision).
   c. Newspapers may not be censored before publishing, except under extreme situations.
   d. Justice Hughes said only times when you can possibly censor the media are for
      i. National security.
      ii. Control of obscenity.
      iii. Incitement to violence.

e. The case established a pattern that the Supreme Court has followed ever since.

2. *New York Times v. United States* (1971; also called the ***Pentagon Papers*** case)
    a. President Nixon versus *New York Times* and *Washington Post.*
    b. The papers published secret documents about the American policy of four presidents whose actions were questionable and which in turn led us into the Vietnam War.
    c. Government papers were copied by Daniel Ellsberg, who was later unsuccessfully tried in criminal court for the act.
    d. *New York Times* was stopped by district court from printing; *Washington Post* was not.
    e. Supreme Court allowed the papers to be published because the government failed to prove the articles would endanger national security sufficiently to justify prior restraint. Much of the material should not have been marked "classified." Supreme Court looked at the facts, not the law.

3. *United States v. Morison* (1988)
Upheld conviction of Stanley Morison, who had given secret info about U.S. military hardware to a magazine (*Janes Defence Weekly*). Court said defendant's claim of First Amendment right to distribute military information was not valid.

4. *United States v. "The Progressive"* (1979; **H-Bomb case**)
    a. Liberal magazine wanted to publish an article about the H-bomb, with an accurate description of its components: information was from nonclassified sources.
    b. The magazine sent the article to the government to verify technical accuracy of the description.
    c. Government said the article posed a danger to the national security.
    d. Court said it might provoke some countries into getting on the nuclear bandwagon.
    e. Also said it violated the 1954 Atomic Energy Act.
    f. Before case could reach any appelate court, however, another magazine published a similar article, so the case was ***moot*** (dead or pointless): the information had already been put out into the public.

5. *United States v. Marchetti* (1972)
    a. Former CIA agent published a book critical of the CIA.
    b. The agency said that the man should have submitted the manuscript to them first for them to censor sensitive material (it was in his employee contract to do so).
    c. Tried to publish a second book: government gets order for prior restraint until agency was allowed to censor book beforehand.

    d. Defendant appealed: Appellate court said that the CIA could censor only the pages that dealt with classified information.

6. *Snepp v. United States* (1980)
    a. Wrote a book alleging CIA ineptness in Vietnam, *Decent Interval.*
    b. He did not submit for approval, as required by his government employment contract.
    c. After publication, the government filed suit for breach of contract.
    d. Supreme Court upheld breach and said the prior restraint issue had nothing to do with this. He had broken his contract first.
    e. This case would not be applicable to other government cases if they did not have this clause in their agency employment contracts.

After this, the government tried to increase restraints to stop federal employees from speaking to the press. President Reagan tried this by ordering a directive that employees sign an agreement consenting to "prepublication review" of their writing.
    a. In sum, 100,000 employees would have been affected.
    b. Did not work, because they could not do this to people who were **already employed**. Also, there was a lot of dissent against it.

7. *United States v. National Treasury Employees Union* (1995)
    a. In 1989, government revised the Ethics in Government Act to state that federal workers could not receive payment for articles written or speeches given, even if subject had nothing to do with government.
    b. Supreme Court ruled that the law was too broad and therefore violated First Amendment rights.

NOTE: Congress also helped expand government workers' free expression by amending the **Hatch Act**. Now workers could participate in political activities, campaigns, and so on, so long as on their own time. Change did not apply to workers in sensitive federal jobs: cops, national security.

Hate Speech

Hundreds of colleges have adopted their own codes addressing this in an effort to eliminate racial tension and promote diversity and understanding. Defenders of the laws cite the **Fighting Words Doctrine** provided by the Supreme Court in *Chaplinsky v. New Hampshire* (1942).

    Chaplinsky meant that when words were used that would likely produce **immediate violence**, they were not protected by the First Amendment. It was a "situational law" in which one had to look at the society and time in which the incident took place. If the words used in relation to situations and ideas of the time caused emotional responses, First Amendment did not apply.

> EXAMPLE: calling someone a "damned fascist" during World War II.

1. *RAV v. St. Paul* (1992)
    a. Supreme Court said that "hate speech" cannot be banned on the basis of its content, although violent action can.
    b. Case involved a white guy who burned a cross on an African American's lawn.
    c. Conviction overturned because court said you cannot punish someone who communicates a message just because it is offensive or emotionally painful for those it targets.
2. *Saxe v. State College Area School District* (2001)
    a. Two Christian students sued because of not being able to demonstrate that they believed homosexuality was a sin because of the school's anti-hate speech code.
    b. Court found that the school's code was unconstitutional on the basis that the school could not prove the code was necessary to protect the rights of other students or maintain order.
3. *Virginia v. Black* (2003)
    a. Supreme Court upheld a state statute that banned cross burning as an act of intimidation, but said burning a cross in an open field, where there is no evidence of intimidation, is protected activity under the First Amendment.
    b. But when an **act of violence** is motivated by hatred based on race, religion, origin, gender, or sexual orientation, the First Amendment does not protect the perpetrator. In the following case, the sentencing of a hate crime could be increased from the normal sentence and the First Amendment did not supply protection for the defendant. (The sentence must be imposed by the sitting jury, not the judge at a later time.) This is called *enhanced sentencing*.
4. *Wisconsin v. Mitchell* (1993)
    a. African American youths beat up a white boy after watching a movie about race hatred.
    b. On conviction, Mitchell's sentence increased because state proved his act was a hate crime.
    c. Supreme Court held "a physical assault is not by any stretch of the imagination expressive conduct protected by the First Amendment."

Flag Desecration

1. *Texas v. Johnson* (1989)
   a. State statute said it was illegal to burn a flag.
   b. As a protest by Johnson at Republican National Convention, he burned a flag.
   c. Supreme Court said the act was protected expression because, even though the act is offensive to many, he is advocating his opinion on public matters without endangering anyone else.

> NOTE: In 1990, Congress and President Bush passed a federal law making it illegal to burn a flag.

2. *United States v. Eichman* (1990)
   a. In 5–4 decision, Supreme Court ruled the law was unconstitutional.
   b. Pointed out that flag burning is an internationally recognized form of political protest.

> NOTE: Courts in California and in the federal circuits have upheld the right of protesters to hang peace signs from interstate highway bridges where U.S. flags had previously hung. That right did not automatically extend to antiabortion protestors.

Prior Restraint of Pickets and Leaflets

content neutrality—rule applies to everyone, regardless of the message they are sending.

time/place/manner restrictions—usually placed by local governments on such things as picketing and demonstrations.

> EXAMPLE: **George Lincoln Rockwell**, American Nazi party leader, marched through area of large Jewish population (Skokie, Illinois). Nazis were denied permit at first because of their message of hatred to Jews and their wanting to march this message through a Jewish neighborhood. Court said city failed to show compelling state interest in denying his request because the city cannot use the possibility of Rockwell's incitement to violence as a reason to deny. Violence can be prevented by city.

> NOTE: So long as a statute is content neutral, a government can have a time/place/manner restriction.
> Courts look for alternatives or other actions that can be taken besides restriction to preserve First Amendment rights.

public forum—sidewalks are traditionally pubic forums, but there may be others.
    a. Hyde Park in London—became a public forum because people had been making speeches there for years at the "Speakers' Corner."
    b. The first public forum was started in Rome.

> EXAMPLE: *RAV v. St. Paul*—Supreme Court said the prosecutors could have filed charges of trespassing; they did not have to charge him and violate his First Amendment rights.

Jehovah's Witnesses

1. *Lovell v. City of Griffin* (1938)
    a. City had ordinance that circulating pamphlets was illegal without administrative approval.
    b. City fined the Witness $50 for violation.
    c. First time where court says there must be content neutrality in ordinance.
    d. Violates First Amendment because of discretion left to city manager who could control content.
    e. Also said the city's defense—that First Amendment applied only to newspapers—was not correct; coverage extends to pamphlets as well.
2. *Schneider v. State of New Jersey* (1939)
    a. City tries to stop distribution by charging the leafleting person with littering.
    b. Supreme Court said city may punish littering and those who litter, but not the distributor.
    c. Also stated that police discretion to issue permits cannot be used to restrict right when people distribute their information. There can be a reasonable time/place/manner, so long as they apply to everyone.
3. *Jones v. Opelika* (1942)
    a. City law said solicitors must get a $10 book agent license.
    b. City manager has discretion as to whose license to revoke.
    c. Supreme Court said this cannot be done because it violates content neutrality.

> NOTE: Lawyers refer to ordinances such as this as an example of cities "trying to do through the back door what they couldn't do through the front."

> EXAMPLE: There is a state veterans memorial building with a basement auditorium, open to almost anyone to use. But, when anti-Vietnam protestors want to use it for a rally, they are denied. A court would probably say they had right to demonstrate there because it was a public forum.

Private Property Literature Distribution

4. *Marsh v. Alabama* (1946)
   a. Chickasaw, Alabama. Company town owned by Gulf Ship Building.
   b. Company said they could bar Jehovah's Witnesses from distributing on "private property."
   c. Supreme Court said it does not matter that they owned it, because in all other respects, it was a city open to the public and near a highway from which motorists were free to enter.

   > NOTE: These company town laws were really put in place to stop organizing by labor unions.

   d. Supreme Court said "ownership does not always mean absolute dominion." More open it becomes to the public, the more open it becomes to the law (looks public? acts public? probably is public).

      Also, private land used for public purposes is often called ***quasi-public*** and treated as public under the law.
5. *Amalgamated Food Employees v. Logan Valley Plaza* (1968; last of the Warren court)
   a. Union picketing on private property thrown off the mall land.
   b. Picketers say the mall is a public forum.
   c. Supreme Court agrees because there is labor dispute with a merchant in the mall, so there is a direct, legal connection between the picketing and a merchant in the mall.

6. *Lloyd Corp. v. Tanner* (1972)
   a. More conservatives are on the court at this time—four Nixon appointees.
   b. Anti-Vietnam protestors want access to shopping mall but are refused.
   c. Supreme Court agrees because there is no relationship between the cause and someone/something in the mall.
7. *Hudgens v. NLRB* (1976)
   a. Federal regulations and state property law are at issue.
   b. **National Labor Relations Board (NLRB)**—started during the Roosevelt era to help deal with the tensions between labor organizations and employers.
   c. Pickets of shoe store at a mall are thrown out by mall owner at request of merchant.
   d. NLRB calls this an **Unfair Labor Practice** and says the protestors should be allowed to picket as a remedy.
   e. Employer says it is private property.
   f. NLRB disagrees citing Logan Valley Plaza as on-point case.
   g. Supreme Court overrules Logan Valley but still allows picketing.
   h. Court says it is not a constitutional right, but there may be statute-created rights so long as they pertain to the question and do not exceed congressional authority.
8. *Pruneyard v. Robins* (1980)
   a. Question of whether state constitutions may extend rights greater than those of the federal constitution.
   b. Supreme Court said they can give greater power than the U.S. Constitution, based on Tenth Amendment: "The powers not delegated to the United States by the Constitution, nor prohibited by it to the States, are reserved to the States respectively, or to the people."
   c. Theory that in a truly federal system there is allotment of power to states and federal government.
9. *First Unitarian v. Salt Lake City Corporation* (2002)
   a. Tenth Circuit Court of Appeals ruled that when a city sells former city street area, including sidewalk, to church, new status as "private property" does not change the nature of the sidewalk from a "public forum."
10. *City of Ladou v. Gilleo* (1994)
    a. Gilleo placed signs in her yard containing political messages.
    b. The signs were either stolen or vandalized.
    c. The city stated the signs were in violation of a city ordinance.
    d. Supreme Court ruled the city ordinance was unconstitutional because it prevented a whole category of speech. It was not content neutral because it allowed FOR SALE signs.

Picketing Rights: Abortion Clinics

11. *Frisby v. Schultz* (1988)
    a. A city in Wisconsin placed a ban on demonstrations held in front of homes after an abortion clinic doctor's home was mass-picketed by protesters.
    b. Supreme Court upheld the ban on picketers protesting in front of a private home because the residents were "captives" in their own home.
    c. The court did state, however, that picketers who keep moving up and down the street are protected by the First Amendment since streets are a traditional public forum.

NOTE: The mass picketers' behavior was seen as ***intrusive*** because it entered into the doctor's private home, contrary to the old English common law policy "A man's home is his castle." When an audience cannot get away from speech, demonstrators are "intruding."

---

12. Freedom of Access to Clinic Entrances Act of 1994 (FACE Act)
    a. Enacted during the Clinton administration after mass demonstrations at abortion facilities during which some demonstrators chained themselves to doors.
    b. Made it a federal offense to limit patient access to be able to exercise their federal rights to obtain abortion services.
    c. It targets only unconstitutional acts, not legitimate demonstrating.

NOTE: In 1995, the Fourth Circuit Court of Appeals ruled in both *Woodall v. Reno* and *American Life League v. Reno* that the FACE Act did not violate the First amendment or the "cruel and unusual punishment" provisions of the Eighth Amendment.

---

13. *Madsen v. Women's Health Center* (1994)
    a. Picketers appealed Florida court injunction that ordered demonstrators to stay at least 36 feet away from any abortion clinic entrance and 300 feet from patients or the residences of clinic workers. It also banned the use of signs displaying "images observable" by patients in the clinic.

b. Supreme Court ruled the 36-foot restriction was reasonable, but the court overturned both 300-foot restrictions and the ban on "observable" signs.
c. Court said a smaller *buffer zone* around the clinic worker's residence with time/place/manner restrictions may be legal. Court also ruled that the ban on the use of signs would be acceptable if it was restricted to only signs that carried threats.

14. *Schenck v. Pro-Choice Network* (1997)
a. Supreme Court determined that demonstrators have right to approach patients on public sidewalk.
b. Court ruled that the New York trial court could not establish a 15-foot **"floating bubble"** around patients and clinic workers, but the court did uphold the judge's ruling that created a 15-foot no-demonstration zone around the clinic entrance.
c. Justice Rehnquist says picketing, leafleting, and loud protesting are legal and protected by the First Amendment.

15. *Hill v. Colorado* (2000)
a. The Supreme Court rules that a Colorado picketing law is not unconstitutional. The law set a 100-foot zone around an abortion clinic's entrance, and within that zone, leaflet distribution, sidewalk counseling, or sign displays were banned within 8 feet of another person unless that person agreed to being approached. The law allowed the display of signs within the 100-foot zone but not within 8 feet of a person.[1]
b. At the time of this ruling, antiabortion protestors had become violent; several clinic doctors were murdered by protesters.

NOTE: One of the most prominent abortion-related cases in the federal courts is *Planned Parenthood v. American Coalition of Life Activists*, 290 F.3d 1058 (2002), a Ninth Circuit case.

The court of appeals upheld part of a jury award of $107 million to doctors and abortion rights activists concerning an antiabortion website, "The Nuremberg Files," which uploaded "Wanted" posters of doctors and clinic workers. Plaintiffs had sued to recover under the FACE Act antiviolence provisions. Court defined a "true threat" as one "where a reasonable person would foresee that the listener will believe he will be subjected to physical violence upon his person," and such threats are unprotected by the First Amendment.

16. *Scheidler v. National Organization of Women* (2003)
    a. Supreme Court rules that federal Racketeer Influenced and Corrupt Organizations Act (RICO) cannot normally be used against abortion protesters to gain treble damages and nationwide injunctions against abortion protestors. Demonstrators can still be sued under the FACE Act.

Issues: Overbreadth, Solicitation, Public Forum

1. *Boos v. Barry* (1988)
   a. Supreme Court overturned denial of right to picket about foreign embassy regarding things that might be "embarrassing" to U.S. government denial on D.C. ordinance.
   b. The law was not **narrowly tailored** (designed specifically to deal with the problem in question) to serve a **compelling state interest**.
   c. Also, it was a ***content-based*** restriction on political speech in a political forum.

content basis—where a law seeks to outlaw specific behavior that is possibly constitutionally protected, must have a ***compelling state interest to justify it***.

content neutral—only a rational relationship is needed between a local or state government's law and the problem it seeks to address.

overbreadth (overbroad)—law is written so that it outlaws protected behavior along with behavior that a government could legitimately control. "You don't throw out the baby with the bath water," or "Don't swat flies with a shotgun."

> EXAMPLE: A city seeks to control door-to-door canvassers going to people's homes at odd hours, sometimes frightening them. An ordinance that prohibited all door-to-door canvassing would be overly broad.

2. *Organization for a Better Austin v. Keefe* (1971)
   a. Keefe was a real estate dealer who sold a black family a house in a white neighborhood.
   b. The dealer then tells the white neighbors, resulting in many of them selling their property. This was known as **blockbusting**. The practice severely damaged many urban neighborhoods during the 1960s and 1970s.
   c. Here, neighbors banded together to stop Keefe, who obtained an injunction on leaflet distributors who were trying to inform the neighborhood of his scheme.

> NOTE: With this case came the idea of a ***heavy presumption*** against the validity of the trial court's action because it affected First Amendment rights. This made it more difficult for local governments to carry the burden of proof to outlaw certain types of behavior.

    d. Supreme Court invalidated the injunction because the act, which was a peaceful distribution, was protected by the First Amendment.

3. *Heffron v. International Society for Krishna Consciousness* (1981)
   a. Hare Krishnas wanted to go to Minnesota state fair and roam freely on the fairgrounds soliciting and proselytizing their beliefs.
   b. The fair board said they could not do this but could set up a booth as everyone else has and do it there.
   c. Supreme Court said this was a reasonable action by the fair board because it was content neutral and a reasonable time/place/manner; showed a rational relationship (required all vendors to do the same thing).

4. *Board of Airport Commissioners v. Jews for Jesus* (1987)
   a. Airport officials put a ban on all First Amendment activities in the airport.
   b. Supreme Court says that restriction is too broad because travelers could inadvertently violate the law.
   c. Court did not rule out regulations that would be more narrowly defined time/place/manner.

5. *Lee v. International Society for Krishna Consciousness* (1992)
   a. Supreme Court allows a ban on fund-raising in airports because it is more intrusive than pamphleting.
   b. Although court says airport is not traditional public forum, less-intrusive First Amendment behavior (leafleting) must be allowed in appropriate areas, such as shopping zones.

6. *United States v. Kokinda* (1990)
   a. Supreme Court says postal office can limit any kind of **soliciting** on its property because it is "inherently disruptive" and impedes the flow of traffic.
   b. Although post office has never been a traditional First Amendment public forum, other forms of protected activity should be allowed if reasonable time/place/manner.

7. *McIntyre v. Ohio Elections Commission* (1995)
   a. State made a law that all distributors of political literature must identify themselves.
   b. Supreme Court said this law is unconstitutional because anonymous political activity has a long tradition in this country, citing James Madison's use of pseudonyms in writing the Federalist Papers.

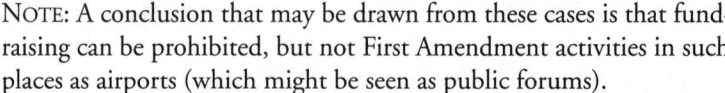

> NOTE: A conclusion that may be drawn from these cases is that fund-raising can be prohibited, but not First Amendment activities in such places as airports (which might be seen as public forums).

Parades and Organizations

1. *St. Patrick's Day Parade in New York* (1993; 814 F. Supp. 358)
   a. **Ancient Order of Hibernians**—Irish Roman Catholic men sponsor the parade.
   b. They refused to allow gays into the parade participation.
   c. Federal judge ruled the group had the right to refuse because it was a private organization. Any city order that sought to force them to accept the gay organization was in violation of the group members' free speech right.
2. *St. Patrick's Day in Boston* (1994)
   a. Veterans group traditionally put on the parade but did not allow gays to participate.
   b. Massachusetts Supreme Court ordered that they be allowed to participate because there was a state law guaranteeing homosexuals equal access to public facilities.
   c. Veterans cancel 1994 parade and turn 1995 parade into a protest while appealing the Massachusetts Supreme Court order.
   d. *Hurley v. Irish American Gay, Lesbian, Bisexual Group* (1995)—Supreme Court overturned the order, stating the veterans had the First Amendment right to choose which groups they would include in the parade.
   e. Said the state could not use the public accommodations law to force a private group to admit anyone with whom it disagreed.
3. *Boy Scouts of America v. Dale* (2000)
   a. James Dale had been a scoutmaster when the organization found out he was gay. He was then dismissed.
   b. Supreme Court ruled 5–4 that the organization had the First Amendment right to freedom of association and had the right to set its own moral code and viewpoint.
4. *Romer v. Evans* (1996)
   a. Colorado ballot initiative banned state and local laws giving legal protection to homosexuals.
   b. In a 6–3 ruling, Supreme Court said a state cannot single out a group for "disfavored treatment" based on "animosity."

    c. Said the proposed amendment "classifies homosexuals not to further a proper legislative end but to make them unequal to everyone else."

    d. The case cannot be seen as granting gays equal rights, but it suggests that laws attempting to legalize discrimination against them will not be upheld.

5. *Thomas v. Chicago Park District* (2002)

    a. City had a 13-point guideline for people wanting to use public parks to stage public events.

    b. Plaintiff's objected to provision requiring groups of more than 50 to have insurance.

    c. Supreme Court rules this to be a reasonable content-neutral time/place/manner because all groups were required to conform to the guideline.

6. *Brown v. Calif. Dept. of Transportation*, 321 F.3d 1217 (2003; Ninth Circuit)

    a. Antiwar demonstrators hung banners on interstate highway overpasses, and state personnel removed them while allowing U.S. flags and "patriotic" banners to stay.

    b. Appellate court says if one type may remain, antiwar types may also, unless they pose a significant safety risk.

Newsrack Ordinances

CONCLUSION: Newsracks are part of a legitimate expression of freedom and cannot be mandated away or regulated with restrictions. The only thing that can be regulated is how many total may be put in a single place. So long as the rule applies to everyone, then a government can mandate the number of newsracks each publication may have.

EXAMPLES: *Honolulu Weekly v. Harris* (2002) allows city to limit newsracks and provide space by lottery. In *City of Lakewood v. Plain Dealer Publishing Company* (1988) Supreme Court said a city cannot base its decisions regarding awarding newsrack space on the content of the publication. In *Cincinnati v. Discovery Network* (1993), Supreme Court said city could not ban commercial literature newsracks while allowing newspaper vending machines.[2]

Censorship through Taxation

NOTE: Taxes have been used as a means of controlling the press for many years. An example of this was the Stamp Act, one of the British acts that brought about the American Revolution.

1. *Grosjean v. American Press* (1936)
   a. Governor Huey "Kingfish" Long of Louisiana put tax on gross receipts on the 13 largest papers, 12 of which opposed him.
   b. Tax was on those with a circulation of more than 20,000 per week.
   c. Supreme Court ruled the tax was unconstitutional because it curtailed advertising revenue and was designed to limit newspaper circulation. Court said this type of tax had a "long history of hostile misuse against the freedom of the press."
2. *City of Corona v. Corona Daily Independent* (1953)
   a. Local government required a mandatory $32 business license fee be paid by all businesses.
   b. Court ruled it was not unconstitutional, because it was content neutral and applied to all businesses, so newspapers had to pay too.
3. *Minneapolis Star and Tribune v. Minnesota Commissioner of Revenue* (1983)
   a. A tax put on the ink and newsprint used by newspapers in 1971.
   b. Smaller papers complained of the cost, so law was amended to exempt the first $100,000 in these items. Thus, it singled out the big newspapers.
   c. Plaintiff was the largest paper in the state and ended up paying two-thirds of the total tax.
   d. Supreme Court overturned the tax law 8–1 because it singled out certain newspapers only.
4. *Arkansas Writer's Project v. Ragland* (1987)
   a. Sales tax applied to general-interest magazines but not to newspapers or to special-interest magazines.
   b. Supreme Court ruled it unconstitutional based on the *Minneapolis* case.
   c. Added offensive element here was that the Arkansas law required government officials to base a tax break on the content of the media.
   d. But court did not rule out a state's imposing taxes on an entire category of media, such as on all newspapers or on all magazines.
5. *Texas Monthly v. Bullock* (1989)
   a. Tax exemption given to religious books, magazines, and papers but not to secular publications.
   b. Court ruled it unconstitutional because of separation of church and state and not on the basis of discriminatory taxation.

6. *Leathers v. Medlock* (1991)
   a. Upheld state tax that applied to cable and satellite television services because it also applied to all utilities and other businesses. It did not single out the press.

Other Censorship Issues

1. *Lowe v. Securities and Exchange Commission* (1985)
   a. Under the Investment Advisers Act, the Securities and Exchange Commission (SEC) regulates the dissemination of investment advice, even in the form of publications. The act exempts **bona fide** newspapers and magazines.
   b. Defendant's registration as an investment adviser is canceled. He continues to publish a newsletter.
   c. The SEC tried to stop him, but Supreme Court said it was a bona fide newsletter and exempt from regulation.
   d. Court says he is not violating his investment adviser regulations, just issuing opinions and analyses of various stocks to which he is not connected.
2. *SEC v. Wall Street Publishing Institute* (1988; court of appeals)
   a. SEC wanted order for the *Stock Market Magazine* to disclose its origin of certain articles that were "**flackery**" (stories that came from stock market public relations people and just flattered stock).
   b. Court says they cannot do that unless they can prove that the magazine is accepting payment for the stories. Accepting payment to publication is a form of advertising and subject to SEC regulation.
3. *Meese v. Keene* (1987)
   a. Justice Department has right to require that foreign films be labeled "**political propaganda**" if attorney general considers them to be such.
   b. Power given under the Foreign Agents Registration Act of 1938.
   c. Meese labeled three Canadian environmental films.
   d. Court said the political label does not violate the First Amendment. It merely gives the public additional information.
4. *Bullfrog Films v. Wick* (1988)
   a. U.S.-made films dealt with nuclear war, use of Agent Orange, and the Nicaraguan Sandinista government.
   b. U.S. Information Agency (USIA) denied Bullfrog the "educational" classification so exposed the films to import taxation overseas. Under the Beirut Agreement, educational, scientific, or cultural films are exempt from high import tariffs. As documentaries, their market was limited.

c. This power gave the USIA free hand to grant the classification to those they agreed with and to deny it to those with which they disagreed.

    d. Court of appeals ruled the USIA (now part of State Department) may not deny a certification that a film is "educational" based on whether the USIA agreed with the content.

    e. Also ordered the USIA to make the regulation content neutral.

    f. USIA reenacted virtually the same standards and threatened to withdraw from the Beirut Agreement.

5. *Ward v. Rock against Racism* (1989; sound-level issue)

    a. Played annually in New York City Central Park and got constant complaints about noise.

    b. City set limits on sound volume; bands constantly went over the limit; city banned them from playing.

    c. City moved in with its own technicians and sound equipment to control the sound on future concerts.

    d. Supreme Court said that sound-level restriction was not a violation but a reasonable time/place/manner.

    e. Court also said the city's use of its own equipment and technicians were reasonable.

NOTE: There are two important holdings that came out of this case. The major holding was that time/place/manner restrictions need not be the least intrusive restrictions available, as courts had held before. The lesser point was that rock and roll was entitled to First Amendment protection.

---

6. *Bernstein v. U.S. Dept. of Justice* (1999; Ninth Circuit)

    a. Court rejected the government's concern that unregulated spread of encoded message capability would aid criminals and terrorists. The government had forbidden the export of encryption technology, such as computer source code.

    b. Said it constituted a prior restraint.

    c. The Ninth decided to hear the case again ***en banc***, but by that time, the government had relaxed its rules.

7. *Simon & Schuster v. New York State Crime Victims Board* (1991)

    a. Movie *Goodfellas* was made from the book written about Henry Hill (Mafia man).

CONCLUSION: Computer and encryption software are protected by First Amendment.

    b. Simon & Schuster wanted to publish *Wiseguy* the book.

    c. New York had a "Son of Sam" law that said authorities could take criminals' publishing profits and give them to a state board for redistribution to the victims of crimes.

    d. Supreme Court said law was unconstitutional because it imposed a special financial burden on communication based on the content of the message. Also said the law was overinclusive in that it could be applied to many works of literature.

8. *California First Amendment Coalition v. Lungren* (1995)

    a. During O. J. Simpson case, several witnesses were paid for their stories in a manner dubbed "**checkbook journalism**."

    b. California passed law forbidding witnesses to receive payment for stories for a year after the criminal act was committed, just long enough that story becomes less newsworthy (and less valuable).

    c. Federal district court said law violated the First Amendment. It was content based.

9. *Keenan v. Superior Court* (1999)

    a. Appellate court overturned "Son of Sam" law against Barry Keenan, the kidnapper of Frank Sinatra Jr., because it was overly broad; could include "real crime" writers.

Media Information Cases

10. *Oklahoma Publishing v. District Court* (1977)

    a. Court held that so long as a reporter does not obtain the names and information of crime victims illegally, even if juveniles, it is not unlawful to print them.

11. *Seattle Times v. Rhinehart* (1984)

    a. Supreme Court ruled a judge can forbid newspapers to publish information obtained during discovery if they are a party to the litigation.

12. *Cox Broadcasting v. Cohn* (1975)

    a. Laws that prohibit publishing the names of sex crime victims cannot stand, so long as the names are obtained from public records.

13. *Landmark Communications v. Virginia* (1978)

    a. Law making the proceedings of a judicial-conduct review board confidential is in violation of the First Amendment.

    b. Reasoning is that judges, personally, have no greater standing under the law than average citizens.

14. *Florida Star v. BJF* (1989)

    a. Crime victim cannot recover from newspaper for publishing name because it was lawfully obtained from police report posted on the pressroom wall.

> QUESTION: Could the victim be able to recover from the police department for having wrongly posted the information?

"Causation Cases"

15. *Rice v. Paladin Enterprises* (1998)
    a. Published a book titled *Hit Man: A Technical Manual for Independent Contractors.*
    b. Explains how to kill people for hire.
    c. Sued by families of victims killed by people using the book as a guide.
    d. Defendant claims First Amendment immunity. Court held that a publisher could be sued by those who are injured in this case because the book was clearly a "step-by-step murder manual, a training book for assassins" and not protected by the First Amendment.
16. *Grabes v. Warner Brothers* (2002; Michigan Appellate Court)
    a. The *Jenny Jones Show* murder. One guest tells another he has a homosexual interest in him. The straight man kills the gay man three days later and a long distance from where the show was filmed. Gay man's family sues. Jury awards $30 million.
    b. Appellate court says there was no legal duty to anticipate and prevent a murder three days later and hundreds of miles away.
17. *Byers v. Edmonson* (1999)
    a. *Natural Born Killers* movie: Victims claimed the movie incited violent acts by "copy cats." They tried to sue the producer.
    b. Supreme Court refused to hear appeal from Louisiana court ruling that said "if you can find a causal connection between the crime and the movie, then fine." Lower court dismissed the case because plaintiffs could not prove that the movie had **intended** to incite violence.
18. *Braun v. Soldier of Fortune Magazine* (1982)
    a. Magazine carried an ad from a man who said he "was discreet and very private" and would consider "all jobs."
    b. Family of a man killed by this "contractor," who was hired by someone else, sued the magazine and obtained a judgment of $4.3 million.
    c. Federal appellate court upholds the judgment, turning aside the magazine's First Amendment argument.

Miscellaneous

19. *Manuel Noriega and CNN*
   a. CNN somehow obtained taped telephone conversation between Noriega (former dictator of Panama, then in a Miami, Florida, jail) and his lawyers.
   b. Federal district court issued—at the government's request—an injunction barring broadcast of the tapes.
   c. Supreme Court refused to hear an emergency appeal.
   d. District court reversed itself and said CNN could broadcast because tapes would not hurt Noriega's chance for fair trail.

> NOTE: It is never a good idea to ignore a judge's order, even if you don't agree with it.

   e. But, CNN was charged with, and convicted of, criminal contempt because they continued airing the tapes while the injunction was in place.

Notes

1. Wayne Overbeck, *Major Principles of Media Law* (Belmont, Calif.: Thomson-Wadsworth, 2004), 88.

2. Overbeck, *Major Principles of Media Law*, 96.

The Student Press in America

T HE FIGHT TO RETAIN the rights of the free press has found a new frontline on the campuses of today's colleges, universities, and high schools. Using all sorts of excuses and justifications, college and high school administrators have tried to shut down or control student newspapers, magazines, and yearbooks. Who is right? What can students do? What can administrators do?

> NOTE: Until the 1960s, censorship was routine on college and high school campuses. In 1969, the Supreme Court first extended First Amendment rights to students in public institutions. During Vietnam War, courts ruled that schools could not censor student expression. But private institutions were exempt because there is no state action involved in the conduct necessary to invade personal freedoms. Then, in the 1980s, the law came full circle and started denying some rights.

Freedom of Speech and the Freedom of the Press

1. *Tinker v. Des Moines Independent* (1969)
   a. Students wore black armbands to school to protest Vietnam War and were suspended.

b. Supreme Court said it was ***symbolic speech*** and did not cause a **disruption of the class atmosphere** and therefore was protected under the First Amendment.

   c. Court said that schools "may not be enclaves to totalitarianism" but also noted that students do not have the same rights as adults when the students' exercise "would materially and substantially interfere with the requirements of appropriate discipline in the operation of the school."

   d. Famous quote from the case: "It can hardly be argued that either students or teachers shed their constitutional rights to freedom of speech or expression at the schoolhouse gate" (associate justice Abe Fortas).

2. *Antonelli v. Hammond* (1970; federal district court)

   a. Antonelli, a student newspaper editor at Fitchburg State College, resigned rather than submit an article by black activist Eldridge Cleaver to the campus review board to be preapproved (a form of prior restraint).

   b. College president Hammond set up the board to precensor the paper for obscenity and to "assure responsibility."

   c. Court said precensorship and Hammond's threat to cut the paper's funding were unconstitutional breaches of the students' First Amendment right.

3. *Trujillo v. Love* (1971; federal district court)

   a. This involved a "laboratory newspaper" produced by the mass communication department at Southern Colorado State College.

   b. The advisors said that an editorial criticizing a local judge and a cartoon that criticized the college press did not meet professional standards, so the editor was removed.

   c. Court ruled that the paper was a ***student forum of expression*** and protected by the First Amendment, despite its in-class status.

4. *Healy v. James* (1972; Supreme Court)

   a. A local chapter of the Students for a Democratic Society sought recognition as a campus group to gain access to campus facilities.

   b. Connecticut State College denied them because the national group was known to be radical.

   c. Court said local group cannot be denied campus privileges because of the national organization's reputation.

5. *Papish v. University of Missouri Curators* (1973)

   a. Papish published an underground newspaper called the *Free Press Underground.*

   b. She angered college administration by distributing the paper when a group of high school students and their parents were on campus.

c. The expulsion edition that followed had a political cartoon about a policeman raping the Statue of Liberty and the Goddess of Justice. The headline of an inside article read "Mother Fucker Acquitted."

d. Court said the expulsion was prohibited because it was her constitutional right to print what she did and distribute it. Neither the headline nor the cartoon were **obscene**.

6. *Bazaar v. Fortune* (1973; Fifth Circuit Court of Appeals)
   a. University of Missouri literary magazine had two short stories dealing with racial themes.
   b. They included "**earthy language**." Magazine was sponsored by English department and printed on campus. When stories were noticed, the printing was halted.
   c. Court said university must publish it because of freedom of speech, even though it was not an official publication of the university because it was produced by a class. Court told the school that it could put a disclaimer on the paper to protect itself.

7. *Joyner v. Whiting* (1973; Fourth Circuit Court of Appeals)
   a. President of North Carolina Central University cut off funds to paper because editor opposed integration of the historically black school and wrote about it. President was worried the school would lose government funding.
   b. Editor (Joyner) declared paper would not accept advertising from white owners nor allow white staff members.
   c. Court said school violated the First Amendment because the editor's stance had not produced **campus disruption**.
   d. Court said a college does not have to create a student newspaper in the first place, but once a paper is established, it cannot be shut down just because the administration does not like its content.

8. *Schiff v. Williams* (1975; Fourth Circuit Court of Appeals)
   a. Three editors at Florida Atlantic University were fired because the university president said that the "level of editorial responsibility and competence had deteriorated."
   b. Court said it was unconstitutional to attempt to impose administrative control on papers because their incompetence does not take away their right to print what they think.

9. *Stanley v. Magrath* (1983; Eighth Circuit Court of Appeals)
   a. University of Minnesota—*Minnesota Daily*—published a "humor issue" in 1979 with an "interview" with Jesus depicted as a "Jewish cult hero."
   b. Article angered many people, so campus allowed students to withhold their fees destined for the paper.

    c. Court said the control of funding was an attempt to control content and unconstitutional.

10. *Hays County Guardian v. Supple* (1992; Southwest Texas State University)
    a. Popular off-campus underground, freely distributed advertiser-supported newspaper that wished to be on campus.
    b. Federal appellate court ruled that administration could not use a rule against commercial solicitation on campus to ban the distribution of a free, advertiser-supported community paper.[1]
    c. Court noted that the presence of ads in a paper does not reduce its First Amendment rights.
    d. Also ruled that campus has **characteristics of public forum**.

11. *Rosenberger v. Rector and Visitors of the University of Virginia,* 515 U.S. 819 (1995)
    a. Court held religious student group should receive same school printing subsidies as other secular groups did.
    b. Held that First Amendment *establishment clause* does not require a university to withhold funding from religious group if the school supports other publications on campus.
    c. Court said university was engaged in "viewpoint discrimination" by not funding the paper.

12. *Board of Regents v. Southworth* (2000; Supreme Court)
    a. Conservative students did not want fee money going to organizations on campus they disagreed with.
    b. Court ruled that a public university may distribute mandatory student fee money to controversial organizations as long as the fee money can be reached by the campus's various student groups on a *viewpoint-neutral* basis (content neutrality?).

High School Freedoms before the Hazelwood Case

1. *Fujishima v. Board of Education* (1972; Seventh Circuit Court of Appeals)
    a. Court overturned suspension of two students who distributed an underground paper called *The Cosmic Frog.*
    b. Court said that just because the principal "predicted" school disruption, it did not give him the right to censor the paper. But, *contra* . . .

2. *Eisner v. Stamford Board of Education* (1971; federal appellate court)
    a. Court said prior restraint is acceptable if certain *procedural safeguards* are available.
    b. Court said there must be a quick *administrative remedy*: If school regulation impedes rights, there should be immediate action by the school

to review the administrator's action. If there is not immediate action taken, then a school cannot just have a blanket censorship on everything. There must be **due process**. Most courts go by this ruling.

3. *Trachtman v. Anker* (1977; Second Circuit Court of Appeals)
   a. Student journalists wanted to distribute survey on sexual attitudes to high school students.
   b. School pulled them; court said this was okay because the information could cause serious psychological harm to some students.

4. *Frasca v. Andrews* (1979; federal district court)
   a. Article talked about a heated discussion between members of the lacrosse team, and the editors and another accused a student body officer of incompetence.
   b. Principal pulled the paper because he said he predicted a disruption.
   c. Court allowed school to censor publication based on a "forecast" of disruption as a justification.

5. *Baughman v. Freienmuth* (1973; federal appellate court)
   a. Court overturned school policy that allowed prior restraint when school officials believed material in the paper was "libelous or obscene."
   b. Court said these were **terms of art** in the practice of law and too vague to be applied by students and principals.
   c. The decision stressed a need for a system of review of such censorship decisions, standards by which the review would take place, and mechanisms to ensure that the review was available in a prompt fashion.

6. *Jacobs v. Indianapolis Board of School Commissioners* (1973)
   a. Supreme Court agreed to review this case but then set it aside as moot because all the students in the case had graduated.
   b. Appellate court had said that use of "earthy language" doesn't make a publication legally obscene and that 4-letter words (or even 12-letter words) do not necessarily make a publication obscene.

7. *Gambino v. Fairfax* (1977; federal appellate court)
   a. Editor whose staff wrote an article for the high school paper on contraceptive methods challenged the school principal's censorship of the article.
   b. Principal said the material was too sensitive and controversial for the students and cut out parts of the piece.
   c. Federal district court held the paper was a public forum protected by First Amendment and the school could not censor it. Appellate court affirmed.

8. *Williams v. Spencer* (1980; federal appellate court)
   a. Student-produced underground newspaper, *The Joint Effort*.

b. School stopped distribution on campus because it contained advertising from a local "head shop" that officials believed would encourage drug use.

c. Court upheld administrator's act to censor articles about illegal drug use.

9. *Bethel School District v. Fraser* (1986; Supreme Court)

a. Washington State high school disciplined a student for giving a speech containing sexual innuendoes, even though the speech contained no four-letter words and was not obscene.

b. The student, Matthew Fraser, was a state champion public speaker.

c. Court said the school "may determine that the essential lessons of civil, mature conduct cannot be conveyed in a school that tolerates lewd, indecent, or offensive speech and conduct such as that indulged in *by this confused boy.*" Decision by Justice Burger.

Landmark Hazelwood Decision

1. *Hazelwood School District v. Kuhlmeier* (1988)

a. Missouri high school paper tried to print stories about birth control and the effects of parents' divorces on students.

b. In a surprising 5–3 Supreme Court decision, it was held that official student newspapers at high schools are not ordinarily protected by the First Amendment and that the school never intended for this paper to be a public forum.

c. Administration may censor papers if what might be said could reflect badly on the school.

d. Court said the principal may censor even though the paper neither violated the rights of other students nor threatened to cause a disruption (contrary to *Tinker*).

e. Court said administration has "editorial control over the content and style of student speech in **school sponsored activities**" (plays, musicals,

NOTE: It was commonly believed that this ruling did not extend to college papers, but since then, the question has more accurately become, Did it?

Also, some states began to give more statutory freedom to the student press in response to this decision, passing a version of a high school students' "bill of rights."

etc.) so long as the administrators' "actions are **reasonably related to legitimate pedagogical concerns**."

f. Justices Brennan, Marshall, and Blackman wrote dissenting opinions.

The Post-Hazelwood Attack in the Colleges

1. *Kincaid v. Gibson* (2001; Sixth Circuit Court of Appeals; *en banc* decision)
    a. Kentucky State University impounded all the university yearbooks in 1994 because of officials' objections to the books: they said the color was wrong; there was a lack of photo captions; there was poor editing; and it included off-campus material.
    b. Students said the real reason was that there were critical articles about the administration.
    c. District court and the federal appellate court three-judge panel first ruled that *Hazelwood* applied to student publications on the college level. Many press organizations from around the country joined in asking the Sixth Circuit Court of Appeals for a hearing *en banc*. The court agreed, and after reviewing many "friend of the court" briefs, the *en banc* court reversed the three-judge panel and the application of *Hazelwood* to college publications.
2. *Hosty v. Carter* (2003; Seventh Circuit Court of Appeals; Governor's State Case)
    a. Here, a student newspaper had been shut down after the vice president of student affairs intervened with the paper's printer, threatening to withhold payment if the administration was not allowed advance review. The students sued.
    b. The representatives for the state and the university were able to convince the district court judge that *Hazelwood* applied at the college level.
    c. On appeal, the same group of pro–college press organizations approached the court as friends of the students, and the Seventh Circuit three-judge panel issued an opinion saying—in no uncertain terms—that *Hazelwood* did not apply to publications at the college level. The court of appeals first issued a prostudent opinion, but after the state requested an *en banc* review, the full court agreed to hear the case and, in the meantime, vacated the three-judge panel's decision. The case is now pending.

Note

1. Wayne Overbeck, *Major Principles of Media Law* (Belmont, Calif.: Thomson-Wadsworth, 2004), 585.

Injury to Reputation: Defamation

J UST AS IN THE "days of old" when one could go to prison or be executed for libeling the king, one could suffer serious harm for libeling or slandering another person. The rule of law was close to what your Mother may have told you at some time, "If you can't say something nice about someone, don't say anything at all." But the law has changed since the "good old days," and this chapter helps you understand how those changes took place.

defamation—act of speaking or writing something that harms someone's
    reputation.
libel—written.
slander—verbal.

Elements Needed for Libel

1. Injury to reputation
   a. *libel per se*—Nazis, corrupt, immoral conduct.
      i. Calling plaintiff a Nazi during World War II.
      ii. Alleging corruption by public officials.
      iii. Immoral conduct by private citizens (preacher's wife, for instance).

b. ***libel per quod***:

        i. adding other facts, circumstances to the situation to be able to prove libel.

        ii. Context in which the words are used.

    c. ***libel by implication***—when you do not directly give the connection between the plaintiff and some action or situation, but a jury can see the connection in context.

> EXAMPLE: Gossip columnist notes film actor is dating so-and-so, which is not libelous until you add the fact that the actor is married.

> EXAMPLE: Same columnist writes, "Guess who our Sicilian city council member, who is in the olive oil business, eats lunch with every day at the same Sicilian restaurant? Yes, it's the only Sicilian construction magnate in town." Mafia affiliation implied.

2. Falsity—a burden shifted from the common law days.

    a. The **burden of going forward.**

        i. Plaintiff goes into a trial and establishes on its face (***prima facie***) that libel was committed. Defendant then calls for a dismissal on the grounds that the plaintiff did not establish the case. The judge reviews and answers that they have. Then defendant has the burden of going forward and proving the story was true and therefore protected.

        ii. The text books and some newer cases say that the plaintiff has the burden of proving untruth of the printed statement, just as the plaintiff must prove all other elements.

> NOTE: *Philadelphia Newspaper v. Hepps* (1986) changed the common law burden of proof.

    a. A defendant published several articles linking beverage distributor Hepps to organized crime.

    b. He could not prove that charges were false, and reporter could not prove they were true.

    c. Court said the plaintiff must bear the burden of proof in such cases to prevent self-censorship of stories by journalists, especially those who deal with public concern.

> NOTE: Although the Supreme Court has ruled that the burden of proof is on the plaintiff to show falsity, a number of state constitutions still contain provisions allowing a defendant to introduce "truth" as an element of the defense at trial.

    d. Court left cases that do not involve public concern up to the states.

    e. Private rather than public persons: publishing false statements negligently or unknowingly is enough to libel someone.

3. Publication

    a. Transmitting information to third party and not the injured person.

    b. You are not protected if you republish something. The burden falls on everyone who publishes it to determine the truth of the information.

4. Identification

    a. Living person or business may be libeled, although Texas constitution says the dead may be libeled as well. Governmental units cannot be libeled.

       i. A product of a business can be libeled. This is also called ***product disparagement.***

    b. Libeled person need not be named.

    c. Identity based on impressions of those who hear or read it.

    d. Libel may apply to small identifiable group ("Everyone knows all the waitresses at that bar have loose moral character").

5. Fault

    a. No longer strict liability, as in common law days.

       i. **Public officials must show *actual malice (AM)***—knowledge of falsity or reckless disregard—before they can sue (*New York Times v. Sullivan*).

         (1) Mere negligence not enough.

         (2) Actual malice applies to public officials (those who affect public policy) or public figures (those who are widely known, such as Madonna).

> EXAMPLE: You write in an article the name and address of a man who committed a crime. It just so happens that another man with the same name but different middle initial lives on the same street. The innocent man can sue you because you neglected to see if there was anyone else on that street with the same name.

> NOTE: These are really *tort* actions—civil wrongs from the common law tried in state courts. It is generally not a constitutional question but one of common law. There are money damages and a jury trial.

(3) Mere negligence standard applies to private citizens if the state so chooses.

(4) What if you invite public attention and comment? Can you be a limited or all-purpose public figure? Can *you* answer this question?

> NOTE: If there is a state statute concerning the required elements of a tort, then the common law requirements are void.

6. Damage or harm
   a. Actual losses (lost job, damaged reputation, psychological treatment) and punitive damages. Punitive damages are awarded to punish the person who committed the act and to discourage others from doing the same.

Defenses against Libel Suits

1. Rhetorical hyperbole
   a. Professor calls it the "Your mama's so fat . . ." defense.
   b. Everyone knows the meaning of what is said and that it is so outrageous when considered in the common language, it is not libel.
2. Fair comment privilege
   a. Statements of opinion versus statements of fact.
      i. When you write or say something and claim it is your own opinion—"In my opinion, the mayor is not doing his job properly"—this is protected.
      ii. When you state something as opinion but it can be taken as fact, then it is not protected—"I think the mayor is having an affair because he was seen leaving the local hotel with a woman late last night."
3. Courtroom privileges
   a. When something is said on a public floor, meeting, and so on, then it is protected.
      i. Includes the court, city council, school board, and so forth.
4. The truth is always a defense to actions in libel.

Who May Sue for Libel

Anyone may sue for libel except state governmental units and (in most states) the dead.

1. Libel usually seen as a *personal right*; means that the right to sue dies with the individual.
   a. Most states follow the common law rule that the heirs cannot sue on behalf of the deceased person unless they were also personally libeled.
   b. Not called a *property right* because with this type of right stays with whatever is being fought over.
2. Group libel
   a. Individuals of the group may sue for libel when a group to which they belong has been defamed.
      i. The group must be small enough that the libel affects the reputations of the individual members.
      ii. Libelous statement must refer particularly to individuals who are suing.
      iii. *class action suit*—filed by an individual for a group of people similarly situated.

distinguishing a case—when you go into court and argue that a harmful precedent used against your case really has no bearing to the circumstances at hand or is inadmissible.

> EXAMPLE: auto accident—if it happened to you, only you can collect from it.

> EXAMPLE: land—if you sell your land, a right to file suit for incursion by a neighbor passes on to the new owner.

> EXAMPLE: Enron—benefit is that, under the trial rules, you can often claim attorney fees in this type of suit.

Cases of Libel

1. The modern era of defamation law starts with *New York Times v. Sullivan* (1964).
   a. County commissioner in Alabama during the civil rights era.
   b. A group of people took out an ad in the *New York Times* in which they made allegations of wrongdoings by local public officials in Alabama.
   c. Some of the facts in the ad were wrong, so Sullivan sued on grounds of libel.

    d. Supreme Court said that "strict liability" is not constitutional in this case.

    e. Introduced the concept of requiring fault in state court libel actions.

    f. Inadvertent errors not enough to allow damage award to "public officials"; showing of *actual malice* required.

        i. "Debate on public issues should be uninhibited, robust, and wide open."

        ii. "Actual malice" means publishing with knowledge of falsity or reckless disregard (serious doubt) of accuracy.

Libel Law Redefined, Post-Sullivan

2. *Curtis Publishing v. Butts* (1967; ruled on jointly with *Associated Press v. Walker*)

    a. Publishing company in Indianapolis published the *Saturday Evening Post.*

    b. Article claimed that Butts, athletic director of University of Georgia, gave Alabama coach information in advance about Georgia's game plans for upcoming game.

    c. Reported by a man who said he had overheard the telephone conversation.

    d. *Post* did not double-check and ran the story.

    e. Supreme Court affirmed judgment of $500,000 because the *Post* had the opportunity to check its source (negligence).

3. *Associated Press v. Walker* (1967)

    a. Major General Edwin Walker, U.S. Army, retired.

    b. Present at the desegregation of University of Mississippi (James Meredith—first black student to enter the school).

    c. Group of whites attacked the marshals; Walker had addressed the crowd before.

    d. Reporter claimed (in early versions of the story) that the ex-general had led the fight.

    e. Walker sued because he was not the instigator but was trying to stop the fighting.

    f. Supreme Court did not uphold plaintiff's verdict because the circumstances were different:

NOTE: These two cases, decided together, helped to establish the requirement of applying "actual malice" to a public figure.

> NOTE: In three other 1971 cases, the Supreme Court failed to find actual malice, thereby setting aside judgments won by public officials *Greenbelt Publishing Association v. Bresler; Ocala Star-Banner v. Damron*; and *Time, Inc., v. Pape.*

      i. The reporter was under intense deadline.

     ii. He was a well-respected reporter with a reputation for accuracy at the scene.

    iii. The conduct the reporter attributed to Walker was consistent with Walker's earlier views on desegregation.

4. *Rosenbloom v. Metromedia* (1971; a blip on the screen that quickly passes)
   a. Plaintiff sued radio station for libel and won.
   b. Appellate court reversed judgment.
   c. Supreme Court upheld appellate court decision because the criteria for applying "actual malice" should be whether the plaintiff was involved in a matter of "public interest." If plaintiff was, the requirement to prove actual malice applies even if they are private citizens.
   d. This was an opinion of the Supreme Court signed by only three judges.
5. *Gertz v. Welch* (1974; *Sullivan v. New York Times* revisited)
   a. Chicago lawyer who represented a family of black man killed by police officer, helped family seek civil damages.
   b. Article in the *American Opinion* labeled him a Communist (Robert Welch, Inc., publisher from Greenwood, an Indianapolis suburb).
      i. Published by the John Birch Society, a group that thought that adding fluoride to water against people's will was a sign of Communist thinking.
   c. Gertz sued and won a $50,000 suit.
   d. Trial judge set it aside because said Gertz was a public figure (since he tried the wrongful death case) and had not proven actual malice.
   e. Supreme Court ruled that Gertz had done nothing to seek public figure status in this context. So he was not required to prove actual malice to win.
      i. Ruling finally approved by appellate court in 1982—eight years after the Supreme Court decision and **14 years after the incident!**
      ii. Ruled that **states may set a lower standard of liability for private citizens**.
      iii. Majority of states set "mere negligence" as standard.
      iv. Plaintiff who does not show actual malice limited to actual damage.

~

Example of "Mere Negligence" Cases

6. *Behrendt v. Times Mirror Company* (1939)
   a. Ralph A. Behrend and R. Allen Behrendt were doctors who worked in the same hospital.
   b. *Los Angeles Times* said that Dr. Behrendt was arrested for theft.
   c. It was actually Dr. Behrend, so Behrendt sued and won.
7. *Washington Post v. Kennedy* (1924; dealt with **identification**)
   a. Two lawyers in the District of Columbia were named Harry Kennedy.
   b. One was arrested for a serious crime, and the *Post* did not include his middle initial, which he used.
   c. The other Kennedy filed libel suit and won.
8. Jonestown Massacre (1978)
   a. Larry Layton implicated in the murder–suicide of several hundred people.
   b. Another man named Larry Layton lived in Los Angeles.
   c. The Los Angeles paper printed an article to tell its readers that the first man was not the same prominent lawyer in Los Angeles.
   d. Did this to save themselves from potential libel suit.

Privilege

Privilege—immunity from legal liability; generally in state court actions.
1. Certain people may not be witnesses for certain reasons: lawyers, doctors, confessors, accountants (some states).
2. Members of Congress, legislature, government officials, government, and so on, have **absolute privilege** for anything they say on the floor of the proceedings.
3. *qualified privilege*—libel defense that allows media to report on government proceedings and records without fear of suit, provided they give fair and accurate account. Sometimes called **conditional privilege** or **fair reports privilege**.
4. Documents that have been filed but have not been reviewed by a judge may not be privileged.
5. A story based on reports may not be protected if it comes from such sources as police case reports in cases that have not been solved yet and that have no criminal defendant indentified.
6. Media has absolute privilege only when broadcasters are required by law to provide equal airtime to candidates for public office.
   a. Broadcaster has no control over content and so cannot be sued for libel with regard to what their opponent might say.

Privilege Cases

1. *Farmer Educational & Cooperative Union v. WDAY* (1959)
   a. Court gave broadcasters absolute immunity in equal-time cases.
2. *DiSalle v. P.G. Publishing Company* (1988)
   a. Said an attorney—later a judge—helped prepare a false will as a favor to a woman he was having an affair with; got information from court deposition.
   b. Published after a court ruled the will was not fraudulent. Paper paid $3 million.
   c. Reasoning: newspapers have a duty to make sure the "privileged" information is accurate.
3. *Hutchinson v. Proxmire* (1979)
   a. "Golden Fleece of the Month Award."
   b. Proxmire gave award to people he felt were wasting tax money on useless research.
   c. Dr. Hutchinson received large grant to study teeth-clenching habits in monkeys.
   d. Proxmire issued a press release stating Dr. Hutchinson was the new winner.
   e. Plaintiff said this was libel because the public relations went beyond the senator's privilege in Congress.
   f. Court agreed and said Proxmire went beyond the floor of the Senate and that Hutchinson was a private citizen and did not have to prove malice.
4. *Dorsey v. National Enquirer* (1991)
   a. "Revealed" that singer Engelbert Humperdinck supposedly had AIDS.
   b. Received information from court document filed by woman seeking support.
   c. Also had a photo caption of Humperdinck saying the charge was false.
   d. Because they did this, they had produced a fair and accurate account of the document.

Fair Comment

1. Protects expressions of opinion about the public performances of persons, such as entertainers and politicians, who voluntarily place themselves before the public.
2. Expression has to be based on facts that are correct and accurate and has to be a critique of person's public performance rather than of their private lives.
3. May use **_rhetorical hyperbole_**.
4. *Milkovich v. Lorain Journal* (1990)
   a. High school coach sued because of story that he lied under oath.

b. Lower court said cannot prove or disprove opinion, so therefore not libelous.

    c. However, Supreme Court said the report also included some factual allegations that could be disproved, so case met requirements for a libel suit under the *Hepps* case.

5. *Moldea v. New York Times* (1994)

    a. U.S. Court of Appeals in District of Columbia said that book reviewers could be sued for expressing the opinion that a book contained "sloppy journalism." A few months later, it quickly reversed the decision to say a book review must be rationally supportable by reference to the actual text the writer is evaluating.

6. *Cochran v. NYPD Holdings* (2000; federal appellate court)

    a. *New York Post* writer, Peyser, wrote unflattering things about O. J. Simpson trial lawyer Johnny Cochran regarding the Simpson trial.

    b. Cochran sued, but court dismissed case because Payser merely exercised her right to criticize this defense strategy, not accusing him of unethical conduct.

7. *Ollman v. Evans* (1985)

    a. Columnists allege teacher was a Marxist trying to use his position to spread his beliefs.

    b. Court said statements were opinions and not actionable.

8. *Janklow v. Newsweek* (1986)

    a. Plaintiff described as having a "long feud" with Indian activist Dennis Banks arising out of Banks's allegation that plaintiff had raped an Indian girl.

    b. Federal court found statements by *Newsweek* to be opinions and therefore not actionable.

    c. Criteria for determining whether statement is libelous fact or protected opinion.

       i. Specificity and precision of the statement.

      ii. Verifiability of the statement.

     iii. Literary context in which the statement is made.

     iv. "Public context" of the statement, as to whether it is made in the political arena or which implicates core value of the First Amendment is more likely to be seen as opinion.

Private Persons and Public Figures

1. *Time, Inc., v. Firestone* (1976)

    a. Tire company heir and wife divorce in a very publicized, "seedy" proceeding.

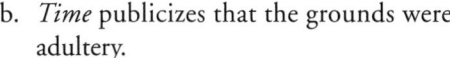

    b. *Time* publicizes that the grounds were adultery.

    c. Obscure Florida law says there could be no alimony ordered if adultery found.

    d. Magazine did not know this and printed.

    e. Wife sued, won; she was considered a private citizen, did not have to prove actual malice.

> NOTE: Many people in the news are not public figures unless they take actions that would cause controversy or public criticism or notoriety.

2. *Wolston v. Reader's Digest Association* (1979)

    a. Narrowing the definition of a public figure.

    b. Wolston had an aunt/uncle who pleaded guilty to charges of spying.

    c. He was also cited for contempt but never convicted.

    d. Years later the *Digest* includes a list of Soviet agents with his name on it.

    e. Supreme Court said he had done nothing to inject himself into a public controversy.

Setting the Limits of Actual Malice

1. *Bose v. Consumer's Union* (1984)

    a. Bose sued *Consumer Reports* for a negative product review.

    b. A 1970 article said that these speakers have music that "wanders around the room."

    c. Fifth Circuit Court of Appeals reversed decision, said the magazine was not guilty of actual malice.

    d. Appellate court reviewed the trial court's **assessment of the facts**.

    e. Supreme Court upheld decision, ruling the media require the additional protection of being able to appeal a trial court's **factual** determination of actual malice.

2. *Dun & Bradstreet v. Greenmoss Builders* (1985)

    a. The defendant was a credit-reporting agency that falsely told clients that the plaintiff (a construction company) was going out of business.

    b. Mistake due to a new worker's error in record checking.

    c. Supreme Court ruled that credit ratings are not matters of public concern and therefore not subject to actual malice rule.

    d. Means that actual malice should apply to cases involving public concern only, not to purely private matters.

3. *Herbert v. Lando* (1979)

    a. Military officer sued *60 Minutes* and sought "state of mind" evidence.

    b. Show's producers refused to cooperate, but court said that First Amendment was no immunity from normal rules of discovery.

c. This meant that plaintiffs are entitled to use the discovery process to check on the journalists' attitudes and thoughts to help prove actual malice.

4. *Newton v. NBC* (1990)
   a. Singer sued over allegations that he was involved in questionable business matters and had ties to organized crime.
   b. Jury awarded $5.3 million.
   c. Ninth Circuit Court of Appeals reversed, saying he had not proved actual malice.

5. *Harte-Hanks Communications v. Connaughton* (1989)
   a. Supreme Court rules *Hamilton Journal-Beacon* falsely reported that Connaughton had wrongfully tried to discredit an election opponent.
   b. Supreme Court ruled that actual malice was present because paper failed to check its sources or listen to tape-recorded interviews that would have cast doubt on the accuracy of the allegations.

6. *Anderson v. Liberty Lobby* (1986)
   a. Magazine articles in which Anderson called Carto, founder of Liberty Lobby, a neo-Nazi.
   b. Trial judge dismissed case because it said Anderson had done extensive research, so the plaintiff cannot say that he had a "reckless disregard for the truth."
   c. Supreme Court ruled that if Carto cannot show "clear and convincing" proof he could win the case, it should be dismissed without subjecting the media to the expense of a trial.

Complexity and Defense of Modern Libel Suits

1. *Philadelphia Inquirer* (1990)
   a. Paper charged Sprague had once dropped a murder investigation as a favor to a police official whose son had been present at the crime.
   b. Jury awarded $34 million, reduced to $24 million by appellate court.
   c. Settled in 1996, event occurred in 1973—23 years of court.

2. *Dallas Television* (1991)
   a. Waco, Texas, jury awarded $58 million to district attorney who was accused by station of accepting payoffs to drop drunk-driving cases.
   b. Verdict was appealed and settled amount out of court.

3. *Wall Street Journal* (1997)
   a. Houston jury awarded $222.7 million to investment brokerage that went out of business after the paper reported on firm's alleged difficulties.
   b. Judge later threw out $200 million punitive damages, and later the rest because the plaintiff's law firm had withheld crucial evidence that would have corroborated the story.

4. *Food Lion v. Capital Cities/ABC* (1997)
   a. ABC had two staff members obtain jobs at the Food Lion under false pretenses.
   b. Used cameras to document mishandling of food.
   c. Jury found ABC guilty of trespass and fraud.
   d. Trial judge reduced the $5.5 million award to $315,000, and then Fourth Circuit Court of Appeals reduced that to just $2 (staffers applied for jobs falsely).
5. *Brown and Williamson Tobacco Company v. Jacobson* (1987)
   a. U.S. Court of Appeals in Chicago awarded $3.05 million against CBS.
   b. Case resulted from broadcasts by Chicago news anchor Walter Jacobson accusing tobacco companies of targeting young people in their advertising. Reporter used an unused ad as his example.
   c. In 1994 ABC had the same type of story but decided not to run it because of fear of suit. Reported that the tobacco companies were spiking their cigarettes to keep people hooked
      i. Philip Morris filed a $10 billion lawsuit.
      ii. In 1995 ABC paid $15 million to drop the case—used cost of defense payment.
         (1) Take the probability of success, multiply by the potential judgment, and add the cost of litigating.
         (2) Although ABC apologized, the reporter and producer did not, because they said they could document their findings.

> NOTE: Rule 11—federal trial rules (not in all states). Allows for the defendant to order the plaintiff to pay for defense cost and attorney fees if the plaintiff files a frivolous lawsuit. Can also be used by the plaintiff if a defendant refuses to cooperate in such things as producing evidence or appearing for questioning. The plaintiff gets an order for the defendant to pay the cost of having the evidence obtained.

6. *Masson v. New Yorker Magazine* (1991)
   a. Psychoanalyst sues *New Yorker* for publishing an article containing six quotes he denied making.
   b. Malcolm (writer) taped their interviews but also had some non-recorded; plaintiff said the misrepresentations of his views injured his reputation.
   c. Lower court dismissed his libel case, but Supreme Court reinstated, saying the quotes were significantly different from the taped conversations.

d. Established that so long as a journalist does not change the meaning of the quotes, minor changes are protected.

e. In 1996, appellate court finally upheld verdict that Masson had not proven his case. This ended a 12-year court battle with legal fees to the defendant of $2.5 million.

Retractions

Most states require that a plaintiff must demand a retraction of the challenged material before filing a lawsuit. If plaintiff does not, then cannot claim punitive damages (in some states). In others, the amount that might be claimed as emotional damages or lost wages can be limited.

The retraction must retract all libelous charges and be as prominent as the original libel. Each state is specific, and local law should be examined.

1. *Carol Burnett v. National Enquirer* (1983)
   a. Trial court ruled *Enquirer* a magazine, not a newspaper, depriving it of the protection of the retraction statute.

Jurisdictional Cases

1. *International Shoe v. Washington* (1945)
   a. This case is known for the rule that any corporation or other business entity may be sued in any state where it has "minimum contacts."
2. *Keeton v. Hustler* (1984)
   a. Even where the publication and the plaintiff had little contact with the state, the Supreme Court would not extend constitutional protection to journalists who argued that they should not be subject to lawsuits all around the country. ***Forum shopping*** was allowed.
3. *Calder v. Jones* (1984)
   a. Supreme Court again allows "forum shopping"—looking for the longest statute of limitations or some other benefit in libel cases.

Suits to Stop Public Action

SLAPP lawsuits—strategic lawsuits against public participation.
   a. Corporations sometimes sue activists (environmentalists) when they speak against a corporate project.
   b. It is an attempt to silence their critics.

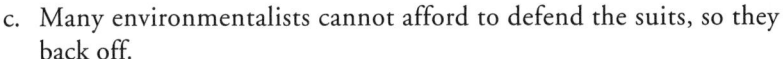

   c. Many environmentalists cannot afford to defend the suits, so they back off.

anti-SLAPP statute—legislation brought into effect that says if a plaintiff files a meritless lawsuit to discourage the defendant, then the defendant can require the plaintiff to pay attorney fees. It also allows the court to dismiss the frivolous lawsuit. This protects public participation. In effect in a minority of states. Differ from state to state.

Libel and Emotional Distress

1. *Hustler v. Falwell* (1988)
   a. Magazine did a parody (satirical version) of a Compari liquor ad, substituting the Reverend Jerry Falwell for the usual type of character used in the ads. Instead of talking about his first encounter with Compari, he talked about his "first sexual experience," allegedly with his mother in an outhouse.
   b. Sues for libel and intentional infliction of emotional distress. Gets jury verdict of $200,000 for emotional distress claim but not for libel.
   c. Lower federal court says plaintiff need not prove actual malice to recover under theory of intentional emotional distress.
   d. Supreme Court overturns verdict, saying public figures must prove actual malice in emotional distress cases, just as they would in libel cases.

Oprah, Product Disparagement, and "Veggie Libel"

1. *Auvil v. CBS 60 Minutes* (1995)
   a. Washington State apple growers sue network because program alleged chemical used by growers was carcinogenic.
   b. Growers contended that big dip in sales followed the broadcast, costing them $130 million.
   c. Suit dismissed by federal appellate court because the growers could not prove the broadcast was false.
2. *Engler v. Winfrey* (2000)
   a. Texas cattlemen sue Oprah after she discussed mad cow disease on her show.
   b. Cattle prices had dropped sharply after the broadcast.
   c. Judge dismissed "veggie law" claim but allowed trial under general theory of business loss.
   d. Jury not convinced that Oprah intended to harm Texas cattle industry.

Libel in Fiction

1. *Pring v. Penthouse* (1983)
   a. Former Miss Wyoming sues magazine over an article dealing with a fictitious Miss America contestant from Wyoming who was skilled in baton twirling and other interesting things.
   b. Jury verdict of $26.5 million set aside by federal appellate court who said the fiction described impossible events.
   c. Court says the writing investigated must be reasonably understood as describing actual facts about the plaintiff or acts in which she participated.

The Right of Privacy

I N THESE MODERN TIMES, it is hard to visualize a period when celebrities and politicians were not hounded by packs of camera crews and reporters and when the perpetrators and victims of crimes were not constantly on television with microphones in their faces. Now, as many people warn us that our privacy is being lost bit by bit, it does a student well to understand how far we have come in establishing these rights and what we stand to lose.

penumbra of rights—this idea arises when the Bill of Rights is taken as a whole and when things such as the right to privacy are implied from the entire view. It says that the Bill of Rights was made to preserve the integrity and sanctity of the home, which means that the bill also protects those unmentioned rights, such as an individual's right to privacy, the right to travel freely, and the right to freely associate with those you choose.

Right of Privacy

1. Violating the right of privacy (**ROP**) is a *tort*, a civil wrong for which an injured party can sue for monetary compensation.
2. Basically a state legal matter and a relatively new legal action.

~

3. Samuel D. Warren and (later) Justice Louis Brandeis first addressed the privacy issue in an 1890 essay in the *Harvard Law Review* that stated there should be a ROP under the common law or state statutory law. This was the origin of the ROP, although it did not become prominent in law immediately.

4. *Roberson v. Rochester Folding Box Company* (1902)
   a. Roberson's picture was used in a flour ad without her permission.
   b. She sued and the New York appellate court ruled that ROP still did not apply in the legal system, but New York legislature enacted the first privacy law soon after.

5. *Pavesich v. New England Life Insurance Company* (1905)
   a. Georgia Supreme Court held that the artist could sue for the use of his likeness in an ad without his permission.
   b. This was the first case that recognized invasion of privacy (IOP) as a tort.

6. *Sidis v. F-R Publishing Company* (1940)
   a. Dealt with the issue of a media outlet being able to write the "where are they now" stories.
   b. Plaintiff sued *New Yorker* magazine for an article that talked about what happened to him after he graduated from Harvard at the age of 16.
   c. The truth was embarrassing to him, so he sued.
   d. He lost because the federal appellate court said **anyone who is a celebrity, even involuntarily, cannot escape the possibility of publicity later in life** ("newsworthy").

7. *Olmstead v. United States* (1928)
   a. Criminal case in which wiretap evidence is used from homes and business.
   b. Louis Brandeis, now on the Supreme Court, says there needed to be a ROP.
   c. Argues that the framers of the Constitution constructed a system wherein people should have a "right to be let alone" by the government.

8. *Griswold v. Connecticut* (1965)—**real beginning to the ROP**
   a. Emphasized the **penumbra of rights** included with the Constitution.
   b. Supreme Court overturned a state law that banned contraceptive devices.
   c. Court stated that the ROP does not allow a state to interfere in an individual's sexual relations in marriage.

9. *Katz v. United States* (1967)
   a. Criminal case. A person's ROP extends to all areas where there is a "justifiable expectation of privacy," according to a concurring opinion by Justice Harlan.

10. *Roe v. Wade* (1973)
   a. Supreme Court overturned state law that banned abortions.
   b. Stated that abortions were private matters between a woman and her doctor.
11. *Webster v. Human Reproductive Services* (1989)
   a. Supreme Court ruled Missouri's ban on abortion in public hospitals, ban on counseling by public employees, and requirement to test fetus for viability were all legal and permissible.
12. *Planned Parenthood of Southeastern Pennsylvania v. Casey* (1992)
   a. Supreme Court upheld Pennsylvania law that required a 24-hour waiting period for women wanting abortions and requiring teenagers to have parental consent before they could receive abortions because the requirements were not "undue burdens."
   b. However, the court overturned the requirement that married women must first tell their husbands before having an abortion.
   c. These decisions, which were handed down by a surprisingly moderate–conservative court, kept *Roe v. Wade* in place.
13. *Stenberg v. Carhart* (2000)
   a. Supreme Court ruled that Nebraska law banning "partial birth abortions" was unconstitutional limitation on women's ROP.
14. On June 1, 2004, a federal judge in the Northern District of California struck down the federal Partial-Birth Abortion Ban Act of 2003, finding the federal statute "vague" and saying it placed an undue burden on the mother in each such case. *Planned Parenthood v. Ashcroft*, 2004 U.S. District LEXIS 9775 (2004).
15. In May 2004, privacy advocates won another battle in the Ninth Circuit Court of Appeals when the court upheld the only law in the nation that allows physician-assisted suicide for terminally ill patients. The court used strong language in rebuking U.S. Attorney General John Ashcroft for interfering in an area historically reserved to the states. *Oregon v. Ashcroft*, 368 F.3d 1118 (2004)

> NOTE: The phrase "partial birth abortion" is not really a medical term. It is a political term coined by abortion rights opponents.

Alternative Lifestyle Cases

1. *Bowers v. Hardwick* (1986)
   a. Supreme Court ruled against privacy rights for homosexuals under the U.S. Constitution by stating that a Georgia law banning sodomy, regardless of gender or marital status, was legal.

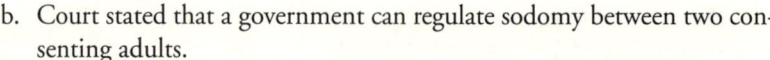

b. Court stated that a government can regulate sodomy between two consenting adults.

c. After this, some state governments enacted their own privacy laws for homosexuals, since they were not covered under federal privacy laws.

2. *Lawrence v. Texas* (2003)

Supreme Court says states cannot, by law, prohibit homosexuals from engaging in sexual activities that would be legal for heterosexuals. This was a criminal case, and defendant was denied equal protection under the Fourteenth Amendment.

The Four Privacy Torts

∼ Commercial Appropriation ∼

1. *commercial appropriation* (of name and likeness)
   a. Someone uses it for **commercial purposes** (trade/self-enrichment).
   b. Also called *misappropriation* or *right of publicity*.
   c. Infringement of the right of publicity, common in advertising and entertainment communications.
   d. The right of publicity does not apply to news situations even though they are commercial.
   e. Virtually every form of commercial advertising falls within the restrictions of the right of publicity, including print and electronic media.
   f. A person may consent to the use of their image for commercial purposes, and this is often done. If the person later challenges the consent form or if circumstances greatly change (i.e., they became very famous), courts will usually examine two issues:
      i. Was there *consideration* or payment for the use of the image (often referred to as *quid pro quo*)?
      ii. Was the person who signed the consent form legally competent to do so (age)?
   g. If the court rules negatively on these issues, the consent may be withdrawn. Note the case of Brooke Shields, *Shields v. Gross*, 7 Med.L.Rptr. 2349 (1981).

Cases Dealing with Commercial Appropriation

1. *Haelan Laboratories v. Topps Chewing Gum* (1953; Second Circuit Court of Appeals)

a. Dealt with baseball players who wanted to control the commercial use of their names on cards and chewing gum.

    b. Court said that they have this "right of publicity." No one should be allowed to use a person's name, likeness, or persona without their consent.

2. *Johnny Carson v. "Here's Johnny"* (1983; federal appellate court)

    a. Identity by reference to part of Carson's public ***persona*** (essence of who he is).

    b. "Here's Johnny" portable toilets, marketing product using Carson's famous line.

    c. Carson sued and won because the phrase was so connected with him, it was a misappropriation.

3. *Sinatra v. Goodyear* (1970; federal appellate court)

    a. Goodyear used Nancy Sinatra's song and her trademark miniskirt and boots in an ad for "Wide Boots" tires.

    b. Court ruled that this was not a misappropriation because neither the song nor the clothing were closely enough associated with her.

    c. The use of the song was actually not an issue because the company had received permission from the copyright holder.

4. *Bette Midler v. Young & Rubicam* (1989; federal appellate court)

    a. Ford Motor Company's ad agency got Midler's longtime backup singer to sing one of Midler's signature songs, imitating her distinctive voice in the commercial.

    b. Midler sued and won, saying her voice was distinctive enough for people to recognize on its own and that they would believe that she endorsed the product.

5. *Vanna White v. Samsung* (1992; federal appellate court; identity by reference)

    a. The company featured an ad with a robot in the same type of clothing and jewelry as Vanna would wear, standing in front of a game board.

    b. Court said she had viable reason to sue (taking of her ***persona***), and she won.

6. *Wendt v. Host International* (1997)

    a. Actors who played Norm and Cliff in *Cheers* sued because a company was placing robot figures that resembled them in airport bars made to look like the *Cheers* bar.

    b. The actors and Paramount (copyright owner of *Cheers* who had allowed the use of the bar scene by Host) settled out of court.

7. *Playgirl v. Muhammad Ali*, 447 F.Supp. 723 (1978)—likeness used

    a. Ali turns down photo request on basis of religious belief. Magazine hires look-alike for a picture shoot.

b. You did not see his face and he did not talk, but they had him in a ring with the same type of boxing gear and gloves worn by Ali.

c. He sues and wins because he did not give them permission to use his likeness for the ad.

8. *Woody Allen Case,* NY 679 F.Supp. 360 (1988)—use of likeness

a. Allen has played clarinet at Manhattan bar every Tuesday night and was well known for this.

b. Advertiser uses a look-alike and the particular type of wooden clarinet in a picture as an apparent endorsement for a product.

c. Allen sues and wins because of the fact that he never endorses anything.

Cases Dealing with Misappropriation and the News

Photographers who use people's images are liable for damages unless they have consent. They may shoot any subject in public places for news purposes, but not for commercial ads, and they must be safe.

1. *Cher v. Forum* (1982; federal appellate court)

a. Cher had granted an interview for the magazine *Us.* However, when the article was rejected, the journalist took the article to *Forum* and *Star,* where it was published.

b. *Forum* ran the article with an ad and her picture and a statement that implied her endorsement of the magazine.

c. Cher sued both papers, but lost to *Star* because the court said *Star* did not violate her ROP by publishing a "newsworthy" story.

d. But she did win against *Forum* because of misappropriation of her image in the ad.

2. *Zacchini v. Scripps-Howard Broadcasting* (1977; Supreme Court)

a. Plaintiff called himself the "Human Cannonball."

b. Television station tapes and airs the man's entire act on the news.

c. He sues and recovers because it was his privacy that was invaded.

d. Court said that a broadcaster who tapes and airs a performer's entire act and shows it as "news" is not protected because of the economic hardship this could cause the plaintiff.

Cases Dealing with Misappropriation and the Deceased

1. *Lugosi v. Universal Pictures* (1979; California Supreme Court)

a. Ruled that a **personal right** dies with the person.

    b. The Lugosi family claimed that Universal was violating their public-ity rights by selling shirts and memorabilia with the likeness of the Dracula actor.

    c. Court said that the "right of publicity" cannot be inherited.

    d. California legislature eventually passed a law that allowed the publicity rights of the deceased to be passed on to heirs for 50 years after the person's death.

2. *Factors v. Pro Arts* (1978; federal appellate court)

    a. Ruled the publicity right of Elvis Presley, "the King," was a **property right** and passed to his heirs.

    b. This was then **overturned by the same court** three years later, which stated that the right does not survive his death (this was in accordance with a Sixth Circuit case interpreting Tennessee law in 1980).

    c. Tennessee legislature then passed an act changing the law, granting rights to the family.

3. *Comedy III Productions v. Gary Saderup, Inc.* (2001; California Supreme Court)

    a. Larry Fine and Mo, Curly, and Shep Howard formed the Three Stooges.

    b. There was a rejuvenation of the show in the 1950s, after Shep and Curly were dead.

    c. Tried to make other movies in the 1950s and 1960s with a stand-in for Curly named "Curly Joe." Made a few bad movies, but old black-and-white reels are still shown on television.

    d. Heirs sued T-shirt maker because he used images without their permission; heirs won. The heirs have control because California now sees **property rights** instead of **personal rights**, and these can be passed on through the estate.

> NOTE: Testates can designate who their estates go to; intestates are settled by the court and usually divided to all relatives based on degree of relation.

intestate—person dies without a will.

testate—person dies with a will.

> NOTE: The California Supreme Court allowed a comic-book maker to do cartoons based on Edgar and Johnny Winters because they were "fanciful creative characters." *Winters v. DC Comics*, 30 C.4th 881.

∼ Intrusion ∼

2. *intrusion*—the "news gatherers' tort"; legal action to compensate a person when a journalist unduly intrudes into his or her physical seclusion or private affairs.

   Elements or indicators of intrusion on physical seclusion:

   a. Entering physical seclusion or private affairs in a manner that is "**highly offensive** to a reasonable person."
   b. Conduct that also violates criminal laws (trespass, harassment).
   c. Disguises, false pretenses, hidden cameras.
   d. Entering into areas where there is an expectation of privacy: home, office, ambulance, hotel room, dressing room, public toilet.
   e. Compare visiting a "quack doctor" in his home versus quack in a public medical center.

Cases Dealing with Intrusion

1. *Dietemann v. Time, Inc.* (1971; federal appellate court)
   a. *Life* magazine undercover reporters investigate a man who "practices medicine" in his home.
   b. It results in prosecution for quackery and an article in the magazine about quackery.
   c. Man sues and wins for IOP; magazine had a right to write the story but not to use hidden cameras and microphones **in the man's house** (common law: "A man's home is his castle").
2. *Florida Publishing Company v. Fletcher* (1976; Florida Supreme Court)
   a. **Contra** to above case (*contra* is the legal form of "contrary").
   b. Photographer takes picture of girl's body outline left on the floor of a burned building.
   c. The mother sues for IOP.
   d. Court rules this is not actionable because the disaster is of **public interest** and that it is normal for a photographer to go to scenes of crimes with police (police asked him to shoot these pictures).
3. *Galella v. Onassis* (1973; federal appellate court)
   a. Defendant photographed Jacqueline Kennedy Onassis and family.
   b. Ordered by court to stay 25 feet away, even in public places.
   c. Eventually found in contempt for continually violating this regulation.
4. *Desnick v. ABC* (1995; Seventh Circuit Court of Appeals)
   a. ABC had people with hidden cameras pose as patients at a cataract clinic.

   b. Found out they did unnecessary surgeries on Medicare patients.
   c. Court ruled that the clinic did not have grounds to sue for IOP; actions
       done in public.
5. *Berger v. Hanlon* (1997; Ninth Circuit Court of Appeals)
   a. CNN and federal wildlife agents teamed up on a raid of a Montana
       rancher accused of killing bald eagles.
   b. Berger was acquitted, and he then sued.
   c. Court said that federal officers should be given qualified immunity from
       ride-along liability because law was not clear at the time, but CNN was
       not offered the same.
6. *Deteresa v. ABC* (1997; Ninth Circuit Court of Appeals)
   a. Allowed a reporter the right to secretly tape a conversation with a reluc-
       tant source on her front porch and use a small part on the air.
   b. Court held that she had no reasonable **expectations of privacy** when
       she talked to a person she knew was a television producer and who was
       on her porch, where anyone could hear.
7. *Shulman v. Group W Productions* (1998; California Supreme Court)
   a. An accident victim sues because news crew shoots the accident and the
       victim being taken care of. The court ruled that media can be sued for
       intruding on accident victims. The most troubling aspect was that the
       crew recorded Shulman's postaccident conversation by having the medics
       wear hidden microphones.
8. *Wilson v. Layne* (1999; U.S. Supreme Court)
   a. Police entered Wilson home with a *Washington Post* reporter/photographer
       in search of the homeowner's son.
   b. While no photos were published, the Wilsons sued officers for allow-
       ing media in.
   c. This case established that media and law enforcement risk liability for
       ride-along.
9. *Sanders v. ABC* (1999; California Supreme Court)
   a. "Psychics" worked in cubicles off-limits to nonemployees. Reporter went
       undercover and used a hidden camera to tape them without their
       knowledge.
   b. Court ruled that ABC could be sued for reporter going undercover as
       a psychic to record conversations of employees who had an **expectation
       of privacy** in the workplace.
   c. But a federal appellate court says that, to recover, the plaintiff must
       be able to show the "intent" to commit a crime. *Sussman v. ABC,* 186
       F.3d 1200 (1999), ***cert. den.***

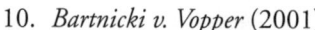

10. *Bartnicki v. Vopper* (2001)
    a. Supreme Court ruled that broadcasters have a right to air newsworthy—but pirated—recorded cell phone conversations. Seen as not violating the wiretap laws.
    b. Concerned a tape of two officials of a teachers' union disgruntled about salaries.
    c. It aired on Vopper's talk show because he said it was of great public interest and dealt with public policy. Media did not encourage illegal taping or participate in it.

∿ Public Disclosure of Private Embarrassing Facts ∿

3. **Public disclosure of private embarrassing facts.**

Cases Dealing with Public Disclosure of Private Embarrassing Facts

1. *Melvin v. Reid* (1931; California appellate court)
   a. Movie showed the past activities of a former prostitute charged with murder but acquitted.
   b. The woman had moved to another town and changed her lifestyle after the trial.
   c. Her new friends knew nothing of her past.
   d. She sued for IOP.
   e. Court said that media could be sued for publishing information about a person's shady past, and it used a "social utility test" to determine whether something is newsworthy.
2. *Briscoe v. Reader's Digest* (1971; California Supreme Court)
   a. *Reader's Digest* had published the name of a convicted man 11 years later.
   b. The man had been rehabilitated and started a family, and no one knew of his past.
   c. Court allowed the lawsuit to proceed, though plaintiff eventually lost the case.
   d. 2003—California court says *Briscoe* may no longer be law because of recent U.S. Supreme Court decisions. *Gates v. Discovery Communications*, 106 C.A. 4th 677.
3. *Cox Broadcasting v. Cohn* (1975)
   a. News broadcast of rape victim's name learned through a copy of court records.
   b. Supreme Court said that the media could not be sued for reporting information that was legally obtained in open court records.

4. *Virgil v. Time, Inc.* (1975; federal appellate court)
   a. *Sports Illustrated* writer did a profile on a surfer.
   b. He had given his consent but then, at the last minute, withdrew consent.
   c. *Time* published it anyway, and Virgil sued.
   d. Court ruled that they had produced a **newsworthy** article and were protected.
5. *Smith v. Daily Mail* (1979; U.S. Supreme Court)
   a. Journalists were indicted after naming a 14-year-old charged with shooting a schoolmate.
   b. Learned the name from eyewitnesses.
   c. Case made it clear that prosecution of media was not an appropriate way to prevent the leak of juvenile names.
6. *Diaz v. Oakland Tribune* (1983; California appellate court)
   a. Student body president had been a boy and had a sex change.
   b. No one knew about it until an article appeared in the paper.
   c. She sued and won, but appellate court overturned verdict and sent it back to the trial court, saying the burden was on the plaintiff to show that the story was *not* newsworthy and that it was not the defendant's burden to show that it was newsworthy.

NOTE: For public disclosure of private embarrassing facts to apply:
a. Disclosure must be "highly offensive to a reasonable person" (fact question for jury).
b. Acts that occur in public places are generally not actionable.

---

   i. **Contra**: Alabama air-jet case, *Daily Times Democrat v. Graham*, 276 Ala. 380 (1964).
      (1) At a carnival a reporter took a picture of a woman coming out of the fun house with her dress flying in the air because of a floor jet at the exit.
      (2) While it was in public, it was not intended for public use and was an embarrassing private act.
      (3) Alabama Supreme Court said exposure was against Mrs. Graham's will and was not newsworthy. Publication therefore outraged the public's sense of decency.
   c. Information lawfully obtained in "a matter of public significance."
      i. But, question the ethics of the act of publication.
   d. Newsworthiness a complete defense . . . public's right to know.

    i. Social value of the information versus depth of intrusion.
    ii. Consider legitimate public interest versus humiliation.
    iii. Consider the lapse of time.

False Light

4. *false light*—a minority rule among the states.

Cases Dealing with False Light

1. *Gill v. Curtis Publishing Company* (1952)
   a. A photo was published in *Harper's Bazaar* and in the *Ladies' Home Journal* of a couple who owned a store at a Los Angeles farmer's market. They were in a tender moment and did not give the photographer permission to take the picture.
   b. The *Harper's Bazaar* article portrayed the picture in a good light. *Ladies' Home Journal,* however, portrayed the picture with an article about the dangers of love at first sight
   c. The couple sued and lost the first case against *Harper* but won the second because there was no basis for the article saying their relationship was built on love at first sight or on instantaneous sexual attraction; thus, it portrayed them in a false public light.

> NOTE: Corporations can sue for defamation (product disparagement) but not for IOP.

2. *Cantrell v. Forest City Publishing Company* (1974)
   a. Newspaper coverage of a fatality victim in an Ohio bridge collapse and how his family was dealing with the loss.
   b. Reporter talked to children while mother was not home, when he was doing a follow-up story that contained a lot of errors and talked about the family's economic condition.
   c. Supreme Court upheld judgment of $60,000 in her favor because the paper knew that it was publishing falsities.

---

a. **false light**—you make people appear other than what they are.
b. Duty to investigate identity.
c. Damages different from those owing to libel: personal embarrassment and anguish, not damage to reputation.

Related Torts

1. Fraud—*Food Lion v. ABC*
   False representation of fact when reporters "applied for work" under false pretenses.
   a. Knowledge of falsity.
   b. Intended to induce reliance.
   c. Justifiable reliance by Food Lion on "employee" representations.
2. Intentional infliction of emotional distress, also known as "outrage."
   Hustler v. Falwell sets the limits by which such a claim may be made by public figures.
   Armstrong v. H&C Communications, Inc. (1991; Florida District Court of Appeals)—broadcast a story of a girl abducted at age three, body found at age six. Unwarned, the family watched the evening news program during which a police officer was shown lifting the child's skull out of a box. Out of court settlement: $175,000.
   Contra: *Florida Publishing Company v. Fletcher* (1976; Florida Supreme Court)—photographer shoots picture of a body outline of a child who died in a fire; puts photo in paper. Photographer had been asked by police to take the picture. Court denies recovery of damages because "the fire was a disaster of great public interest and it is clear that the photographer and other members of the news media entered the burned home at the invitation of the investigating officers."

Related Criminal Statutes

Some states have information-gathering statutes—Freedom of Information Acts (FOIAs)—that allow ways to get government documents. Thus, criminal statutes regarding reporter misbehavior have been held constitutional.

Wiretap laws . . . nearly as old as the phone.

Many states ban tapping unless both parties are aware it is occurring.

Some states require only one person in the conversation to know.

Defenses

1. Incidental use **(misappropriation)**
   Person is just in the picture but not important to the message.
2. Consent
   a. In consent cases, look for *quid pro quo*/age.

> EXAMPLE: picture of a shopping mall with people walking in front of it.

     i. *quid pro quo*—"something for something."

     ii. **consideration**—has the subject received something of value for their picture?

       (1) Publicity is a valid form of consideration.

       (2) Is what you gave the same value as what you get?

     iii. Must be voluntarily entered into.

       (1) A written consent is always better than an oral one.

       (2) Must be broad enough to apply to any situation where likeness might be used.

3. *Age*—one cannot get an eight-year-old to endorse a movie contract without consent of an adult or parent, or sometimes, approval from the court.

   a. Usually informed consent starts as 18.

NOTE: Photographers should not get consent for the publication of only one paper at one time. Make sure it is for subsequent uses by all media, including publications' Web pages.

Internet and Privacy

1. *TBG Insurance Services v. Superior Court* (2002; federal appellate court)
   If an employer provides an employee with a home-use computer with the understanding that it will be used for business purposes only, employee has no reasonable expectation of privacy that would deny the employer access to the computer's files.

2. *Intel Corporation v. Hamidi* (2003; California Supreme Court)
   Employer could not block former employees antiemployer messages to current employees under a theory of trespass, because it interfered with his free-expression rights.

   The 1998 Online Children's Privacy Protection Act was passed by Congress to limit the collection of information about children under the age of 13 without parental consent. It also limits the child's ability to have e-mail without parental consent.

   While United States has no Internet privacy law, Europe does. The European Union (EU) requires member countries to implement data-protection standards to avoid improper use of personal information gained from the Internet.

If countries outside the EU do not have such standards, then the EU does not allow companies from those countries to do business in Europe. Companies in countries that do maintain such standards are also barred from transferring information to another country that does not have these standards.

Employees' E-Mail

Employers have the ability to intercept e-mail that coworkers send to one another through corporate servers. But, there has been discussion about the legality of intercepting e-mail between workers that are sent through outside message systems.

Intellectual Property

T HE FOUNDERS of this country were very much in favor of the government's encouraging and protecting writers, composers, artists, and inventors. Thus, early in the Constitution, Congress is given the power to grant "for limited times" the rights we now know as patents, trademarks, service marks, and copyrights. Patents and inventions are not covered in this chapter. To do so would require another book entirely.

Intellectual Property Law

1. *Intellectual property law*—the law governing copyright, trademark, and patent.
   a. *copyrights*—protect books, papers, manuscripts, music, film, software, art.
   b. *trademarks*—protect words, phrases, symbols identifying products or services.
   c. *patents*—protect inventions and scientific processes.
      i. Initially evolved from the English common law.
      ii. It was written into the U.S. Constitution in Article 1, section 8.
      iii. Shortly after ratification of the Constitution, Congress enacted the Copyright Act of 1790.

iv. Copyright protection is now automatic: once material is **fixed in a tangible medium of expression**, it is copyrighted.

(1) Also called *common law copyright*.

v. A copyright lasts about 95 years—more or less—as stated in the **Berne Convention**.

See *Elderd v. Ashcroft*, 537 U.S. 186 (2003).

2. Copyright law gives the owner the **exclusive right** to reproduce the work, create derivative works, distribute copies, or perform or display it.

a. *exclusive right*—only the holder of the copyright can determine how the work is used or copied. He or she can shorten, lengthen, rewrite, or rearrange the work; or perform or display the work or any derivative work he or she may choose to create. The owner can sell or give away any or all of these rights, in part or whole.

b. *derivative work*—a product of the original, such as a movie made from a book.

c. The news itself cannot be copyrighted; only the description of it. This means the information cannot be copyrighted, only the way it is put together by the journalist, broadcaster, and so on (protects the style of the information, not the actual information).

d. A news medium cannot take all of its news from one source, change it around, and send it out as its own so that they do not have to hire a news staff. This is called *unfair competition* as well as *news piracy*.

e. Historical or scientific information, ideas, processes, or inventions cannot be copyrighted.

3. *compulsory licensing*—when the owner gives others the right to arrange and perform a work in return for the payment of royalties. The law actually **requires** that the owners of musical works allow anyone to make a sound recording of their work once it is publicly performed. The second artist pays the royalties specified by law for each copy that is sold and agrees that there will not be any major changes to the piece without the owners' approval. The owner cannot allow one person to use the copyrighted work and not another.

Compulsory licensing does not include **synchronization rights**, the process of combining the music and visuals in a video or karaoke performance.

works made for hire—when a person creates a work for their employer, the copyright is the employer's, not the creator's. Courts will look to the facts to determine the type of relationship it is.

4. Registering a work

a. Complete the form and pay $30 fee.

b. Send in copy of work to the copyright office at the Library of Congress.

> NOTE: If you have not registered your copyright and it is infringed on, you may still sue, but you must first register the copyright. As a result of not registering before an infringement occurs, you lose the ability to collect the same amount of damages.

    a. When it is registered, your remedies include
        i. injunction;
       ii. court-ordered impounding of all offending copies;
      iii. court-ordered payment of the owner's attorney fees; and
      iv. actual or statutory damages, whichever is greater.
    b. When it is not registered, the copyright owner may not get an award of attorney fees or a choice of taking statutory damages.
5. Displaying a copyright notice—you must have three things displayed when you claim copyright of a work:
    a. (C) or the copyright symbol © ;
    b. date (year); and
    c. author's name.

Proving Copyright Infringement

Plaintiff must show:
    a. a ***substantial similarity*** between the original and the copied work;
    b. a **valid copyright of the original**; and
    c. that the accused must have had **access** to the original.
1. George Harrison case—*Bright Tunes Music Corporation v. Harrisongs Music, Ltd.*, 420 F. Supp. 177 (1976) . . . good example of all elements.
    a. Plaintiff claimed that Harrison's song "My Sweet Lord" was copied from "He's So Fine" by a group called the Chiffons of the early 1960s. They have virtually the same melody.
    b. Harrison argued he did not know of the earlier song and did not mean to plagiarize it.
    c. The court ruled that the song must have influenced him in some way, even on an unconscious level, so he lost.
2. *Feist Publications v. Rural Telephone Services Company* (1991)
    Supreme Court said that only an original arrangement of facts can be copyrighted, not the facts themselves (telephone book information cannot be copyrighted).

> NOTE: In the end, the court ordered Harrison's former manager to sell
> Harrison the rights to "He's So Fine" so that Harrison ended up with
> the rights to both songs and could keep selling his own as well as the
> original. Also, it should be noted that much of the Beatles' early musi-
> cal influence came from American rhythm and blues, so it was unlikely
> that Harrison had never heard "He's So Fine."

3. *Fogerty v. Fantasy* (1994)
   a. Supreme Court said that **both** the plaintiffs and the defendants may ask
      the court to order the other side to pay their attorney fees if they win.
   b. Singer Fogerty was sued by his former manager because, according to
      the manager, Fogerty's new songs were too much like the old ones he
      had sung for his old label.
   c. Fogerty won, and the other side was ordered to pay attorney fees.
4. *Feltner v. Columbia Pictures Television* (1998)
   Supreme Court ruled that a defendant has the right to a jury trial in a copyright case since the case dealt with ***statutory damages***—sum of money a
   court may award, based on the copyright statute, when actual damages are
   either hard to prove or are nominal.

Cases Explaining Elements of Copyright

1. *Stewart v. Abend* (1990)
   a. Actor Jimmy Stewart and a group wanted to rerelease the movie *Rear
      Window*.
   b. Abend had purchased the rights to the original short story from which
      the movie was made, from the heirs of the author.
   c. After the 28-year copyright term had expired, the heirs renewed the
      copyright before Abend purchased it from them.
   d. The Supreme Court held that Abend was right in saying that Stewart
      had to renegotiate for the rights to the original story to release the movie
      because the right to release the movie died with the expiration of the
      first copyright term.
   e. As a result of this case, there was a **derivative works exception** put into
      the copyright act, which says that owners of derivative works do not lose
      their rights in the derivative works when the copyright of the original
      work is renewed.

2. *Batjac Productions v. GoodTimes Home Video Corporation* (1998; federal appellate court)
   When the copyright of a movie expires and the movie enters the public domain, the screenplay for the movie also enters the public domain.
3. *Community for Creative Nonviolence v. Reid* (1989; Supreme Court)
   Dispute arose because the organization had hired Reid to do a sculpture.
   a. The organization argued the copyright belonged to them because they had paid him for the work as a "work for hire." Reid claimed that he did it under contract.
   b. The court said Reid owned the copyright because he was not on the organization's regular payroll and not an employee (working as an independent contractor almost always gives the creator the sole ownership of the copyright, unless otherwise specified in a contract).
   c. The copyright will likely belong to employers if
      i. they are withholding taxes;
      ii. they provide the tools; and
      iii. they tell the person when to work and when not to.

   The 1976 Copyright Act—the latest total revision of U.S. copyright law—did away with the **state common law copyright** system for works published after January 1978. As of that date, all state laws relating to copyrights were preempted, superseded by federal law.

Fair Use Doctrine

Must look at four things to decide if a secondary work is *fair use*:
   a. purpose of the secondary use;
   b. the nature of the original work;
   c. the percentage of total original work used in the secondary work; and
   d. the effect the use will have on the profit-making capability of the original work.
1. *Basic Books v. Kinko's Graphics Corporation* (1991; federal appellate court)
   Large-scale use of printed copies to make "course booklets" was seen as not being fair use. This idea reinforced by an *en banc* ruling in the Sixth Circuit, *Princeton University v. Michigan Document Services*, 99 F.3d 1381 (1996).

NOTE: As a result of this case, Congress included a provision with complicated rules for libraries in 1976 act. Consult your textbook and confer with your teacher if you have questions.

---

2. *Williams and Wilkins v. United States* (1973; federal appellate court)
   Court ruled medical journal knowledge was so important that a hospital medical library could copy the journals and pass them around to medical staff (purpose of secondary use).
3. *Rosemont Enterprises v. Random House* (1966; federal appellate court)
   Court refused to stop unauthorized autobiography of billionaire recluse Howard Hughes although it was based—in small part—on a magazine article he owned the rights to. Court saw a ***legitimate public interest*** in the doings of the rich and powerful (purpose of secondary use).
4. *Time, Inc., v. Bernard Geis Associates*, 293 F.Supp. 130 (1968)
   a. *Time* owned the Abraham Zapruder film of the JFK assassination.
   b. Geis wanted to use a few frames in a book. They denied him permission.
   c. He used drawings of the photos instead.
   d. Court says it is an infringement, but there is a **legitimate public interest** in knowledge concerning the president's assassination, so this was fair use (all four elements of fair use).
5. *Estate of Martin Luther King v. CBS*, 194 F.3d 1211 (1999)
   a. Federal appellate court rules that King's "I Have a Dream" speech was his creative work and that the copyright passed to his family.
   b. CBS could not, therefore, use it in its entirety (nature of original and percentage used).

Unpublished Works

1. *Harper & Row Publishers v. The Nation Enterprises*, 471 U.S. 539 (1986)
   a. *The Nation* gets hold of 300 words from the autobiography of Gerald Ford before the book's release.
   b. Court rules it was the heart of the book—about Ford's pardon of Richard Nixon—and interfered with the marketability of the book.
   c. Court said it was piracy, not fair use.
2. *New Era Publications v. Henry Holt & Company*, 873 F2d 576 (1989)
   a. Church of Scientology moves to block publication of 41 unpublished writings by its founder, L. Ron Hubbard, in an unauthorized biography.
   b. Court says it was not "fair use," as material had not been published.

NOTE: Congress reacts to case by amending the fair use portion of the Copyright Act in 1992 to extend fair use protection to previously unpublished material.

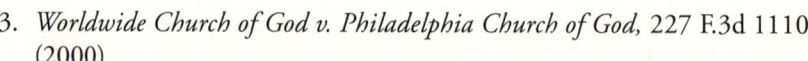

3. *Worldwide Church of God v. Philadelphia Church of God,* 227 F.3d 1110 (2000)

   Court says holder of a copyright may later bar use by anyone else, even if the holder chooses to no longer publish the work.

NOTE: See also, *Salinger v. Random House,* 811 F.2d 90 (1987) certiorari denied, 108 Supreme Court 213.

Television News, Clipping Services, and Fair Use

1. *Georgia Television Company v. Television News Clips of Atlanta,* 983 F. 2d 238 (1993)

   "Video clipping" services that copied stories from news programs for clients were not seen as engaging in fair use.

   1993—the "Rodney King beating tape" was seen to be of such great public interest that its copying and reuse by others was seen as fair use.

   But 1997—*Los Angeles News Service v. KCAL-TV,* 108 F.3d 1119, said that the videotape of the beating of Reginald Denny during the riots that followed the King–police officer trials riots (filmed by LANS and used by KCAL for its own television news program) was not fair use because it was unauthorized and therefore illegally copied.

   But 2002—Court TV was allowed to use a few seconds of the Reginald Denny tape in a nonnews fashion (promotion of its coverage of the trial of the perpetrators of the beating) because of the brevity of the segment.

Fair Use and the Parody Doctrine

1. *Fisher v. Dees,* 794 F.2d 432 (1986)

   "When Sonny Sniffs Glue" seen as a legitimate *parody* of "When Sunny Gets Blue." It was clear, the court said, that the second "poked fun at the composers" and at Johnny Mathis's rather singular vocal range and was not intended to tap the same market as the original.

2. *Campbell v. Acuff-Rose Music, Inc.* (1994)

   a. Supreme Court says 2 Live Crew's "Pretty Woman" was a **parody** of Roy Orbison's "Oh, Pretty Woman."

   b. Distinctive bass line and first line of lyrics were the same.

   c. Song seen as having "transformative value."

> NOTE: Consider the percentage of the original taken and whether the second tapped the market for the first. A **parody** can be defined as "a humorous imitation of a serious piece of literature, music or other writing." It makes fun of a particular work.

3. *Dr. Seuss Enterprises v. Penguin Books,* 109 F.3d 1394 (1997)
   a. Reporter and artist who used the distinctive Seuss styles of writing and drawing to poke fun at the O. J. Simpson trial were *not* engaged in fair use.
   b. *The Cat NOT in the Hat, a Parody by Dr. Juice* was not a **parody** of the well-known *The Cat in the Hat.*

   Advertising and fair use—two Circuit Courts have held that it is permissible to use images of a competitor's product in advertising of your own.

   Sony Computer Entertainment v. Bleem, 214 F.3d 1022 (2000; Ninth Circuit)

   Triangle Publications v. Knight-Ridder Newspapers, 626 F.2d 1171 (1980; Fifth Circuit)

> NOTE: 2001, *The Wind Done Gone.* The Eleventh Circuit Court of Appeals ruled that the slave-oriented version of *Gone with the Wind* had new characters and plot lines and was not an infringement on the original as an unauthorized derivative work but more likely a parody. A suit by the estate of Margaret Mitchell was not entitled to an injunction because it served as a prior restraint and censorship. The parties settled the dispute, and the second book was published and sold.

Copyright and Music

1. ***Royalties*** for playing another's music go to the author or copyright owner, not the performer.
2. ***compulsory licensing***—anyone can record copyrighted music simply by paying the specified royalties. 2 Live Crew's "Pretty Woman" is an example of this policy.
3. **BMI** and **ASCAP**—two large groups that collect royalties, then pay them to the copyright holders.
   a. Even from night clubs, radio stations, churches, marching bands, and so forth.

b. A series of cases have resulted in the rule that retail stores that play music over only one stereo unit with nearby speakers do not have to pay royalties, regardless of the store size.

4. Recording technology

a. *Sony Corporation of America v. Universal Studios* (1984)—in a 5–4 decision, the Supreme Court said videotaping something from VCR is not necessarily copyright infringement. **Noncommercial** use is seen as "time shifting," which the court said was **fair use**.

5. Audio Home Recording Act (1992)—a fee is placed on the sale of all digital recording equipment and tapes or discs that took the place of actual copyright royalties. Consumers are allowed to make one copy for **noncommercial** use.

Copyright in the Age of Computers and the Internet

1. Personal computers have posed many problems for federal regulators and courts, including the question of whether software can be patented or copyrighted. Apple Computers won two big early cases that said the programming language that created the program and the system could be copyrighted, *Apple Computer, Inc., v. Franklin Computer Corporation,* 714 F.2d 1240 (1983; Third Circuit).

   See also, *Apple Computer, Inc., v. Formula International,* 725 F.2d 521 (1984; Second Circuit), where court found that the computer program was "an original work affixed to a tangible medium."

   But Apple had filed a series of lawsuits designed to protect the "look and feel" of the Apple user system. In 1995, Supreme Court refused to review all of the dismissals of the Apple suits, leaving Microsoft open to continued efforts to copy the Apple look. By and large, the courts are not too keen on making rulings that would keep new ideas out of the market place.

2. In 1992, two federal courts allowed decisions to stand wherein one toy maker made "Game Genie," which allowed players to extend speed, ability, and "lives" in Nintendo games, *Galoob Toys v. Nintendo of America,* 964 F.2d 965 (1992). Competitors may also "tear down" the computer code of others and use it to make modifications for compatible games of their own, *Sega Enterprises v. Acolade, Inc.,* 977 F.2d 1510 (1992).

3. 1998 Digital Millennium Copyright Act—requires VCR manufacturers to place software in their VCRs that will disable copying attempts. Also gives protection to "cookies" on the Internet. Allows those claiming copyrights to shut down infringing websites unless they acknowledge the owner's site as well. Established new rules for digital copyrights for pictures, sound, and

so on. Banned technology that could work around encryption software on tapes and discs that barred them from being copied.

4. File sharing and the Digital Millennium Copyright Act—problems brought around by the formation of Napster and others. Copy-coded formats are being tested that would bar reprinting of new-music CDs. Lawsuits are also being filed against hundreds of the leading offenders. The act found not to violate First Amendment, *Universal City Studios v. Corley*, 273 F.3d 429 (2001).

5. Sound Recording Act of 1995 made many broadcasters leery of broadcasting through the Internet—or webcasting—because of the high cost of having to pay two royalties. Act allows payment of one fee large enough to cover all the royalties that might have arisen from college radio stations playing a lot of music and webcasting, too. A copyright arbitration royalty panel arrived at a proposal that frightened many college radio stations, but the final figures were finally arranged.

6. Freelancers and online publishing—*New York Times Company v. Tasini*, 533 U.S. 483 (2001).

   Supreme Court sides with freelance writers and says newspapers were paying only for "first publishing rights" and not for the rights to publish the writers' stories in the Internet version of the paper or in anthologies.

7. Copyrights apply to Internet sites—*Playboy Enterprises v. Sanfilippo*, U.S. District Lexis 4773 (1998). Defendant operates website with 7,500 *Playboy*-owned photos. *Playboy* gets $3.74 million judgment for infringement. *Playboy* also won other suits in the late 1990s. But in *Playboy Enterprises v. Welles*, 162 F.3d 11 (1998), 279 F.3d 796 (2002), court said defendant could use the title "former Playmate of the Year" because it is a title she would hold for life, like Heisman winner or ambassador to the Court of St. James.

Copyright and the International Community

United States joined the Berne Convention in 1989, adding copyright protection for U.S. materials in 24 countries. Congress also passed the Sonny Bono Copyright Term Extension Act in 1998. Other treaties were also signed, the two main results being the following.

NOTE: Instructors will have varying standards by which they expect their students to know some or all of these periods. We can assume for general purposes that a period of approximately 95 years will apply, give or take a few years.

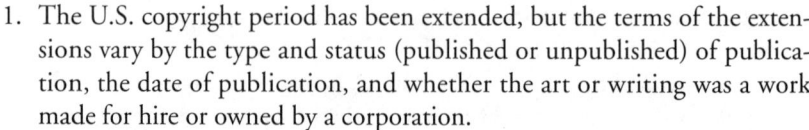

1. The U.S. copyright period has been extended, but the terms of the extensions vary by the type and status (published or unpublished) of publication, the date of publication, and whether the art or writing was a work made for hire or owned by a corporation.
2. By signing the Berne Convention, the United States agreed in principle to acknowledge the **moral copyrights** that stay with the creators of works. These allow the creator some say in how the piece is subsequently used, even if the copyright is sold to someone else.

Internet Domain Names

1. The Internet was developed and paid for by the U.S. government. Originally called **ARPAnet**, until the U.S. military withdrew to form a more secure network in the late 1960s.
2. ICANN, Internet Corporation for Assigned Names and Numbers, now oversees the operation.
   Network Solutions, Inc., is in charge of all domain-name registration.
3. In the beginning, "cybersquatters" registered the trademarks and trade names of others, then demanded large sums to release the names to the rightful owners.
4. *Panavision International v. Toeppen,* 141 F.3d 1316 (1998)
   Court rules defendant was in violation of the Federal Trademark Dilution Act for engaging in cybersquatting.
5. *Brookfield Communications v. West Coast Entertainment,* 174 F.3d 1036 (1999)
   Court says trademarks have priority over registration of domain names. Company that held the trademarked name the longest was given the domain name.
6. *Toys R Us v. Akkaoui,* U.S. District Lexis 17090 (1996)
   Adult entertainment site named "AdultsRus.com" was ordered to stop using the name because it would tarnish or dilute plaintiff's trademark.
7. *Bally Total Fitness v. Faber,* 29 F.Supp.2d 1161 (1998)
   Site expressing anger toward the plaintiff—which included the plaintiff's logo on the site with the word *sucks*—is held not to be a trademark infringement but is seen as protected First Amendment activity.

Unfair Competition

1. Also called *misappropriation* (not to be confused with violation of privacy).
2. It is a violation if one news outlet routinely uses another as a source of information, then passes the information off to others as though it were its own

work, *International News Service v. AP,* 248 U.S. 215 (1918); *Pottstown Daily News Publishing Company v. Pottstown Broadcasting* 192 A.2d 657 (1963; Pennsylvania Supreme Court).
3. It is not infringing to broadcast sports scores while game is still going, *NBA v. Motorola* 105 F.3d 841 (1997).

Trademarks

1. Short phrases, logos, designs symbols, and names—can be either state (intrastate) or federal (interstate). Federal good for 10 years but may be renewed in perpetuity. "Coca-Cola," "Kleenex," and "Xerox" are closely guarded trademarks. Aspirin, cellophane, cornflakes, yo-yo, and linoleum once were but expired.

> NOTE: Unlike copyright, no such thing as a common law trademark exists.

2. Plexiglas, Styrofoam, and Dolby are all trademarks. So is the MGM lion's roar and the three-note NBC chime but not the sound made by Harley-Davidson motorcycles.
3. The Supreme Court said that Taco Cabana could stop Two Pesos restaurants from using the same design of its interior because some "looks" may have "inherent distinctiveness" that can be protected, *Two Pesos v. Taco Cabana,* 505 U.S. 763 (1992).

> NOTE: If the trademark is properly registered, it will usually bear the ® mark. If it is claimed but not registered, it can be shown as ™.

4. The Trademark Law Revision Act of 1988 allows for **treble damages** for plaintiffs who have been the victim of false comparative advertising. The Federal Trademark Dilution Act of 1995 allows a suit for "blurring" or "tarnishing" a trademark. EXAMPLE: "Cocaine" in "Coca-Cola" lettering.

> NOTE: It can be anticipated that copyright and trademark problems on the Internet will multiply in the future because of the development of Internet II—the fastest-ever version of the Net—and the expansion of the number and types of domain extensions (.gov, .com, .edu, etc.). This expansion will allow much greater opportunity for cybersquatting.

5. *Mosely v. V Secret Catalogue, Inc.,* 537 U.S. 418 (2003)—Supreme Court
   bars Victoria's Secret from stopping Victor's Little Secret, a Kentucky sex
   shop, from using the name. Court notes "no showing of a lessening of
   plaintiff's capacity to distinguish its own good and services" from Victor's
   Little Secret's.

Internet II is now being developed at a limited number of universities. The
hardware is centered on the campus of Indiana University–Purdue University
at Indianapolis.

Prejudicial Publicity and Fair Trial Issues

T HERE ARE TIMES when courts are faced with true conflicts between provisions of the U.S. Constitution, which is itself supposed to be the highest arbiter of any conflicts in American law. So how do we work out two provisions of a document that seem to be in opposition to each other? In this chapter, we review how the courts have balanced the public and press's "right to know" with a criminal defendant's right to a fair trial by a jury of his or her peers.

The Balancing of First and Sixth Amendment Rights

Opponents to the Press's Involvement in the Judicial System

A jury's job is to find one guilty or not guilty in a criminal case, not to find whether the defendant has good moral character. So, past records are considered irrelevant in courts of law. But sometimes the media bring past events to the attention of the public, such as by reporting unsubstantiated information or rumor or by "revealing" the existence of a confession when there was not one. Because of this, it can be quite difficult to find an impartial jury who has not been influenced by the media.

Supporters of the Press's Role in the Judicial System

The media keep the public informed about society and the people in it. The press is a "watchdog" that monitors the justice system. In addition, the media's right to cover the news is constitutionally protected.

> EXAMPLE:
> O. J. Simpson case.

1. A criminal jury acquitted Simpson of killing his ex-wife and her friend, but a civil jury found him liable for the deaths, a verdict that was upheld on appeal, *Rufo v. Simpson* 86 C.A. 4th 573 (2001).
   a. In sum, 95 million people watched the vehicle pursuit (the white Bronco) live, and incriminating details were widely publicized.
   b. In 1994, a judge disqualified the Los Angeles County grand jury from hearing evidence to issue an indictment because they might be prejudiced by the widespread publicity.
   c. Instead, the case went to a preliminary hearing, with live news coverage broadcast as far away as the Arctic Circle in the Yukon Territory.
   d. Viewers saw scenes the trial jury was not permitted to.
   e. The jury was sequestered during the actual criminal trial.
   f. The criminal court jury verdict was viewed by the largest television audience in history.
   g. Many people believe the real trial took place in the media and not in the courtroom.
2. The case altered the justice system.
   a. California legislature barred witnesses from selling their stories to the media because of the large amount of money some of the O. J. witnesses received prior to actually testifying.
   b. The California First Amendment Coalition won an appeal that found this law unconstitutional.
   c. California restricted what lawyers can say to the media.
   d. Judges wrestled with the idea of continuing television coverage of celebrity trials.
   e. South Carolina television was banned from covering the Susan Smith trial (drowned her sons).
   f. California barred cameras from the Richard Allen Davis case (celebrated murder case).
   g. Cameras barred from the Menendez brothers trial (murder of wealthy parents).
   h. Cameras were also barred from the civil lawsuit for O. J.
   i. Heavy limits on cameras for Timothy McVeigh, Oklahoma City bomber.

3. Rodney King case
   a. The videotape of his beating and the rioting after the police officers were acquitted became major media stories.
   b. Videotape caused racial tension in Los Angeles because it was a black man beaten by white officers.
   c. The police trial was moved out of Los Angeles to a white suburban town.
   d. Jury concluded that there was not enough evidence beyond a reasonable doubt.
   e. The media were blamed for a large share of the uproar because it was said that the media failed to explain the beating in its actual context (King's offenses and criminal history).

Fair Trial and Free Press Become Issues

Supreme Court has struggled with this issue for more than 50 years.
1. *Irvin v. Dowd*, 366 U.S. 717 (1961)
   a. First case to reverse a state murder conviction because of ***prejudicial publicity***.
   b. Leslie Irvin convicted of murdering six people in Kentucky and Indiana.
   c. He had been arrested on suspicion of writing bad checks and burglary.
   d. Under pressure to name a murder suspect, the local prosecutor called Irvin the "mad dog" and said he had confessed to the murders, which Irvin denied.
   e. He was widely known as "the mad dog killer."
   f. There was a ***change of venue*** to a nearby county that had also seen extensive media coverage of the case and the alleged confession.
   g. A request for a second change of venue (farther away) was denied.
   h. In total, 430 potential jurors were examined; 370 had formed an opinion about his guilt; of the 12 jurors seated, 8 said that they thought he was guilty but promised to be fair.
   i. Irvin's lawyer could not keep them off the panel because he had already used all of his ***peremptory challenges***.
   j. Supreme Court reviewed the case five years later and found he had received an unfair trial.
   k. He was retried 1962, convicted of one murder and sentenced to life.
2. *Rideau v. Louisiana*, 373 U.S. 723 (1963)
   a. Wilbert Rideau arrested and charged with robbing a bank and killing an employee.
   b. He confessed during jailhouse interrogation.

   c. The session was filmed and shown on local television.
   d. The Supreme Court said it was a denial of his right to a fair trial not to grant him a change of venue since the public had been repeatedly exposed to this information.
   e. He was retried, convicted, and sentenced to life.
3. *Sheppard v. Maxwell* (1966)
   a. Called "the trial of the century."
   b. In 1954, the wife of Dr. Sam Sheppard, an osteopath in Ohio, was murdered in their home while he was there asleep.
   c. He claimed it was the "bushy-haired intruder" who had done it.
   d. The local papers demanded Sheppard's conviction.
   e. They took over the courtroom and even published the jurors' home phone numbers as pressure to gain a guilty verdict.
   f. Sheppard was convicted, and it was upheld in the Ohio courts.
   g. Supreme Court first declined to review the case.
   h. In the 1960s, his lawyers asked the Supreme Court to again look at his case after the issue of free press/fair trial became important.
   i. In 1966 the conviction was reversed; in a new trial, he was acquitted.
   j. Four years after acquittal, at age 46, he died, having spent more than ten years in prison.
   k. In the 1990s, the case was reopened with Richard Eberling as the suspect.
   l. DNA testing and other evidence pointed to him as the real killer.
   m. The doctor's son, Sam Reese Sheppard, filed a lawsuit for wrongful conviction.
   n. The media sympathized with the son, but the court did not; it rejected his suit in 2000.
4. The Sheppard case was the **landmark** Supreme Court decision on free press/fair trial:
   a. In an 8–1 opinion, court ruled that the state trial judge had not done his duty in protecting Sheppard from the prejudicial publicity.
   b. The court instructed trial judges what they must do to ensure a fair trial.
      i. Adopt rules to curtail in-court misconduct by reporters.
      ii. Issue protective orders (or **"gag" orders**) to control out-of-court statements by trial participants, such as parties, witnesses, and lawyers.

NOTE: These rules are designed to compensate for potentially prejudicial publicity or eliminate such publicity.

---

iii. Grant a continuance of the trial until community prejudice has had time to subside.

    iv. Grant a change of venue to where there has been less-prejudicial publicity.

    v. ***Admonish the jury*** to disregard the media publicity about the case.

    vi. ***Sequester the jury***—that is, remove a jury panel from the regular community for the duration of a trial.

Gag Orders

Also called "protective orders" or "restrictive orders"—the most controversial remedy that came out of the Sheppard trial.

Fall into two categories:

a. Those directed to the participants in the trial, ordering them not to reveal prejudicial information to the public or the media (usually holds up in court).

b. Those directed against the media, ordering them not to publish prejudicial information, even if they obtain it lawfully (usually do not hold up well in higher courts).

Other Remedies to Be Used before Gag Orders

1. Change of venue
    a. Can be expensive.
    b. And with today's media, the new venue may have been just as saturated with the case as the venue where the crime had been committed.

2. Postponement of a trial
    a. Denies right to speedy trial.
    b. Witnesses often become unavailable after a time.
    c. There is no guarantee the publicity will not start up again as the new trial approaches.

3. Sequestering the jury
    a. Many jurors are not willing to serve on a case when they are isolated.
    b. Can be very expensive.
    c. Becomes almost impossible to completely isolate jurors from the media.

4. Questioning the jurors about the prejudices during *voir dire*
    a. They may say they are impartial when they really have strong feelings.

5. Admonitions to the jury to disregard publicity
    a. People realistically cannot do this. They will take everything they know, whether they are supposed to or not, and draw a conclusion from it.

Gag Orders as Prior Restraints

Gag orders were widely used in 1970s. Most courts would issue orders to those involved to avoid speaking with the press about the case or any information regarding it. But some judges would even try to bar the media from publicizing information they already had. From 1967 to 1975, 174 such orders were issued, including 50 that involved some prior restraint of the media.

1. *Nebraska Press Association v. Stuart*, 427 U.S. 53 (1976)
   a. Rule virtually eliminated gag orders that restrained the press.
   b. Erwin Simants murdered six people in their home; he turned himself in and confessed.
   c. There were major questions about his mental state (IQ 75).
   d. Preliminary hearing judge ordered the media not to publish any of the testimony.
   e. The media appealed to district court judge Stuart.
   f. Stuart said the media could not publish certain prejudicial information.
   g. Nebraska Supreme Court refined order to ban publishing Simants's confession or any information that strongly implicated the suspect.
   h. Media appealed to Supreme Court, which ruled that the order was a violation of the First Amendment because it imposed prior restraint on the press.
   i. But the court did not completely rule out orders against the media in the future. It said that in extraordinary cases, the orders could be imposed, but **there must be enough evidence** to conclude that
      i. there will be intense and pervasive publicity covering the case;
      ii. no other alternative measures will mitigate the effects; and
      iii. the restrictive order will effectively prevent prejudicial information from reaching potential jurors.
2. *United States v. Cable News Network* (1994)
   a. Judge ordered the taped conversations between Manuel Noriega and his lawyers—in CNN's possession—not be broadcast.
   b. The order was appealed by CNN, but the Supreme Court refused to hear the case.
   c. The original judge later reviewed his order and decided that the broadcast of the tapes would not interfere with Noriega's right to a fair trial and thus removed the gag order.
   d. In 1994 U.S. Attorney's office filed contempt of court charges against CNN for broadcasting the tapes while the order was in effect, and CNN was fined.

> NOTE: When a federal judge tells you not to do something, don't do it.

Protective Orders and Trial Lawyers

1. Although the *Nebraska Press* case placed limits on the power of judges to "gag" the press, it did not limit the inherent power judges have to control the actions of trial participants.
2. In all, 40 states have rules on what lawyers can publicly say concerning a newsworthy case.
3. American Bar Association (ABA) has a set of guidelines that are voluntary but upon which many states base their mandatory rules.
   a. ABA rule 3.6 states that lawyers may not make out-of-court statements they know may reasonably cause prejudice in the case.
   b. This rule applies only to lawyers involved in the case and while the case is pending.
   c. ABA rule 3.8 bans prosecutors from making "extrajudicial comments that could heighten public condemnation of the accused."
4. *Gentile v. State Bar of Nevada* (1991)
   a. Gentile was a criminal defense lawyer who was disciplined for making improper public comments after a client was indicted.
   b. He appealed, and the Supreme Court held that the Nevada rules were too vague and thus violated his First Amendment rights.
   c. The ABA eventually set new limits on what trial lawyers could say on pending cases.

Voluntary Guidelines Constructed by the Press

1. In the 1960s and 1970s, many state media groups joined with the state bars and developed voluntary guidelines on coverage of newsworthy cases.
2. ABA created committee under Massachusetts Supreme Court justice Paul C. Reardon to develop these guidelines.
   a. Came to be known as the Reardon Report.
      i. Urged restraint by all parties in releasing prejudicial information to the press.
      ii. Urged judges to hold lawyers and those who release information in contempt.
      iii. Endorsed closed preliminary hearings if the information presented might hinder the right to a fair trial.
      iv. Urged local groups of lawyers, judges, and journalists to set their own guidelines.
      v. While they were widely opposed, these guidelines formed the basis for similar local rules in 23 states.

3. *Federated Publications v. Swedberg* (1981)
    a. Washington judge forced journalists to abide by the voluntary guidelines if they wanted to be allowed into the court for certain courtroom proceedings.
    b. This meant reporters could not report on things overheard in an open courtroom.
    c. Appealed to the **Washington Supreme Court**, which said the order was a reasonable means of avoiding a closed hearing. Court found no prior restraint.
4. *Seattle Times v. Ishikawa* (1982)
    a. Said a judge must weigh certain factors before barring journalists or sealing records.
    b. Must consider alternative means to protecting the defendant and must allow anyone to object to the closure.
    c. If the reason behind the closure is anything other than the right to a fair trial, there must be much stronger justification for the closure.[1]

Courtroom Closure

1. Courts can be closed for several reasons:
    a. to protect a defendant's right to a fair trial;
    b. to protect individual's privacy;
    c. ensure secrecy of information affecting national security;
    d. to keep the police investigation details confidential; and
    e. as in the 1970s, to hinder the release of prejudicial publicity.
2. *Gannett v. Depasquale* (1979)
    a. Supreme Court upheld an order barring newspaper reporter from a pretrial evidentiary hearing in New York.
    b. Two men charged with murdering a policeman.
    c. Allegedly confessed to the crime and were indicted.
    d. Both the defense and the prosecution decided to close the pretrial hearing because of the intense publicity.
    e. Gannett newspapers appealed to the state Supreme Court, which upheld the order.
    f. In 5–4 U.S. Supreme Court decision, the court said the Sixth Amendment right to public trial belongs to the defendant, not the public, and the defendant has the right to waive public trial.
    g. This case stood as precedent to allow judges to at least close pretrial hearings if the danger of prejudicial publicity outweighed the public's right to attend.[2]

3. *Richmond Newspapers v. Virginia* (1980)
   a. County judge closed court at the fourth trial of a man who had been charged with the murder of a hotel manager.
   b. First trial had been invalidated "by a technicality," and the other two were mistrials.
   c. The judge closed the trial based on a Virginia statute.
   d. The defendant was acquitted.
   e. Richmond papers appealed the decision; Virginia Supreme Court upheld ruling.
   f. The U.S. Supreme Court overturned closure in a 7–1 decision saying that the public's right to attend trials was a legitimate right even if it was not specifically stated in the Constitution.
4. *Globe Newspaper Company v. Superior Court* (1982)
   a. Supreme Court overturned Massachusetts law that closed all trials involving juvenile sex crime victims.
   b. A judge had closed the rape trial where the victims were three girls under 18.
   c. *Boston Globe* challenged the closure; state supreme court upheld it.
   d. In a 6–3 decision, the U.S. Supreme Court said that each judge must evaluate each case before making the decision to close. There cannot be an automatic law allowing this.
   e. Justice Brennan said the right of the public of access to trials is not absolute; that act can close a trial if
      i. there is a "compelling government interest" that requires it; and
      ii. the law requiring the closure is "narrowly tailored to serve the interest."[3]
5. *Press Enterprise Company v. Superior Court* (1984; PE I)
   a. Supreme Court unanimously overturned a California judge's decision to close six weeks of jury selection and to make no transcript of the selection public in a 1981 murder trial.
   b. The judge had refused to make a transcript of the jury selection public after the defendant was convicted of raping and murdering a 13-year-old girl and the death sentence imposed.
6. *Waller v. Georgia* (1984)
   a. Supreme Court overturned an order to close a pretrial evidence-suppression hearing where the police had searched homes and done wiretaps to uncover gambling. Court again cites rights of the press and public to be present and says they may be barred only for some compelling reason.
   b. The defendant had argued that the evidence had been obtained unlawfully.

~

   c. Defendant requested that the trial be open to the public; the judge refused.

   d. The judge then admitted much of the challenged evidence and convicted some defendants of various crimes.

7. *Press-Enterprise Company v. Superior Court* (1986; PE II)

   a. Supreme Court ruled that preliminary hearings and other pretrial proceedings must be open unless it can be shown "(a) there is a substantial probability that the defendant's right to a fair trial will be prejudiced by publicity that closure would prevent, and (b) reasonable alternatives to closure cannot adequately protect the defendant's fair trial rights."

   b. The *Riverside Press* appealed the closing of a 41-day preliminary hearing concerning a male nurse charged with killing hospital patients.

8. *El Vocero de Puerto Rico v. Puerto Rico* (1993)

   a. A journalist tried to attend a closed preliminary hearing and was turned down.

   b. He appealed the Puerto Rican trial rule.

   c. The U.S. Supreme Court held that the law was unconstitutional and that they must allow access.

> NOTE: All of these cases up until now involved criminal proceedings; we now look at civil court proceedings, starting with Clint Eastwood's case.

9. *NBC Subsidiary v. Superior Court* (1999)

   a. California Supreme Court overturned restrictions that a judge imposed on the press and public during the "palimony" trial of Clint Eastwood and Sondra Locke.

   b. State supreme court recognized a constitutional right under the First Amendment that allows the public to attend civil trials.

   c. First time any state Supreme Court recognized this right.

Courtroom Documents

1. Many lower courts have ruled that public has a right to see and copy court documents.

2. They have normally been open to the public, except in child custody investigations, but recent decisions have established a First Amendment right to this.

3. *Associated Press v. District Court* (1983; federal court of appeals)

   a. Federal judge closed some pretrial proceedings and sealed documents in John DeLorean case (set up cocaine deal to save his automobile company).

   b. The court ruled that the order violated the First Amendment right to access.

    c. The decision also included recognition that the First Amendment also covers court documents.

    d. Court said this right must be balanced with defendant's right to fair trial: judge must determine if

        i. allowing public access would cause "a substantial probability" that irreparable damage to the fair trial would result;

        ii. there are not alternative ways to protect the right;

        iii. there is a substantial probability that the secrecy will actually prevent the defendant's rights from being violated; and

        iv. as in this case, there had already been extensive coverage.[4]

4. *Valley Broadcasting Company v. United States District Court* (1986; federal court of appeals)

    a. Case involving the racketeering trial of Mafia man Anthony Spilotro.

    b. Held that broadcaster had a limited right of access to taped evidence.

    c. Trial judge refused to allow KVBC to copy taped evidence, but the appellate court ordered the judge to reconsider because of KVBC's common law right of access to the material.

    d. Appellate court said there was no risk of evidence being destroyed because the court's tapes were only copies.

5. *Phoenix Newspapers v. United States District Court* (1998; federal court of appeals)

    a. Case involving former Arizona governor Fife Symington.

    b. The media appealed the sealing of transcripts of hearings that concerned alleged jury tampering in the ex-governor's trial.

    c. Court ruled that federal courts in the Ninth Circuit had to follow specific guidelines in determining when the press and public can see sealed transcripts of closed court hearings and review court records.

6. *United States v. Kaczynski* (1998)

    a. Ninth Circuit Court of Appeals held that the public had the right to see psychiatric evaluation of "Unabomber" Theodore Kaczynski.

Cameras and Courtrooms

Bruno Richard Hauptmann trial in 1935 revealed the debate over cameras in court. While the trial did not take place until three years after the murder of Charles Lindbergh's son, the courtroom was packed, and there was a lot of inflammatory publicity. The trial had been preceded by the John Scopes "monkey trial" in 1925, the first ever broadcast over the radio.

The ABA in 1937 introduced the Canon 35 to its judicial ethics, which prohibited broadcasting and taking photos in court. This was later amended to prohibit television coverage. After the Sheppard case in the 1960s, it was amended again in the 1970s and given the designation of rule 3A(7). It permitted some television coverage of court proceedings with consent of all parties but only for use in educational institutions. It was again later amended to allow much more extensive television coverage.

By the 1960s, every state except Colorado and Texas had rules prohibiting cameras and broadcast coverage.

1. *Estes v. Texas* (1956)
   a. Texas grain dealer convicted of swindling group of investors; conviction was reversed by Supreme Court because two days of the preliminary hearing and part of trial were televised.
   b. Court said the coverage was "obtrusive" because everyone knew the cameras were there in the courtroom.
   c. By 1980, 10 states allowed broadcast coverage, even without the consent of the defendant.
2. *Chandler v. Florida* (1981)
   a. Two police officers convicted of using a squad car and their radios in a restaurant burglary.
   b. The court had allowed television cameras. Two defendants appealed the convictions, citing an unfair trial because of the televisions.
   c. In an 8–0 decision, the Supreme Court refused to overturn convictions saying there was no constitutional prohibition against allowing cameras in the courtroom.
   d. But, it also did not say that the broadcast media had a special right of access to courts.
   e. Instead, it said the states can allow cameras if they wish.
   f. The ABA revised rule 3A(7) to say that judges may allow cameras if they meet certain requirements, in that coverage
      i. "must be consistent with the right of the parties to a fair trial," and
      ii. "must be unobtrusive, not to distract trial participants, or interfere with the administration of justice."

> NOTE: By 2003, 47 states allowed some coverage with the approval of a judge. At least 35 of these allowed coverage without the consent of the defendant.

Federal Court Rules Regarding Cameras

In 1991, the federal courts began a three-year trial period on allowing cameras into trial courts and courts of appeal, although not in criminal proceedings.

The trial ran through December 1994, but after that there was a period in which cameras were not allowed.

New rules were adopted in 1996 allowing each federal appellate court to choose whether to have cameras in appellate proceedings. District courts were discouraged from doing so and were forbidden to allow the cameras in criminal proceedings.

Congress has considered legislation since that time to allow cameras in federal courts, but at this time there is still limited access.

Notes

1. Wayne Overbeck, *Major Principles of Media Law* (Belmont, Calif.: Thomson-Wadsworth, 2004), 308.

2. Overbeck, *Major Principles of Media Law*, 310.

3. Overbeck, *Major Principles of Media Law*, 312. See a lengthier discussion of case requirements in Kent R. Middleton, William E. Lee, and Bill F. Chamberlin, *The Law of Public Communication* (Boston: Allyn & Bacon, 2004), 471–73.

4. Overbeck, *Major Principles of Media Law*, 316–17.

Reporters, Shield Laws, and Other Protections

SOMETIMES REPORTERS who engage in investigatory journalism find themselves in need of using anonymous sources and then having to protect the identity of those sources. Sometimes, journalists run afoul of judges simply for what stories they have covered or what words they have used. And sometimes, journalists find themselves on the receiving end of a subpoena for their private notes and tapes. Is there any protection? Any law to guide us?

civil contempt of court—not a punishment but more a form of coercion where the person who is disobeying the court order is put in jail until he or she decides to obey. This can lead to long, indefinite sentences. Reporters who refuse to reveal their sources to a court often face this type of action.

criminal contempt of court—a punishment for an act of severe disrespect for a court. Often heard by a judge other than the judge who was insulted or treated disrespectfully. May result in the imposition of either a fine or jail time, or both.

direct contempt of court—when someone disrupts the courtroom or shows disrespect for the legal process in the presence of the judge, such as in refusing to be seated.

> NOTE: Many people criticize the contempt-of-court process because the judge alone defines the violation, tries and convicts the person, and sets the sentence—sometimes all in a matter of minutes.

indirect contempt of court—when someone does a disrespectful act away from the courtroom, as in refusing to answer a subpoena.
1. *Bloom v. Illinois* (1968) and *Baldwin v. New York* (1970)
    a. Both of these cases were heard by the Supreme Court.
    b. The court said that with criminal contempt-of-court cases, if the sentence lasts longer than six months, the judge cannot hear the case without a jury.
2. *Bridges v. California* (1941)
    a. Bridges was a union leader who threatened a West Coast dock strike if a court followed through and enforced a ruling unfavorable to him.
    b. The *Los Angeles Times* was also writing unpopular editorials about some judges.
    c. They were both held in indirect contempt of court, but the Supreme Court ruled that the findings were contrary to the First Amendment.
    d. The court said the justice system could no longer issue contempts of court unless the publishings presented a "clear and present danger" to the justice system.
3. *Pennekamp v. Florida* (1946)
    a. Florida Supreme Court ruled that *Miami Herald* was in contempt of court because it had published articles saying several judges were soft on criminals.
    b. The U.S. Supreme Court reversed the decision based on the clear-and-present-danger test.
4. *Craig v. Harney* (1947)
    a. The Corpus Christi *Caller-Times* was held in contempt of court for criticizing a judge's handling of a landlord–tenant case.
    b. The Supreme Court reversed this citation on the same grounds (clear-and-present-danger test).

Privilege

Privilege—an exemption from a citizen's normal duty to testify when ordered to do so in court or in another official information gathering proceeding.

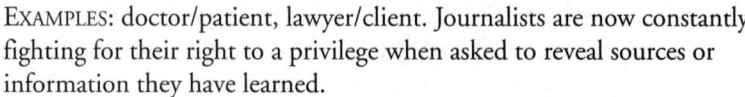

> EXAMPLES: doctor/patient, lawyer/client. Journalists are now constantly fighting for their right to a privilege when asked to reveal sources or information they have learned.

1. *Garland v. Torre* (1958)
   a. Torre wrote unfavorable comments about Judy Garland that came from a CBS executive.
   b. Garland sued and demanded to know who said these things.
   c. Torre refused and was cited for contempt of court; he lost and was sentenced to 10 days in jail. She appealed.
   d. Federal appellate court said that the source's identity was a direct link to the very basis of Garland's claim of libel; thus, the right to protect the source had to give way.
2. *Branzburg v. Hayes* (1972)
   a. Supreme Court ruled that there is no constitutional privilege for journalists.
   b. There were three cases consolidated in this decision:
      i. *U.S. v. Caldwell*
         (1) *New York Times* reporter who had interviewed leaders of the Black Panther movement.
         (2) A California grand jury subpoenaed him to testify and also subpoenaed his notes and tapes. Caldwell refused, saying it would undermine his relationship with the group.
         (3) *New York Times* and Caldwell asked district court to quash subpoena. Their request was granted in part. Ninth Circuit Court of Appeals granted the request, citing Caldwell's First Amendment rights.
      ii. *In re Pappas*
         (1) Pappas was a television journalist invited to the Black Panther headquarters.
         (2) He was summoned by a grand jury and asked what he had seen, and he refused to answer on First Amendment grounds.
         (3) The state supreme court refused his argument, and he appealed to the U.S. Supreme Court.
      iii. *Branzburg case (Louisville Courier-Journal)*
         (1) He had seen two guys processing hashish and wrote a story about drug use in Kentucky.
         (2) He was later subpoenaed and refused to testify on First Amendment and state ***shield law*** grounds.

> (3) The state court rejected the argument, and he appealed to the Supreme Court.
>
> c. The court was divided 5–4 on the decision and ruled that each journalist must comply.
> d. Three of the dissenting justices thought there ought to be a **qualified** journalist's privilege; but to justify requiring a journalist to reveal sources, the government should have to show three things:
>> i. there is probable cause to believe the journalist has relevant information regarding a violation of the law;
>> ii. the information cannot be gotten in any other way; and
>> iii. there is a compelling interest in the information.[1]

NOTE: Even though these guidelines were in the dissenting opinion, numerous courts and judges have used them to establish qualified privilege in state and federal cases.

Post-Branzburg Rulings

1. *Baker v. F & F Investment* (1972)
   a. Journalist was asked to reveal his source on an article he wrote about the "blockbusting" practices of real estate agents, but he said he could not, because the source was a member of the real estate community and would be subjected to harassment.
   b. But this was in a civil lawsuit between black homebuyers and the firms.
   c. The Second Circuit Court of Appeals said journalists do have a constitutional right to keep their sources under certain circumstances, as in a civil lawsuit to which he was not a party.
2. *United States v. Cuthbertson* (1980)
   a. CBS was ordered to submit to the court all tapes and material that appeared on a *60 Minutes* story about a food chain and possible criminal activity.
   b. Several of the chain's executives were indicted on criminal charges
   c. CBS refused, was cited for contempt of court, and they appealed.
   d. The U.S. Circuit Court of Appeals upheld the order, and the Supreme Court refused to hear the case.
3. *Riley v. Chester* (1979; Third Circuit Court of Appeals)
   a. A police officer had an argument with his chief, sued him, and made news.

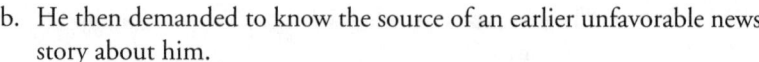

b. He then demanded to know the source of an earlier unfavorable news story about him.

c. The journalist refused to answer when subpoenaed and was held in contempt of court.

d. The appellate court overturned the order because it said the information was not relevant enough to the case to override the reporter's qualified privilege.

4. *United States v. Criden* (1980; Third Circuit Court of Appeals)

a. The court held a journalist at the *Philadelphia Inquirer* in contempt of court because she refused to testify about her conversations with a U.S. attorney about the "Abscam" case (FBI agents posing as representatives of Arab oil interests who gave large cash bribes to members of Congress and others, ostensibly to gain favorable position in Washington).

b. The appellate court upheld the contempt-of-court charge because they said the more prevailing issue was the conduct of the U.S. attorney who had leaked information to the press about the case.

5. *Silkwood v. Kerr-McGee* (1977; Tenth Circuit Court of Appeals)

a. Said the reporter's privilege applies to documentary filmmakers.

b. Trial court was ordered to weigh

   i. the relevance and necessity of the information sought;

   ii. whether it went "to the heart of the matter";

   iii. its possible availability elsewhere; and

   iv. the type of case involved.[2]

> NOTE: The case of Karen Silkwood's death is very interesting, and students are urged to do some research on their own regarding the case's historical aspects.

6. *Bruno & Stillman v. Globe Newspaper Company* (1980)

a. First Circuit Court of Appeals dealt with this civil libel case.

b. The court ruled that the reporter's privilege still exists but that there must be a balancing of the press's First Amendment rights and the plaintiff's **need to know**.

7. *Miller v. Transamerican Press* (1980)

a. The Fifth Circuit said that the reporter's privilege does exist but that it had to give way for a libel plaintiff's need for information; otherwise, plaintiff would not be able to prove actual malice in a case against a magazine.

8. *United States v. Hubbard* (1979)

a. The court said a *Washington Post* reporter had the qualified privilege because the Church of Scientology could have retrieved the information they wanted about an FBI investigation into the church directly from the FBI.

9. *Zerilli v. Smith* (1981)
   a. The Justice Department leaked information to the *Detroit News* about wiretapped conversations of underworld leaders.
   b. The men sued and demanded to know the sources; the judge refused and they appealed.
   c. The appellate court for the District of Columbia circuit refused because the men did not try to acquire the information from some other source first.
   d. The court said that to override the reporter privilege in a civil suit, the party must show that
      i. the lawsuit is not frivolous;
      ii. the information is crucial to the case; and
      iii. all other sources for the information came up with nothing.
10. *Dillon v. City and County of San Francisco* (1990)
    a. The federal district court decided that there was no privilege for a television cameraman to avoid testifying concerning a fight he witnessed between a citizen and a group of police officers, who the citizen was suing.
    b. Instead of being tried in state court, the case was tried in federal court, where privilege does not generally apply.
11. *Gonzales v. NBC* (1999; Second Circuit Court of Appeals)
    a. A *Dateline* story about police misconduct in Louisiana led to a lawsuit by a couple who requested "outtakes" from the NBC show.
    b. The appellate court recognized the existence of the reporters' privilege but ruled that the outtakes were relevant to the case and not available elsewhere.
12. *Ashcroft v. Conoco, Inc.* (2000; Fourth Circuit Court of Appeals)
    a. Recognized the existence of reporter privilege and overturned a contempt-of-court citation for a North Carolina reporter who received copies of "sealed" court documents and who refused to reveal his source for the documents.
    b. Circuit court said trial judge erred in the manner by which he sealed the documents, thereby invalidating any "compelling interest" that would require him to reveal the source. Also, the documents were seen as newsworthy.
13. *Shoen v. Shoen* (1993/1995; Ninth Circuit Court of Appeals)
    a. Feud in the family of the U-Haul founder, who commented that he thought two of his sons were responsible for the death of the wife of a third son.

b. The father is quoted in a book called *Birthright,* and the two sons sued father for libel.

c. Sons demanded interview tapes from author, who refused and appealed the subpoena.

d. Court says authors, like other reporters, may invoke the privilege when plaintiff does not exhaust all other possible sources.

e. Sons get father's deposition and again subpoena author's notes and tapes.

f. He again refuses and is cited for contempt of court, but the federal appellate court reaffirms the reporter's privilege, saying he could not be forced to turn over his research materials unless it was a last resort.

g. Court devises new test to be used only when
   i. reporter is not a litigant in the suit;
   ii. there are no confidential sources; and
   iii. the reporter's sources do not object to disclosure of the information.

h. If these conditions have been met, then to overcome the journalist's privilege, it must be shown that the information
   i. is "unavailable despite exhaustion of all reasonable alternative sources";
   ii. is not cumulative (i.e., repetitive to what is already there); and
   iii. is "clearly relevant to an important issue in the case."[3]

State Court Privilege Rulings

1. *Winegard v. Oxberger* (1977; Iowa Supreme Court)
   a. The court followed the *Branzburg* three-part test and found a First Amendment right of privilege for a reporter, with the added requirement that the pending lawsuit cannot appear to be "patently frivolous."

2. *Zelenka v. Wisconsin* (1978)
   a. Wisconsin Supreme Court ruled that the reporter privilege is visible in its state constitution as well as in the federal constitution.
   b. In a murder case, the defendant wanted the name of the source for a story that had run claiming the victim had been cooperating with a narcotics officer.
   c. State court said defendant had not shown that information sought would aid his defense.

3. *New Hampshire v. Siel* (1982)—another murder case
   a. Two student journalists at the University of New Hampshire refused to reveal their sources about a story that talked of a victim's connection with drug dealings.

b. The court said the information would not help to change the outcome of the case.

4. *Mitchell v. Superior Court* (1984; California Supreme Court)

    a. The court had ordered a trial judge to reconsider an order requiring the journalists at a small newspaper to reveal their sources for a series of stories critical of the practices of a drug rehabilitation center.

    b. The center had sued for libel. The California Supreme Court had previously said that the shield law did not protect journalists when they are defending against a libel case.

    c. However, the court said that if the case appears to be without merit or if protecting the identities outweighs the need for the information, then reporters need not reveal their sources.

    d. This ruling came about because the center really only wanted to know who ratted them out.

5. *Caldero v. Tribune Publishing* (1977; Idaho Supreme Court)

    a. A police officer was criticized in the paper for shooting a person fleeing from a crime.

    b. The officer wanted to know the identity of the source, and the paper refused.

    c. The court held the paper in contempt of court, not acknowledging any reporter privilege whatsoever.

6. *Sierra Life v. Magic Valley Newspapers* (1980; Idaho Supreme Court)

    a. A life insurance company sued the paper for libel and demanded to know the sources for a story about the legal actions being taken by other states against the company.

    b. The trial judge ordered the paper to name its sources; it refused.

    c. The judge found for the plaintiff on the libel question and awarded $1.9 million without any proof of the elements of libel.

    d. The Idaho Supreme Court reversed the decision saying plaintiff had to prove the journalist's information was relevant before it could be discovered.

NOTE: Congress has tried to create federal statutory shield laws but has run across some problems:

1. deciding who should be covered;
2. resolving the "prescient witness" question: whether someone who witnessed a crime should have to testify;
3. determining the definition of a journalist; and
4. deciding if the law should be weak or strong.

But, more than 30 states have shield laws that fall into three categories:
1. absolute privilege law;
2. laws that allow the privilege only if the information is published; and
3. qualified or limited laws.

Shield Laws and the Courts

Shield laws are statutes passed by the states that serve to protect journalists from being forced to identify their sources of information. These laws generally keep a reporter from being jailed for contempt of court for refusing to identify those sources.

1. *WBAI-FM v. Proskin* (1973)
   a. New York court ruled that a journalist did not have the right to use the shield law if the information was not a confidential communication.
2. *Farr v. Superior Court* (1971; California appellate court)
   a. Said that the privilege did not apply if a judge wanted to know who had disobeyed a "gag" order.
3. *CBS v. Superior Court* (1978; California appellate court)
   a. Said the shield law does not apply if the information requested could help someone be found innocent of a crime.
4. *KSDO v. Superior Court* (1982; California appellate court)
   a. Ruled that the shield laws were able to protect journalists only from contempt of court, not from anything else.
5. *Delaney v. Superior Court* (1990; California Supreme Court)
   a. The court said that the shield law applies to eyewitness observations and both nonconfidential and confidential information; however, if the material could help free an accused of a crime, then the information must be presented.
6. *Miller v. Superior Court* (1999; California Supreme Court)
   a. Ruled that while the shield laws do not apply when a defendant needs the information to free himself or herself, it does apply to the prosecution who would like the information.
7. *New York Times Company v. Superior Court* (1990; California Supreme Court)
   a. Ruled that in civil case where the journalist is not one of the parties, the shield laws provide absolute protection from revealing sources.
   b. But journalists can encounter other problems, such as being sued by the loser for the monetary damages since they would not release information that might have helped the loser to win the case.
8. *In re Farber* (New Jersey Supreme Court 1978)
   a. Court said that in a criminal case the journalist must give information that the defendant wants and that the shield law will not apply.

b. The court and the legislature later strengthened their shield law; the court said the law is nearly absolute in libel cases.

  9. *Steaks Unlimited v. Deaner* (1980)

    a. A Pennsylvania federal court upheld the shield law because it dealt with a "diversity of citizenship cases," where federal courts usually apply state law in large part.

  10. *State of Minnesota v. Turner* (1996; Minnesota State Supreme Court)

    a. Court said the shield law protected only the names of the sources and not any other information the reporter may have.

    b. In 1998 the legislature strengthened the shield law to say that a reporter must give over information only if it is relevant, if it cannot be obtained elsewhere, and if a compelling interest requires disclosure.

  11. *People v. Pawlaczyk* (2000; Illinois Supreme Court)

    a. Ruled the state's law did not protect two reporters called to testify to a grand jury.

    b. The point was that the court had to find out if a city official had committed perjury by denying that he was one of the sources.

Significant Shield Cases

The Farr Case

1. Farr was covering the Charles Manson murder trial as a reporter.
2. Some of the attorneys gave Farr a copy of a statement by a prosecution witness, and he ran it in the *Herald Examiner.*
3. The judge demanded to know who had violated the gag order, but Farr refused to tell, citing the California shield law; the judge accepted the response.
4. Farr later left the paper and went to work for the Los Angeles County district attorney's office, and the judge again demanded the sources; he still refused.
5. He was cited for contempt of court because, according to the judge, the law applied only to those who were currently employed journalists.
6. Four appellate court decisions emerged from this.

    a. *Farr v. Superior Court* (1972)

       i. Court said the legislature had no authority to pass a law to prevent a judge from finding out who violated a gag order; thus, the shield law was invalid as it applied to Farr.

      ii. Farr went to jail for contempt of court for 46 days.

    b. *In re Farr* (1974)

       i. With this appeal, the appellate court recognized that Farr might continue to stay in jail.

    ii. The court recognized the need to set up a system for releasing contempt-of-court prisoners who based their violation on "clearly articulated moral principle."

    iii. Appellate court said the trial court had to determine whether Farr refused to cooperate because of a principle and if added jail time would not get him to obey the order.

    iv. If these answers were positive, the trial court had to change the contempt of court from civil to criminal, which in Farr's case had a maximum sentence of five days.

  c. *Farr v. Pitchess* (1975; U.S. Court of Appeals)

    i. Rejected Farr's claim that the new criminal contempt-of-court citation issued by the trial judge was unconstitutional.

    ii. The court said that the need to know the violators' names outweighed Farr's rights.

  d. *In re Farr* (1976; California appellate court)

    i. Set aside a new criminal citation saying Farr was being charged multiple times for the same offense.

The Farber Case

1. Farber worked for the *New York Times* and wrote several stories about mysterious deaths at a New Jersey hospital 10 years earlier.
2. One Dr. Mario Jascalevich was indicted, partially because of the stories.
3. As the case went on, the defense obtained an order for Farber and the *Times* to release information from interviews about the deaths, but they refused.
4. Farber was fined and sent to jail; the *Times* was also fined per day until they cooperated.
5. The paper and Farber appealed, but the New Jersey Supreme Court said the shield law and First Amendment did not apply when a criminal defendant needs the information to defend himself.
6. They still refused and continued paying the fines and serving jail time.
7. Eventually, the case was dismissed, and the governor pardoned Farber and the *Times* and repaid to the *Times* all the money paid in fines.

The Vanessa Leggett Case

1. Jailed 168 days in 2001–2002 for refusing to reveal her notes and sources to a grand jury investigating a murder trial.
2. She was writing a book about the murder of Houston socialite Doris Angleton.

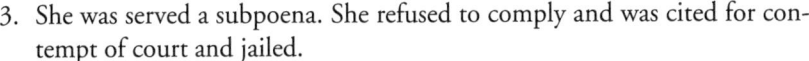

3. She was served a subpoena. She refused to comply and was cited for contempt of court and jailed.
4. A Houston attorney defended her, but both the trial judge and the Fifth Circuit Court of Appeals refused to accept her First Amendment claims.
5. Federal appellate court said journalistic privilege does not reach grand jury investigations or criminal proceedings in federal court.
6. She was released only because the jury had adjourned without handing down any indictments.

Suits Filed by the News Sources

1. *Cohen v. Cowles Media Company* (1991)
   a. Cohen, a public relations man for Republican candidate for governor of Minnesota, gave material to reporters showing misdeeds years earlier by Democratic candidate for lieutenant governor.
   b. The papers published the story with his name, even though they promised confidentiality.
   c. He was fired. He sued the papers for breach of contract and won.
   d. The papers appealed and the Minnesota Supreme Court overturned the jury verdict, saying the First Amendment protects media from liability when publishing a name with a newsworthy story.
   e. The court said the only thing he could have done was use the doctrine of ***promissory estoppel***, something people can do when they agree to do something for someone else relying on the second party's promise and the promise is broken, injuring the first party in some way. But, even that remedy is available only if the case is not covered by the First Amendment
   f. The U.S. Supreme Court overturned this decision saying that estoppel is a general doctrine of law that applies to the mass media despite the First Amendment, so Cohen won.
2. *Zurcher v. Stanford Daily* (1978)
   a. Demonstrators at the university hospital were forcibly ejected by the police.
   b. The student paper covered the event, which included a lot of violence.
   c. They ran a special edition with a lot of photographs of the demonstration.

NOTE: The Privacy Protection Act of 1980 bars police from searching and seizing "documentary materials" held by news organizations, except under limited circumstances, and outlaws most newsroom searches.

---

d. The police issued a search warrant and searched the newspaper office.
e. The staff filed a civil action against the police.
f. The Supreme Court said such a search is constitutional so long as the search is by warrant, is reasonable, and is specific in what it seeks.

Four exceptions to warrant requirement:
1. person holding the information is suspected of a crime;
2. reason to believe information must be seized immediately to prevent a death or serious bodily injury;
3. there is reason to believe that giving notice of intent to seize the information would result in its destruction, alteration, or disappearance; or
4. the information was not produced in response to a court order that had been confirmed on appeal.

A journalist's **work product** cannot be seized unless the journalist is a crime suspect or the seizure could prevent someone's death or bodily injury.

Anyone searched in violation of the act may sue the federal, state, or local government; but the evidence seized may still be used in court against them.

Police must obtain subpoenas instead of search warrants to get material from journalists. This allows journalists the opportunity to challenge the subpoena in open court.

Notes

1. Wayne Overbeck, *Major Principles of Media Law* (Belmont, Calif.: Thomson-Wadsworth, 2004), 331–32.
2. Overbeck, *Major Principles of Media Law*, 336.
3. Overbeck, *Major Principles of Media Law*, 338–39.

Transparency and Freedom of Information

I T IS A NECESSITY in a free society that people have access to the records of their government and the functions that take place. Since 1966, the Freedom of Information Act has contributed greatly to the openness or transparency of the federal government and many state governments. But it hasn't always been easy.

The movement for something resembling the Freedom of Information Act (FOIA) began in the latter part of the 1960s. The act itself was passed in 1966. The main users of the act are corporations, academic researchers, and private individuals because they have the time to spend waiting for the request to go through, unlike journalists, who work on deadlines. Despite the growing need for information regarding the government, in 1996 Congress extended government agencies' response time from 10 working days to 20.

In addition, in 1995 more than 3.5 million documents a year were declared "secret" for national security reasons alone. But the movement of people seeking open access to government information—*transparency*—is so great that all

50 states now have laws that require most agencies of state and local government to hold open meetings and grant public access to many government records. More than one million requests filed under the FOIA act occur per year.

Freedom of Information Act

1. Provisions of the FOIA
   a. Declares a number of records kept by federal administration agencies to be open to the public.
   b. Copies are to be provided to the public at a reasonable cost.
   c. 1974 amendment to the law required agencies to furnish lists of their records and post their fee schedules for making copies for FOIA requests.
      i. The fees may be waived or reduced if an agency believes the documents would benefit the general public and not just one individual or company.
      ii. Some have criticized this process because it places the discretionary power of whether to charge in the hands of the agency.
   d. In 1986 Congress amended the act to reduce the fees government agencies may charge news organizations and nonprofit educational or scientific institutions, while increasing the fees charged to commercial businesses.[1]
2. *Department of Defense v. Federal Labor Relations Authority* (1994)
   a. U.S. Supreme Court stated that an agency might not release a document based on the requester's identity or the purpose for it.
3. *Long v. Internal Revenue Service* (1980; federal appellate court)
   a. The IRS claimed that filling a request would be prohibitively expensive ($160,000) and so exempted themselves from the requirement to provide the documents.
   b. The court said the IRS must give requested information, even if it would be costly.
4. *Fiduccia v. Department of Justice* (1999; federal appellate court)
   a. Ruled that an eight-year delay in responding to an FOIA request is too long.
   b. But, the courts have often excused government agencies from the time limit of 20 working days, ruling that the limit is "directory" not "mandatory."
   c. If a request is denied, the person then has the right to appeal, first through the agency's appeal process and then through the federal courts.
   d. Because of amendments in 1974 and 1976 federal judges can review the requested information *in camera* (in private, in chambers) and examine reasoning behind the agency's denial.

e. The agency must have filed a denial based on one of nine statutory exceptions:

    i. documents properly classified as **confidential** or **secret** in the interest of **national security** or U.S. foreign policy;

    ii. documents relating to "internal personnel rules and practices" of federal agencies;

    iii. matters that are specifically exempted from public disclosure by some other statutory law;

    iv. trade secrets and other financial and commercial information gathered by government agencies;

    v. interagency and intra-agency memoranda that involve the internal decision-making process;

    vi. personnel and medical files and similar documents that should be kept confidential to protect individual privacy;

    vii. investigatory files compiled for law enforcement purposes but only when the disclosure of such files would interfere with law enforcement, deprive a person of a fair trial, constitute an unwarranted invasion of personal privacy, disclose a confidential source, disclose investigative techniques (and thereby permit someone to circumvent the law), or endanger the life or safety of any individual;

    viii. documents prepared by or used by agencies regulating banks and other financial institutions; and

    ix. oil and gas exploration data, including maps.[2]

Implementing the FOIA

When using the FOIA, you should make it clear in writing, using the actual citation of Title 5 of the United States Code, section 552. The request should be very specific, naming the desired document exactly as it is defined by the agency. This information can be found in the Federal Register. The FOIA request should first be directed to the person in charge of receiving the requests inside the agency involved. If the request is denied, it should then go to the agency head. If it is also denied at that level, the requester will have to go to court.

When a request is denied, the requester is supposed to receive a Vaughn Index, a list of documents being withheld with the explanations or the legal justifications for withholding them. This is a result of the case of *Vaughn v. Rosen*, 484 F.2d 820 (1973).

In 1995, President Bill Clinton signed an executive order that revised the rules under which agencies could classify documents as "secret" for national security. The order required that most documents 25 years old be open to the public. Exceptions are to be made to this rule only with the approval from a committee set up to review the request. The rule exempts CIA documents that would reveal names of spies, as well as Defense Department documents relating to such things as war plans.

In the post–September 11 atmosphere in Washington, the Bush administration replaced much of the content and intent of the Clinton policy. The new policy opts for secrecy over disclosure whenever there is a "sound legal basis" for doing so. The administration also postponed the document disclosure provisions of the 1995 order by three years.

Enforcement of FOIA in Court

The act states that a court can require the government to pay the requester's attorney fees and court costs if the lawsuit is successful. It also states that if the agency acts arbitrarily in denying requests, the Civil Service Commission must hold a proceeding to decide if disciplinary action should be taken against the persons involved.

1. *Bell v. United States* (1977; federal appellate court)
    a. Court said that an affidavit submitted by the agency that justifies the need for keeping the document secret should be given "substantial weight."
2. *Schaffer v. Kissinger* (1974; federal appellate court)
    a. Said Red Cross reports on South Vietnamese prison camps had been improperly classified and must be made public; if documents need to be kept secret, it must be done properly.
3. Assassination Records Review Board
    a. Created by Congress to review all the classified documents about the JFK assassination.
    b. The board concluded in 1998 that the government had "needlessly" withheld some records. It was noted that this secrecy is what led many to believe the government had something to hide about the assassination.
    c. While the national security exception can be very dangerous because it can withhold many documents from public examination and knowledge, the other exceptions have also caused problems.
    d. Trade secrets and private business exception have caused a lot of double lawsuits.
        i. One side is seeking information that may be covered by the exception.
        ii. The other, the private company that originally submitted the information, is suing to persuade the government to keep the material confidential. This is called a "reverse FOI suit."

e. Law enforcement information, internal personnel rules, and internal working documents exception has also caused problems (see next case).

4. *Department of the Air Force v. Rose* (1976; Supreme Court)
   a. Legal researcher requested air force academy records of honors and ethics code violation hearings at the academy with the names of alleged violators deleted.
   b. Court ruled that where there is a genuine and significant public interest in agency policies, they should be made public unless it would harm an investigation or prosecution.
   c. This type of information should be made public so long as no personal privacy right is threatened.

5. *Kissinger v. Reporters Committee for Freedom of the Press* (1980)
   a. Supreme Court ruled that former secretary of state Henry Kissinger could keep his diary of official phone calls private because he took the book home with him. It was personal.

6. *Forsham v. Harris* (1980)
   a. Supreme Court ruled private research organizations using government grants do not have to make their research data public.

7. *FBI v. Abramson* (1982)
   a. Supreme Court ruled that some of the information gathered by the Nixon administration about its critics was exempt from being public because it had originally gathered the information for investigatory purposes.

8. *Department of State v. Washington Post* (1982)
   a. Supreme Court said records stating whether a person holds a passport fall under the "personnel, medical, and similar files" exception.
   b. The *Post* was trying to find out if two Iranian nationals living in Iran held American passports. The State Department refused the information. The *Post* appealed and lost.

9. *Bibles v. Oregon Natural Desert Association* (1997)
   a. Supreme Court ruled that a government agency's mailing list should not be open to the public because of the balance between the public's right to know and the privacy of the people on the list.

10. *CIA v. Sims* (1985)
    a. Supreme Court ruled that the CIA may keep its intelligence sources secret even when national security is not an issue.
    b. The Ralph Nader Public Citizen Health Research Group wanted to know the names of researchers and institutions that had taken part in CIA project with mind-altering drugs.
    c. The CIA released some the names, those who had agreed to be identified, but kept the rest secret.

    d. The Nader organization sued, but the CIA used the third exception to justify and the court agreed.

11. *U.S. Department of Justice v. Reports Committee for Freedom of the Press* (1989)
    a. Supreme Court ruled out public access to FBI criminal histories on millions of Americans.
    b. Court pointed to the personal privacy exception under the FOIA.

12. *John Doe Agency v. John Doe Corporation* (1989)
    a. Supreme Court ruled that many documents obtained by the FBI from other government agencies are also exempt from being public.
    b. Grumman Corporation requested documents from the Defense Contract Auditing Agency during a federal grand jury investigation of aerospace industry accounting practices. The auditing agency responded by turning the documents over to the FBI, which then refused to release copies under the act because they were "compiled for law enforcement purposes."[3]

13. *U.S. Department of Justice v. Landano* (1993)
    a. Supreme Court said the exception for police records does not give the FBI an automatic right to deny requests for the release of information that might identify a source.
    b. There is no legal presumption that this information is always confidential.

14. *Department of the Interior v. Klamath Water Users Protective Association* (2001)
    a. Supreme Court ruled the Bureau of Indian Affairs cannot keep correspondence with Indian tribes confidential under the fifth FOIA exception.

Other FOIA Considerations

1. In addition to problems posed by the exceptions, requesters may face high court costs and attorney fees.
    a. If the requester wins, the government pays the fees; but if the requester loses, he or she is liable to pay the bill.
    b. *Baez v. United States Justice Dept.,* 684 F.2d 999 (1982)
        i. Government won an order that required Joan Baez to pay the government's court costs when she sued to get additional information the government had kept secret about her.
        ii. She lost, and a federal appellate court ordered her to pay the bill.

2. "Legally sanctioned censoring" of documents.
    a. Lets agencies delete parts of documents that fall within an exception while releasing the rest of the document intact.

3. Federal bureaucracy has made an attempt to weaken the FOIA.

4. In 1986 Congress said the FBI and other law enforcement agencies may deny a request for information without confirming or denying the existence of the material sought.
   a. This was important because before this ruling when the FBI chose to deny a request, it had to justify the denial, which served to prove the document's existence.
   b. Congress passed the Intelligence Identities Protection Act, which made it a crime to engage in activities that might lead to identifying covert agents.

Freedom of Information in an Electronic World

1. Electronic FOIA Amendments of 1996
   a. Requires agencies to make it easier for the public to identify and access government records.
      i. Indexes and guides to explain available records and how to find them.
      ii. Divided all government records that fall under the FOIA into three categories:
         (1) Must be published.
         (2) Must be available in agency reading rooms or placed online, even without a request.
         (3) Must be made available when there is a request.
   b. Brought about the computerization of the FOIA compliance process.
      i. Agencies must set up "electronic reading rooms" so anyone, anywhere can access the information when needed.
      ii. Information must be provided in different computer formats.
      iii. Required electronic "*redacted*" records to show where deletions were and how much was cut.
   c. Reformed timetable and procedures that agencies must follow in responding to FOIA requests.
      i. Gives agencies 20 working days to respond.
      ii. Journalists are to be able to have their request expedited.
      iii. If someone's request is long and complex and demands a lot of time, the requester must be given the option to go back and simplify the request.
      iv. Those who face delays must be notified and given estimated time of completion.
   d. Required that agencies figure out which information is repeatedly requested and to make it available to the public so that they can stop duplicating the same request.

Limited Boundaries of the FOIA

1. Executive privilege
   a. Often asserted by presidents when they want to withhold information, such as military or diplomatic secrets and internal documents.
   b. The secrets were classified on three levels:
      i. confidential
      ii. secret
      iii. top secret
   c. The Pentagon Papers are an example of how the claim of executive privilege was used to cover up former administrations' errors concerning the Vietnam War.
      i. The Supreme Court ruled the papers were allowed to be published.
   d. The FOIA recognizes executive privilege, in a sense, because it exempts matters of national security and internal working documents of agencies from being disclosed.
2. *United States v. Nixon* (1974; Supreme Court; unanimous decision)
   a. Narrowed the scope of the executive privilege.
   b. Ruled the privilege is absolute only with regards to military and diplomatic information that must be kept secret to protect national security.

Privacy Act of 1974

1. Intended to protect individuals from their personal information being made public by the government.
2. Applies to all information in government records, placing restrictions on the manner in which they can be used.
3. Does not allow information to be made public or even transferred to another agency without the permission of the individual.
4. Gives people the right to see their own government records and to correct any errors.
5. Officials who mishandle the records can be sued for damages, attorney fees, and court costs.
6. There are a few exceptions to the requirement that the government must have the person's permission: law enforcement purposes, census matters, and congressional reasons.
7. In 1988 Congress passed the Computer Matching and Privacy Protection Act, which handles the transfer of information between agency databases.
8. In 2003 new rules required that medical field and health care providers obtain written permission from patients to share their records with others, even for billing or insurance purposes. There are also more stringent limits

on the release of information regarding celebrity hospital patients or those admitted after an accident, disaster, crime, or terrorist attack.

There are criminal penalties involved for violation of the rules.

Buckley Amendment

1. Also known as the Family Education Rights and Privacy Act.
2. Gives parents the right to see their children's school records and does not allow the school to release records without the parents' consent.
3. Allows students over 18 to see their records and does not allow the release of them without written consent.
4. Schools that do not keep grades and records confidential are ineligible for federal funds.
5. It does not prohibit student newspapers from publishing a student's grades to prove that he or she is ineligible for a position or a sport he or she has been involved in.
6. Many schools have used this rule to keep campus crime statistics a secret.
   a. The 1990 Crime Awareness and Campus Security Act says that all colleges and universities that receive federal funds must make an annual report of crime statistics and that the reports must be open to the public.
   b. Does not require campus police records to be open.
7. *Bauer v. Kincaid,* 759 F.Supp. 575 (1991)
   a. Traci Bauer, editor of Southwest Missouri University paper, sued the administration to open campus crime records.
   b. Federal judge ruled the that Buckley amendment cannot be used to justify keeping these records closed when state law says they must be open.
8. *United States v. Miami University* (2002; federal appellate court)
   a. Federal judge ruled that the Buckley amendment forbids the release of student disciplinary proceedings on college campuses.
   b. Said such records are educational and not to be released.
   c. Also ruled that the Department of Education has the right to bring forth lawsuits to enforce the Buckley amendment.
9. *Gonzaga University v. Doe* (2002; Supreme Court)
   a. Students cannot sue schools under the Buckley amendment for divulging personal information.
10. *Owasso Indiana School District v. Falvo* (2002; Supreme Court)
    a. Buckley amendment does not rule out everyday activities, such as having students grade one another's papers. It is intended to cover only permanent records.

11. 1998 Higher Education Act
   a. States that the school must keep a log of criminal incidents reported to the campus police and must make it open to the public.
   b. Known as the Jeanne Clerry Disclosure of Campus Security Policy and Campus Crime Statistics Act.

The Federal Advisory Committee Act and "Open Meetings"

The Federal Advisory Committee Act was enacted in 1972. It required, for the first time, that nongovernment organizations that gave advice to the government had to hold open meetings and have public records.
1. *Public Citizen v. Department of Justice* (1989)
   a. Supreme Court limited the usefulness of the act by ruling that it did not cover privately funded bodies, such as the American Bar Association.
   b. The effect was that other private groups could meet secretly as well.
2. *Association of American Physicians and Surgeons v. Hillary Rodham Clinton* (1993; federal appellate court)
   a. Court had to decide if the task force on national health care reform headed by Hillary Clinton was subject to Federal Advisory Committee Act by seeing if she was an employee of the government or a private citizen.
   b. The court ruled that she was an employee of the government, so the task force could meet in secret.

Criminal History Information

1. In 1976 the Law Enforcement Assistance Administration issued guidelines to restrict the release of information by law enforcement.
2. Required that agencies receiving federal aid must set up policies about the release of personal information on people arrested or charged.
3. It eventually said only that the agencies must have consistent policies; it did not say what the policies had to be.
4. Many states seal records of arrests that do not lead to convictions.
5. At least 47 states have such laws that restrict access to criminal history.

Federal Driver's Privacy Protection Act

1. Enacted in 1994, it required every state to close motor vehicle registration and driving records to the public and press.
2. Any state may opt out of the federal secrecy requirements as long as individuals can request to have their records kept confidential.

3. The act was passed because Congress wanted to keep criminals from obtaining information about their victims from these records through a private investigator or other means.
4. Journalists opposed this because they said private investigators are already exempt from the requirements.
5. *Reno v. Condon* (2000)
   a. Supreme Court upheld Congress's power to use the law to keep these state records secret by way of the commerce clause of the Constitution.

Federal Legislation and Open Meetings

In 1976 came the enactment of the "Government in the Sunshine Act." It requires 50 federal administrative agencies to conduct some of their meetings in public. In addition, they must announce the time and place in advance and indicate that the public is invited.

But closed sessions are permitted for 10 reasons, with the first nine being the same as the FOIA exceptions and with the tenth involving an agency's pending litigation.

Before there is a closed meeting, the board must vote on it and the vote must be recorded. The agency must then keep accurate records of the meeting. It must then quickly publish the results of any votes taken and how each person voted.

A person may sue an agency that he or she believes violated the act, and a federal court is required to issue injunctions ordering the federal agency to comply with the law. The court is required to order the government to pay the fees and court costs when a complainant wins a case.

But there are no civil or criminal penalties for officials who violate the law. The court cannot invalidate any actions completed during the closed meeting. The act applies to the central policymaking boards but not to the staff meetings, cabinet-level departments, or advisory boards. It also excludes informal gatherings and unofficial meetings.

1. *Federal Communications Commission v. ITT World Communications*, 466 U.S. 463 (1984)
   a. Supreme Court ruled that it was okay for the majority of the members of the Federal Communications Commission to meet in private with corporate communication leaders from other countries at an international conference because it was not an official meeting.

States' Open Records and Meetings Laws

State open-meeting laws usually apply to state and local governments. All state meeting laws provide for closed sessions for carefully described reasons, including personnel matters and discussions of pending lawsuits. Many of these laws allow any citizen to sue the government body for an injunction against further closed meetings. A number of states invalidate actions taken during the illegal closed meetings.

Unlike the federal law, some state laws have criminal sanctions for knowing violations.

State Public Record Laws

Most of these allow public access to any person without a "need to know." Most provide for judicial review when access is denied. Most apply criminal sanctions to officials who improperly deny access. About one-third require government agencies to pay fees and costs when the person sues successfully.

1. *Los Angeles Police Department v. United Reporting Publishing Company* (1999; Supreme Court)
   a. Court upheld rule in the California public records act that did not allow the release of addresses of crime victims and persons arrested for a crime for commercial use (attorneys, driving schools, drug counselors, insurance companies, etc.).
   b. Court said California had the right to release these addresses to noncommercial users while denying them to those who might use the information commercially.

General Access Laws

1. *Saxe v. Washington Post* (1974) and *Pell v. Procunier* (1974; Supreme Court)
   a. Ruled that rules against interviewing individual prison inmates were not a violation of the First Amendment.
   b. Started when a California policy to allow journalists to interview inmates was eliminated.
   c. Court said that neither journalists nor citizens have the right to interview inmates.
2. *Houchins v. KQED* (1978)
   a. Television journalist wanted to visit a part of a jail where an inmate committed suicide.

NOTE: Public record laws do not always govern the release of court records, and open-meeting laws do not always guarantee access to the court's records and proceedings crime scenes.

---

b. Jail denied access to the reporters, who sued, saying that prison conditions were a matter of public concern.

c. Federal district court agreed.

d. Ninth Circuit Court of Appeals affirmed decision, but Supreme Court reversed it.

e. There is no constitutional right of access for the press to places not generally accessible by the general public.

3. *California First Amendment Coalition v. Calderon* (1998; federal appellate court)

a. Court upheld a prison's restrictions on the viewing of executions in California.

b. Journalists do not get to see anything more than the inmate on a gurney, already sedated, and the last few seconds before the prisoner is declared dead.

c. Court did say it was possible that a First Amendment right, though very limited, to witness capital punishment did exist and so ordered the lower court to review whether the prison's security standards justified excluding the media. But consider the following case.

d. *California First Amendment Coalition v. Woodford* (2002; federal appellate court)

i. Court ruled that prison's exclusionary standards had not been justified and so upheld the right of witnesses to view the full process of executions.

4. *Los Angeles Free Press v. City of Los Angeles* (1970; California appellate court)

a. An underground newspaper, *Free Press*, sought the same press credentials as other newspapers, but the request was denied.

b. The denial was upheld by the court, saying the weekly alternative paper was not generally involved in the collection and coverage of hard police news.

5. *Quad-City Community News Service v. Jebens* (1971; federal district court)

a. Court overruled the practice of denying an underground paper access to police information that was available to other newspapers.

b. Said there was no showing of a compelling interest to justify the police actions.

6. *Ludtke v. Kuhn* (1978; federal district court)

a. A female reporter could not be denied access to a portion of a city owned baseball stadium where men were allowed (i.e., the teams' locker rooms) because the privacy of the players could be protected while alternatives to total exclusion could be found.

7. *Sherrill v. Knight* (1978; federal appellate court)

a. Secret Service had denied press credentials to two underground newspaper reporters.

b. The court overturned the action because the agency did not have any policy for granting press passes and could not demonstrate a reason why reporters were "a security risk."

c. Court said agency had to establish some procedures, explain any denials to reporters, and give them the right to appeal the decision.

Access to Courtroom Proceedings and Records

NOTE: Grand jury proceedings are almost always closed to the press and to the public because a great many things are discussed that would never be admissible at a trial. Even the grand jury transcripts are closed in most states, usually for the same reason. Court records that involve highly personal matters (such as the reports of child welfare agencies regarding proposed custody or adoption orders) are sealed in many states. Juvenile court proceedings are almost always closed to the press and public, at least until a juvenile is remanded to adult criminal court in some crime situations.

A Constitutional Right of Access to Private Organizations?

When a private company is the target of a takeover bid, that fact must be disclosed in a timely manner. But for purely private companies (family owned?) there are few regulations for the release of information.

NOTE: The right of access to enter private business enterprises is usually nonexistent. They do not have to admit reporters to their meetings, and their records are rarely open to public inspection. But, those corporations whose stock is publicly traded must adhere to the Securities Act of 1933 and the Securities Exchange Act of 1934. The 1933 act requires most companies to file extremely detailed reports on their management and business prospects with the Securities and Exchange Commission before offering any stock to the public. The 1934 act requires publicly traded corporations to continue providing information on their business and finances, even when they are not issuing new stock.

Notes

1. Wayne Overbeck, *Major Principles of Media Law* (Belmont, Calif.: Thomson-Wadsworth, 2004), 361.

2. Overbeck, *Major Principles of Media Law*, 362.

3. Overbeck, *Major Principles of Media Law*, 369.

Obscenity and America

BSCENITY HAS BEEN a constant topic of American law since the days of the Mayflower and Plymouth Rock. But what is "obscene"? What is "pornography"? How should the law coincide with the beliefs of the various American faiths? This is a hot potato and one that is not likely to cool down soon.

Supreme Court has said that legally **obscene** material is not protected by the First Amendment. Court said that government cannot ban nonobscene material from the media, even if it is **indecent** and offensive to people. The 1996 Communications Decency Act attempted to ban not only obscene material but also indecent material from Internet sites accessible to minors. But:

1. *Reno v. ACLU* (1997)
   a. Supreme Court overturned the decency act because the Internet has the same First Amendment rights as the rest of the media (more like press than broadcast).
   b. In 1999, the Supreme Court upheld a lower court ruling that allowed the banning of e-mail under the 1996 act only if the e-mail was obscene.
2. *Luke Records v. Navarro* (1992)
   a. Florida federal judge called a 2 Live Crew album obscene and banned it.
   b. An appellate court overturned the ban.

> NOTE: A large part of the history of obscenity law has been simply the attempt to define *obscenity*, both in England and in the United States. Even when a standard has been established, the courts continue to examine the rights of citizens to possess it. The courts also continue to examine allegedly obscene material as it exists in the various media.

3. *National Endowment for the Arts v. Finley* (1998)
   a. Following the furor caused by the Robert Mapplethorpe exhibit in Cincinnati, Ohio (see note below), Congress made restrictions on the types of work that could be financially supported by the National Endowment for the Arts.
   b. Artists who received grants under the new guidelines were required to sign antiobscenity oaths under the legislation passed by Congress.
   c. Supreme Court said that the National Endowment for the Arts decency standards were not an unconstitutional form of viewpoint discrimination by the government.

> NOTE: In Ohio, the director of the Cincinnati art gallery was prosecuted for showing works by Robert Mapplethorpe that were considered obscene (the most notorious of which was a crucifix mounted in a beaker of urine). The director was acquitted in the case.
>
> All the states have rules that govern obscenity, including laws that make producing, performing, or selling obscene works a crime. Under federal law, the importation and mailing of obscene works is prohibited. Federal law also prohibits minors, or adults appearing to be minors, in sexually explicit works. Federal law allows for large fines and prison sentences for violators. Among the weapons that have been used against child *pornography* producers is the Racketeer Influenced and Corrupt Organization Act, which allows for the seizure of assets of businesses that deal in obscenity.

Early Efforts to Define Obscenity

As is often noted in discussions of American pornography and obscenity matters, the early history of Massachusetts is linked with the settlement of the Puritans. So, it should be no surprise that a Massachusetts law was passed in

> NOTE: This was known as the "Hicklin rule": whether the tendency of the matter is to corrupt "the most susceptible members of society."

1712 making illegal the publishing of "any filthy, obscene, or profane song, pamphlet, libel, or mock sermon." The Tariff Act of 1842 was the first federal law that tried to control obscenity by prohibiting the importation of obscene works.

In England, Lord Campbell's Act of 1857 was passed to help shape obscenity standards by prohibiting obscene books and prints. It was followed in America for many years.

1. *Regina v. Hicklin* (1868)
   a. Judge took the copies of an anti-Catholic pamphlet by Henry Scott that was considered obscene.
   b. Scott appealed to the recorder of London, who ruled in his favor.
   c. The chief justice reversed this decision because of how certain passages, taken out of the context of the work, might affect susceptible readers.

> QUESTION: children or "village idiots"?

Anthony Comstock and the "Comstock Law"

Anthony Comstock came along as a crusader for morality in the media and in the country. His efforts in Washington brought about the "Comstock Law," or officially, the Antiobscenity Act of 1873. It gave the post office the power to seize any mail that was obscene. Comstock organized groups to suppress "immoral" books, even if they were not obscene, and he became the man in charge of seizing material from the mail. He is said to have bragged about taking more than 160 tons (320,000 pounds) of "obscene" material from the mail. He also believed that birth control information was obscene. This led to a prolonged battle with the early women's rights activist Margaret Sanger, who actually fled the country to avoid Comstock prosecution. She finally returned to challenge Comstock at trial in 1915; but he died shortly after her arrival, and the federal district attorney chose to drop the case.

A New Century and New Standards

1. *Halsey v. New York Society for the Suppression of Vice* (1920)
   a. A New York appellate judge ruled that a book must be looked at **as a whole**, rather than in just its parts, before it can be determined to be obscene.

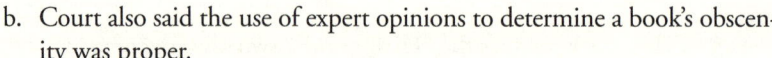

    b. Court also said the use of expert opinions to determine a book's obscenity was proper.

2. *One Book Entitled "Ulysses" v. United States* (1934)

    a. In 1933, a federal district court judge said he would not allow the use of the part of Hicklin rule that said the work would be judged on the affect it had on susceptible readers.

    b. He said the opinion must reflect the work's effect on a person of "average sex instincts."

    c. The court of appeals, with federal judges Augustus and Learned Hand, upheld the decision, and this pretty much did away with the Hicklin test.

The Warren Court and the Roth Case: Seeking a New Definition

1. *Butler v. Michigan* (1957)

    a. Overturned a Michigan law that prohibited the sale of books that might cause minors to commit depraved or immoral acts. Supreme Court said standards of juvenile innocence could not be used to keep books from being read by adults.

2. *Roth v. United States* (1957)

    a. Defendant was convicted of mailing material that was considered obscene.

    b. The Supreme Court upheld the conviction.

    c. The court also **for the first time** gave a definition of *obscenity*.

    d. Whether to the **average person**, applying **contemporary community standards**, the **dominant theme of the material taken as a whole** appeals to *prurient interest*.

The Roth Rule Is Expanded

3. *Manual Enterprises v. Day* (1962)

    a. Post office attempted to ban magazines from mail that was intended for gays.

    b. Majority opinion called them "dismally unpleasant" but not obscene.

    c. Court said they were not ***patently offensive***, and **mere nudity is not obscenity**.

4. *Jacobellis v. Ohio* (1964; Supreme Court)

    a. Theater manager convicted of showing an allegedly "obscene" French film that had been shown elsewhere.

b. The court overturned the ruling, applying **national community standards**: "The federal Constitution would not permit the concept of obscenity to have a varying meaning from county to county or town to town" (Justice Brennan).

5. "Fanny Hill" and "Social Value": *Memoirs of a Woman v. Massachusetts* (1966)

a. Book called *Memoirs of a Woman of Pleasure*, or *Fanny Hill*, was banned because it was thought obscene, but the Supreme Court said it was not and suggested a three-part test for obscenity: The **Roth test** *plus* **"patent offensiveness"** *plus* **"utterly without redeeming social value."** This case made it constitutionally required to test for the social value of a work and made prosecution of obscenity cases very difficult.

Government Alternatives to the Burden of Proving Obscenity

6. *Ginzburg v. United States* (1966; Supreme Court)

a. Upheld obscenity conviction of a pornographer, not because of the content of the material, but because of the way he promoted his works—in a sense, they looked at *pandering*. "The business of purveying textual or graphic matter openly advertised to appeal to the erotic interests of the customers."

b. He mailed his material from cities with certain types of names, such as Middlesex, Blue Ball.

7. *Redrup v. New York* (1967; Supreme Court)

a. Reversed three state obscenity convictions.

b. Listed three categories of marketing that might justify state prosecutions without requiring the works to be obscene:

i. sale of sexually titillating material to juveniles;

ii. distribution of such material in a manner that assaults individual privacy; and

iii. sales made in a pandering way.[1]

8. *Ginzburg v. New York* (1968; Supreme Court)

a. Upheld conviction of Sam Ginzburg because he sold obscene material to a minor.

b. The court accepted "variable obscenity"—being able to prosecute someone who sells material to minors that may not be obscene to adults.

The Warren Court Reaches Its Peak

9. *Stanley v. Georgia* (1969; Supreme Court)

a. Overturned conviction that came from what the court saw as a "fishing expedition."

b. Police searching Stanley's house looking for betting materials but came across some films; they watched them, then arrested him for possessing obscene material.
c. The court said people have a constitutional ROP in their home and the **right to possess obscene material in their home**. But:

10. *United States v. Reidel* (1971; Supreme Court)
a. Upheld federal obscenity law banning **mailing** of obscene material to consenting adults.

11. *United States v. Thirty-Seven Photographs* (1971)
a. Supreme Court said customs officials could seize obscene materials brought back from overseas by travelers, even if they were intended for private use.

12. *United States v. Twelve 200-Foot Reels of Super 8-mm Film* (1973; Supreme Court)
a. Restated that First Amendment does not give the right to bring obscene material back from abroad.
b. Court said once a person is home with the material they are safe; until then, they are exposed.

A New Standard Is Established

1. *Miller v. California* (1973)
a. The Supreme Court revised the Roth–*Memoirs* test.
i. Did away with the "redeeming social value" concept.
ii. Did away with the idea of nationally uniform "community standards"; said each state could adopt its own.
b. Miller had conducted a mass mail campaign to sell "adult" material.
c. Some of his brochures were sent to a California restaurant, and some of the people complained to the police.
d. Miller was convicted of violating the California obscenity law and appealed.
e. Court created a new test that said that a work was obscene if
i. an **average person**, applying **contemporary community standards**, would find that **the work as a whole** appeals to the **prurient interest**;
ii. the **work depicts or describes, in a patently offensive way, sexual conduct**, and the **applicable state law specifically defines what depictions or descriptions are prohibited**; and
iii. the **work, as a whole, lacks serious literary, artistic, political, or scientific value**.[2]

2. *Pinkus v. United States,* 436 U.S. 493 (1978)
   a. Children are not part of the "community" when determining community standards.
3. *Pope v. Illinois,* 481 U.S. 497 (1987)
   a. Measurement of "serious value" must be based on **objective standards**.
   b. **"Reasonable man"** test is used to determine whether a work has serious value.
   c. **Expert witnesses** can be used to establish the presence of value.
4. *Jenkins v. Georgia* 418 U.S. 153 (1974)
   a. Theater owner could not be convicted for showing *Carnal Knowledge,* an R-rated film, because it did not depict sexual acts in a "**patently offensive**" manner.

NOTE: How much can local parochial standards affect national law? By allowing the prosecution of national porn figures in venues that will be "friendly" to the prosecution.

---

5. *United States v. Blucher* (1978)
   a. Porn distributor in Oregon convicted in a Wyoming court for mailing porn to Wyoming at the request of the local postmaster. Case later overturned by Supreme Court on other grounds. ***Forum shopping*?**
   b. Defendant had not done business in Wyoming before. Was he **entrapped** by the phony invitation from the postal officials?
6. *Luke Records v. Navarro* (1992)
   a. Federal court conviction of 2 Live Crew, based on the album *Nasty as They Wanna Be,* is overturned by court of appeals because the prosecuting sheriff offered no expert testimony regarding "serious value."

   NOTE: In the 1980s and 1990s, federal officials prosecuted Los Angeles porn makers in Dallas and Tulsa because of conservative local standards.

7. *United States v. Thomas* (1996)
   a. San Francisco couple sells Internet porn, downloaded in Tennessee. Conviction upheld.

Child Pornography

1. *York v. Ferber* (1982)
   a. Supreme Court upholds child porn statutes in at least 20 states by allowing for use of someone of legal age who looks younger.

> NOTE: Traci Lords made porn flicks at age 17, but two federal court cases said producers could not be held liable if they did not know the performer was under 18, contrary to 1977 Protection of Children against Sexual Exploitation Act.

2. *Osborne v. Ohio* (1990)
    a. Child porn illegal, even in the home. Some argued Ohio statute could make parents' nude baby pictures illegal, which court denied.
3. *Ashcroft v. Free Speech Coalition*, 535 U.S. 234 (2002)
    a. Supreme Court overturns provisions of the Child Pornography Prevention Act of 1996, which outlawed material that "appeared" to depict children, either by using older but younger-looking actors or computer-generated images.

Other Matters

Since 1971, people have had the power to remove their names from mailing lists of adult materials. Before that, people might be surprised in their homes by receiving vivid pornographic advertising.

Military Honor and Decency Act of 1996 was the basis for barring *Penthouse* and *Hustler* from military bases. *Playboy* was allowed. Statute has been upheld twice in courts of appeals.

Films were not seen as protected by the First Amendment originally (1915 case), but protection was granted in 1952 for Roberto Rosselini's film *The Miracle*. Film review boards were not uncommon from the 1920s through the 1960s, usually as a part of local government. Increasingly, the Supreme Court required more and more safeguards to protect films from arbitrary prior restraint, such as the installation of an appeal board that would hear a filmmaker's case within a few days. The Supreme Court has never said that such film censorship is unconstitutional when such safeguards are in place.

In 2003, the Supreme Court said that the Children's Internet Protection Act did not violate the First Amendment, saying it was not unconstitutional to add language requiring independent libraries to get screening software to be eligible for federal grants. But this act was later ruled unconstitutional by a federal circuit court of appeals because it lacked any distinction between materials inappropriate for teenagers and those inappropriate for young children, *ACLU v. Ashcroft*, 322 F.3d 240.

Cities and Pornography Regulation

Supreme Court said that Texas cannot label porn shops "public nuisances" to shut them down, *Vance v. Universal Amusement* (1980).

After certain items in a retail outlet have been ruled obscene, federal officials can go in and shut down the store, but seizure of all assets could be deemed **cruel and unusual punishment**, *Alexander v. United States* 509 U.S. 544 (1993) and *Austin v. United States,* 509 U.S. 602 (1993), decided on the same day.

1. *Hudnut v. American Booksellers* (1986)—court said cities could not identify pornography as violating the civil rights of women in the community, thereby allowing the city to shut down pornography outlets. Federal appellate court said city's ordinance was too broad, and the Supreme Court agreed.
2. *Schrad v. Mt. Ephraim* (1981; Supreme Court)—although cities may control the zoning locations of pornography shops and "strip joints," they may not zone them out of existence without violating the First Amendment.
3. *Renton v. Playtime Theatres* (1986)—Supreme Court said it was okay for local governments to use zoning ordinances to exclude adult businesses in all but remote areas, even if this kept the business from making a profit. Cities could prohibit such businesses within 1,000 feet of a park, school, church, or private residence. The court said that as long as there are some sites available for the businesses and as long as the city is not trying to run them out completely, the zoning is permissible.
4. *Barnes v. Glen Theater* (1991; Supreme Court)—Indiana was free to ban nude dancing, even though it was marginally self-expressive, to protect the public morals.
5. *City of Los Angeles v. Alameda Books* (2002; Supreme Court)
   It was constitutional for the city to ban adult businesses that combined video "viewing booths" and the sale of adult-oriented material because, according to the court, the concentration of the two could cause "more crime and urban blight than a single business would."

Notes

1. Wayne Overbeck, *Major Principles of Media Law* (Belmont, Calif.: Thomson-Wadsworth, 2004), 403.
2. Overbeck, *Major Principles of Media Law,* 406.

Regulation of Electronic Media

BECAUSE OF THE possible wide-ranging strength of the broadcast media, Congress found it necessary to begin to control the airwaves, or radio band, as early as the 1920s. As the media grew ever stronger and invasive of American life, the role of the Federal Communications Commission is also bound to grow over the coming years.

1. Electronic media must deal with the same legal issues as print does: libel, invasion of privacy, copyright infringement, advertising regulation, antitrust law, restrictions on their access to information.
2. Must also deal with other government regulations.
   a. A broadcaster must get a license from the Federal Communications Commission (FCC) and renew it periodically; licenses and franchise renewals are not automatic.
3. FCC gained its power over the electronic media because of the *radio spectrum*.
   a. Because only a limited number of frequencies exist, only a limited number of stations can broadcast.
   b. Therefore, the FCC claimed this problem justified government regulations—*scarcity rationale*.
4. Telecommunications Act of 1996
   a. Function was to increase the amount of competition among broadcasters, cable, telephone, and other communication services.

b. It relaxed many of the rules the electronic media had in the past but added new rules on content.

International Regulation

International Telecommunications Union

1. Responsible for a majority of the decisions made regarding broadcasting because of the lack of international boundaries for broadcasters and because of the spectrum.
2. The union issues the frequencies to the different broadcasters, whereas each country decides which broadcasters transmit on which channels in the AM, FM, and television bans.
3. The union has authority over three regions:
   a. Region 1: Europe, Africa, countries of the former Soviet Union
   b. Region 2: North America and South America
   c. Region 3: Asia and the Pacific
4. The countries within each region meet regularly to discuss the frequencies for that region.

EXAMPLE: In the 1980s, the Reagan administration tried to transmit "Radio Marti" to Cuba over an AM frequency. Cuba saw this as trying to send propaganda, so they began jamming several AM frequencies used by U.S. stations.

Radio Frequencies and the Origin of Broadcasting

1. Division of the radio spectrum
   a. AM (amplitude modulation) frequency: below 2 megahertz.
   b. Shortwave: 2–30 megahertz.
   c. VHF (very high frequency): 30–300 megahertz (television channels 2–13).
   d. FM (frequency modulation) frequency: 30–300 megahertz.
   e. UHF (ultrahigh frequency): 300–3,000 megahertz.
   f. Microwave: 3,000-plus megahertz.
2. Characteristics of the spectrum
   a. *hertz*—measurement unit for the frequency of the spectrum; 1 hertz = 1 electrical cycle per second, stated as hertz, kilohertz, megahertz.

b. The *service area* for each broadcaster must also be determined when issuing a license.

    i. This is determined by measuring the strength of the transmitted signal at different places and then drawing a circular plot. The area inside the circle is the *primary service area*, also called the Grade A contour.

    ii. The Grade B contour is a larger circle where the signal is weaker but still receivable.

c. Different frequency stations have different service areas even though they overlap.

    i. AM signals can have a different service area at night than during the day. This is because AM signals travel by *groundwave* during the day—traveling along the surface of Earth—but can also travel by *skywave* at night, traveling out into space and being reflected back to Earth by the ionosphere. This became a problem because the use of the skywave increased the AM signal, causing interference for other night broadcasters, who then had to fight with the AM signal.

    ii. As a result, the FCC had to require many radio stations to either reduce their night power or go off the air at night.

NOTE: This effect did, however, contribute to the growth of some early AM stations in the 1940s and 1950s, particularly those in Nashville (Tennessee), Shreveport (Louisiana), and Chicago, leading to the first "superstations" of that era. As a result, programs such as *The Grand Ole Opry* and the *Louisiana Hayride* became widely known and contributed to the success of such stars as Hank Williams and Elvis Presley.

How Broadcasting Began

Wireless transmission began as a useful way of communicating for the navy and commercial ship lines.

1. Radio Act of 1912 was the beginning of broadcasting regulation in the United States.

    a. In charge of licensing for shore stations and those at sea.

    b. Was enacted partly because of *Titanic* tragedy.

        i. Required wireless communication and full-time operators on large ships

        ii. Established qualifications for the operators.

        iii. Set technical standards and reserved wavelengths for government and distress signals.

2. In 1921–1922, the request for broadcasting signals became overwhelming, and the act of 1912 did not allow for the government to refuse anyone, even if there was no more space available.
   a. The interference became so bad that broadcasters lobbied the government to take over regulation and bring order.
   b. Radio Act of 1927—Congress established the Federal Radio Commission (FRC), which had the authority to issue licenses to broadcasters on certain frequencies and to deny applications for licenses when there was no more space available.
3. *United States v. Nelson Brothers*, 289 U.S. 266 (1933)
   a. FRC authority was based on the Interstate Commerce Clause.
   b. Some broadcasters claimed they were not subject to FRC regulation because they did not cross state lines.
   c. But the FRC said it had jurisdiction because even local broadcasters could interfere with other stations' signals that did not cross state lines.
   d. Supreme Court upheld FRC's claim.
4. Communications Act of 1934
   a. Gave the FRC broader authority and an administrative staff separate from the Department of Commerce.
   b. The FRC was changed to the Federal Communications Commission (FCC).
   c. Its authority then included broadcast, long-distance telephone service, and nongovernmental uses of the spectrum.
   d. It was not allowed to censor broadcasting, but it was given the power to grant and deny licenses.
   e. The FCC retained from its FRC days a list of goals to pursue when determining who would receive a license or have one renewed:
      i. must ensure that everyone in America could receive at least one radio signal;
      ii. must provide service to as many people as possible from as many different sources as possible; and
      iii. must provide a place for local self-expression.
5. *NBC v. United States*, 319 U.S. 190 (1943)
   a. The FCC had released a set of regulations detailing what broadcasters could not do with regard to content and business practices.
   b. The major networks said the FCC had gone too far.
   c. The Supreme Court held, on basis of the scarcity rationale, that the FCC could regulate these areas.
   d. This decision gave the FCC greater authority over the entire broadcasting spectrum.

$\sim$

Federal Communications Commission

1. Layout
   a. Consists of five members appointed by the president and approved by the Senate for a five-year term.
   b. Only three may come from the same party.
   c. It is like most administrative agencies in that it has the power to make the rules, enforce them, and judge the violators.
   d. But the decisions by the FCC are not absolute; they can be appealed up to the Supreme Court.
2. Functions of the FCC
   a. To authorize individuals and organizations the authority to transmit within the spectrum.
   b. To regulate those licenses once given.
3. Procedures
   a. Notice of inquiry—when particular information is needed on a subject, the commission must publish a notice of inquiry, then wait for responses.
   b. Notice of proposed rule making—this notice is published by the FCC on its website, and the commission then awaits responses.
   c. After the comments are received, the FCC may then have a hearing to hear oral arguments.
   d. The FCC then votes on the proposed rule; if it is passed, it becomes part of the official regulations.
4. *Structure*—the FCC does the majority of its work through internal bureaus.
   a. Media bureau—oversees radio and television stations and cable systems.
   b. Wireline competition bureau—handles the telephone communications.
   c. Wireless telecommunications bureau—deals with wireless and two-way communications, such as cellular phones, paging, public safety communications, and so on.
   d. *International bureau*—handles the shortwave stations that cross international boundaries.
   e. Enforcement bureau—enforces the FCC regulations for everyone.
   f. Consumer and governmental affairs bureau—deals with consumer-related matters.

Broadcasting Licensing and Court Decisions

Minority Preference

1. *Metro Broadcasting v. FCC,* 497 U.S. 547 (1990)

a. The FCC gave preference to minority groups and women when deciding whom to issue licenses to.

b. Many white males challenged this preference, but the Supreme Court
ruled in favor of the FCC because the preferential treatment was mandated by Congress. But:

2. *Adarand Constructors, Inc. v. Pena,* 515 U.S. 200 (1995)

a. The Supreme Court overturned *Metro Broadcasting,* stating there must
be justified proof to use such an action and then only as a solution for a
specific instance of previous discrimination.

b. Such a program would be under ***strict judicial scrutiny.***

Equal Employment Opportunity

3. *Lutheran Church-Missouri Synod v. FCC,* 141 F.3d 344 (1998)

a. The FCC tried to penalize two Lutheran church–owned radio stations
for not following equal employment opportunity (EEO) regulations by
hiring only Lutherans. The stations claimed the rules were violating their
freedom of religion.

b. Court of appeals in Washington declared the FCC's equal employment
opportunity program was unconstitutional because it required the
church stations to modify their message by hiring nonbelievers.[1]

4. *MD/DC/DE Broadcasters Association v. FCC,* 236 F.3d 13 (2001)

a. In 2000 the FCC created new EEO rules that said broadcasters must
create outreach programs to obtain more minorities and women and
must file regular reports with the FCC.

b. The National Association of Broadcasters and all state broadcasting associations challenged the new rules.

c. The federal appellate court in Washington declared the rules unconstitutional because they forced employers to hire on the basis of race alone,
and it was hard for them to determine if they were in compliance, a violation of the due process clause of the Fifth Amendment.

License Renewal

The process of obtaining a license renewal has changed greatly since the FCC's
inception.

5. *Office of Communication of the United Church of Christ v. FCC,* 359 F.2d
994 (1966) and 425 F.2d 543 (1969)

a. A public interest group protested the renewal of a Mississippi television
station because its programming was racially prejudiced, but the FCC
refused to grant a hearing.

    b. The appellate court ordered the FCC to hold a hearing and allow the protesters to appear.

    c. The FCC complied with a hearing where the burden of proof was on the group.

    d. On appeal again, the court said the burden should have been on the broadcaster.

    e. The station lost its license on rehearing.

    f. This case created a surge of similar protests of license renewals that were won; the broadcasters could no longer assume their renewals would be granted.

6. *Greater Boston Television Corp. v. FCC*, 444 F.2d 841 (1970)

    a. The FCC denied a Boston television station a renewal on the basis that a challenger could do a better job than the current owners.

    b. The FCC used the **comparative hearing process**, which allowed that if the current broadcaster had an average service record, it had preference over challengers.

    c. But granting the license to the challenger instead, the FCC ruled that the licensee, even though of average service, showed little interest in the station since he also owned the *Boston Herald-Traveler* newspaper.

NOTE: Throughout the 1980s and 1990s, Congress and the FCC worked to loosen the strings on the renewals. They lengthened the license terms and put limits on financial settlements of renewal disputes.

Content Regulations

Equal Time Rule

This set out the rules for broadcasters when dealing with political candidates, parties, elections, and so on. It stated that each candidate running for a public office should have equal access to the airwaves during a campaign. It also provided that this equal access did not include "bona fide" news coverage (actual reporting on an election, campaign, or political candidate). That meant a station could run a news story about one candidate and not have to run stories on the others. This exemption was also applied to talk shows in 1984.

The rule did not say that politicians must be given free advertising time but that they had to be treated the same. If one candidate was sold a certain amount of time at a certain broadcasting time for a certain price, then all other candidates had to be given the same options (if they could afford them).

The Clinton administration and the FCC wanted the networks to give major party candidates free airtime without journalistic controls. The networks could not refuse all political ads since the communications act stated that broadcasters must provide reasonable access to candidates in federal elections (but not elections for state and local offices).

1. *CBS v. FCC,* 453 U.S. 367 (1981)
   a. During the Carter–Mondale presidential election campaign, the three networks refused to provide airtime about a full year before the election.
   b. In 1981 the Supreme Court agreed with the FCC that the networks had failed to meet the provision of reasonable access and that the campaign had begun even in December 1979.
2. *Kay v. FCC,* 443 F.2d 638 (1970)
   a. A federal appellate court interpreted the equal time provision to say that in a general election, all candidates running for the same office had to be given the opportunity to buy comparable airtime at the same rates. In a nonfederal primary election, the broadcaster had to sell airtime to only the Democratic and Republican candidates and not the minor party candidates, because the minor parties were not yet facing election opposition.

Lowest Unit Charge

States that broadcasters must charge all candidates (federal candidates included) their lowest rate charged to their most preferential commercial advertiser for any advertising done within 45 days of a primary and 60 days of a general election. The rule was later revised to say that broadcasters must tell candidates about all rates and classes of airtime and then allow them to purchase the least expensive airtime available. And, if the ads are preempted, the broadcaster must have a "make good" policy.

1. *Miller v. FCC,* 66 F.3d 1140 (1995)
   a. The FCC said it had exclusive jurisdiction over cases concerning lowest unit charge disputes.
   b. The Eleventh Circuit Court of Appeals dismissed this statement, saying that courts could still hear lowest unit charge disputes. But:
2. *Wilson v. A. H. Belo Corporation,* 87 F.3d 393 (1995)
   a. Ninth Circuit Court of Appeals said FCC's statement was valid and that courts have no jurisdiction.

Debates

The courts ultimately approved FCC rule that broadcasters could air debates without having to have a third-party sponsor (such as the League of Women Voters) and could be exempt from the equal time rule, *League of Women Voters v. FCC*, 731 F.2d 995 (1984).

1. Supreme Court ruled that all television stations (even government owned) do not have to include all candidates, *Arkansas Educational Television Commission v. Forbes* (1998).
2. The federal appellate courts ruled that broadcasters must let candidates include offensive material in their ads, *Becker v. FCC*, 95 F.3d 75 (1996).

Fairness Doctrine

Established in 1949 and abolished in 1987, it stated that broadcasters must keep their public affairs programming reasonably balanced: when they covered one side of an issue, they had to seek out and broadcast the opposing side as well.

The three main reasons for its abolishment are as follows:

1. It gave the government the power to second-guess the judgments of journalists, allowing for the opportunity to infringe on First Amendment rights.
2. It deterred rather than encouraged full and equal news coverage of an issue. Often, the broadcasters would avoid a controversial story altogether or downplay it to avoid having to give free airtime to the numerous arguments over the issue.
3. It led to a belief held by many that the scarcity rationale was no longer relevant to the electronic media because of the numerous news sources available to the public.

Cases Involving the Fairness Doctrine

1. *Red Lion Broadcasting v. FCC*, 395 U.S. 367 (1969)
   a. Supreme Court ruled that First Amendment rights of the people outweigh the rights of the broadcasters.
   b. A radio host attacked Fred Cook, author of a book attacking Republican candidate Barry Goldwater. Cook demanded time to reply. Red Lion refused; the courts ruled that he must be given the time.
2. *Miami Herald v. Tornillo*, 418 U.S. 241 (1974)
   a. Supreme Court ruled that the print media is not subject to the Fairness Doctrine or the personal attack rule; print may choose to publish only one side of an issue and attack people without giving them the space in print to reply.

3. *CBS v. Democratic National Committee,* 412 U.S. 94 (1973)
   a. Supreme Court said the First Amendment did not give anyone a right to advertise on controversial subjects.
   b. Eventually this approach led to what is now almost complete editorial freedom for broadcasters.
4. *Serafyn v. FCC,* 149 F.3d 1213 (1998)
   a. CBS aired a *60 Minutes* show about the Ukraine that said the people are mostly uneducated and anti-Semitic. During the taping, CBS had only interviewed those people who agreed with this description, and it refused to interview those who opposed it. The segment had factual errors about the country's history and allegedly quoted a chief rabbi out of context.
   b. CBS refused to respond to numerous protests from Ukrainian American citizens.
   c. A complaint was brought to the FCC but was dismissed without even a hearing on its merits.
   d. Federal appellate court ruled FCC must reconsider the complaint. While the court did not say FCC had to change its decision, it did show that broadcast is still subject to some government regulation.

Regulating "Decency" and Children's Programming

Indecency—the courts have said that the FCC has the authority to determine what material is considered "indecent" for the airwaves, to set rules on this matter, and to fine those broadcasters who do not comply.

One of the most talked about actions taken by the FCC concerning indecency involved Howard Stern's radio show, in which all stations that carried his program were fined by the FCC to a total of about $2 million.

> NOTE: This matter has become of particular importance since the Janet Jackson "wardrobe malfunction" during the Super Bowl halftime show in January 2004.

1. *Action for Children's Television v. FCC,* 58 F.3d 654 (1995)
   a. Court of appeals in Washington ruled *en banc* that the FCC has the authority to ban indecency from airwaves during most of the day. There is a "safe harbor" window from 10 PM to 6 AM for broadcasters to air adult content because few children are awake at this time.
2. *FCC v. Pacifica Foundation,* 438 U.S. 726 (1978)
   a. Supreme Court ruled that the FCC could ban indecent material from the airwaves, even if it can be legally used in other media.

∽

b. The case began because a George Carlin monologue containing the "seven filthy words" was played at 2 PM on one of Pacifica's radio stations. A man complained to the FCC, who in turn placed a warning in the company's file.

c. Pacifica appealed, but the court ruled that the material was not obscene but inappropriate during the daytime hours.

d. As of 2004, the FCC still has the rule that all obscene material is banned from airwaves, whereas indecent material is banned from the airwaves during the day when children are likely to be listening. The "safe harbor" policy is still in effect.

Children's Television

The FCC has rules requiring that all television stations offer a minimum of three hours per week of regularly scheduled children's programming that meets their "educational and informational needs." The rules state that each segment must be at least 30 minutes long and air between 7 AM and 10 PM. The segments are not to be preempted more than 10 percent of the time.

1. Not surprisingly, broadcasters have become more concerned each year with the FCC's mandatory children's programming because the government is basically telling broadcasters what type of material the government believes children should be watching. This type of control raises First Amendment concerns and potentially interferes with advertising-driven programming, such as some Saturday-morning cartoon shows.

2. These concerns began with the Children's Television Act of 1990.

3. Congress required that advertising on children's shows be limited to 12 minutes per hour on weekdays and 10.5 minutes per hour on weekends. This rule applied to all material for children 12 years and younger. These limits also applied to cable networks and local programming.

4. The law also required that all broadcasters had to provide "quality children's programming" as part of their license renewal qualifications.

Violence

The biggest controversy in this area has been the V-chip. The Telecommunications Act of 1996 required all television sets, except the 13-inch models, to have the V-chip installed by the manufacturer. The FCC then ruled that the industry must come up with a rating system to help block out violent and sexually oriented programming. The V-chip would then allow parents to monitor and program their home units to limit children's access to mature

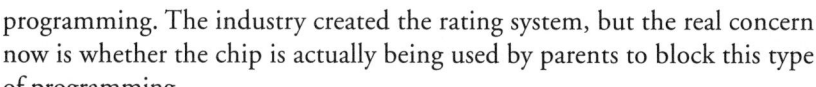

programming. The industry created the rating system, but the real concern now is whether the chip is actually being used by parents to block this type of programming.

Format

The Supreme Court has ruled that radio station format changes are not within the FCC's power to control. The court ruled that such changes are the broadcaster's choice, *FCC v. WNCN Listeners Guild*, 450 U.S. 582 (1981).

Other Regulations

FCC ruled that broadcasters must identify ad sponsors and the sponsor of a nonadvertising material (entertainment programming).

FCC banned hoaxes on airwaves that could "cause substantial harm to public health and welfare," but there was no requirement of this for other forms of media.

There has also been no real clarity in the rules on ads promoting gambling.

1. Charity Games Advertising Clarifications Act of 1988—said casinos and others whose gambling is an end in itself (for profit) were by federal law not allowed to advertise.
2. *United States v. Edge Broadcasting*, 509 U.S. 418 (1993)
   a. Supreme Court ruled that nonlottery-state broadcasters cannot have ads for a nearby state's lottery, even if a large percentage of that broadcaster's audience is in the state that has the lottery.
3. *Greater New Orleans Broadcasting Association v. United States*, 527 U.S. 173 (1999)
   a. Supreme Court ruled that the government cannot ban advertising by a private casino.
   b. This ruling opened up broadcast advertising to almost all gambling ads.
   c. The FCC said it would no longer enforce the lottery ad rule, but the *Edge Broadcasting* decision still stands.

Cable Television

Basic information: Cable systems do not need an FCC license to operate, because they do not use the over-the-air signals. The number of channels provided by cable is limited only by the television receiver. Cable systems must pay royalties for copyrighted programming on nonlocal stations (thanks to the 1976 Copyright Act); they must also at least get broadcasters' consent to carry some local stations. In 1966 the FCC decided to put some regulations on cable. The FCC claimed it had ***ancillary jurisdiction*** since the cable systems were affecting on-the-air broadcasters. Cable had the ability to carry distant signals of network affiliate stations. FCC put a strict limit on the importing of distant signals by cable systems. The Supreme Court affirmed the FCC's authority in *United States v. Southwestern Cable Company,* 392 U.S. 157 (1968).

Regulation

1. The regulation of cable has changed drastically over the past 30 years. In the 1970s, cable had a list of regulations set out by the FCC that were affirmed by the Supreme Court in *United States v. Midwest Video Corporation,* 406 U.S. 649 (1972).
    a. Must provide local public and government channels if more than 3,500 subscribers.
    b. Must originate a minimum amount of local programming.
    c. Must not be allowed to "leapfrog" over a local affiliate to use a more distant signal.
    d. Must respect syndication agreements to not air a show if a local station has exclusive rights to the show.
2. The FCC also made a new rule regarding public access in that the cable system must provide at least 20 channels. The Supreme Court invalidated these rules in *FCC v. Midwest Video,* 440 U.S. 689 (1979). This began a period of deregulation.
    a. With this came the abolishment of the syndicated exclusivity rule in 1980. It had required cable to black out syndicated shows shown by distant stations when a local station had rights to the same show. But it was restored by the FCC in 1988 with a few changes, such as it then allowed "superstations" to obtain exclusive rights to syndicated shows. The court of appeals said the FCC could issue such a rule, *United Video v. FCC,* 890 F.2d 1173 (1990).
    b. In *Capital Cities Cable, Inc. v. Crisp,* 467 U.S. 691 (1984), the Supreme Court stated that federal laws preempt state and local laws that conflict with the federal laws. An Oklahoma law banned cable from advertising wine and liquor ads, and a federal law required that cable must air station programming without interruption.
3. Also in 1984, Congress passed the Cable Communications Policy Act, which abridged local governments' rights in regulating cable. It deregulated subscription fees and banned local government from charging franchise fees over 5 percent of the cable's gross revenues. It said the local government

could still give franchises, but it protected cable systems from "subjective" franchise renewals.

   a. In 1988 the Supreme Court ruled in *City of New York v. FCC*, 486 U.S. 57, that a local government could not create stricter technical rules on cable than those created by the FCC.

4. Regulation began again with the Cable Television Consumer Protection and Competition Act of 1992. Some of the new rules included:

   a. Rate regulation, rate rollbacks, proportional rates, service standards, nondiscriminatory program access for cable competitors, must-carry rule, retransmission consent, and channel repositioning.

      i. A test of this act came with *Turner Broadcasting System v. FCC*, 512 U.S. 622 (1994) and 520 U.S. 180 (1997).

        (1) In the first case, the Supreme Court said the FCC had the authority to require **must-carry rules**, which stated that a television station could request a cable system to carry its programming but that the station would not receive payment for the carriage. The Supreme Court upheld the decision yet again.

        (2) The station could also choose **retransmission consent**—that is, a cable system could only carry the programming with consent from the station and likely with some sort of payment to the station.

   b. In *Time Warner Entertainment v. FCC*, 56 F.3d 151 (1995), the court of appeals in Washington finally killed cable's basic argument that the rules violated its First Amendment rights.

Franchises

5. *City of Los Angeles v. Preferred Communications*, 476 U.S. 488 (1986)

   a. Supreme Court upheld a court of appeals ruling that said local governments cannot subjectively abridge cable operators First Amendment rights.

   b. Case arose because Los Angeles was granting only one company the right to communicate by cable while denying the applications of all others. Preferred Communications challenged this by stating that the utility poles were a First Amendment forum and therefore permit rivals to deliver their communications by them as well. The city was violating the amendment by allowing only one company to operate in the area. The court agreed.

6. *Denver Area Educational Telecommunications Consortium v. FCC*, 518 U.S. 727 (1996)

a. Addressed indecency on cable.
b. Supreme Court affirmed the section of the 1992 act that said cable operators had the choice whether to ban patently offensive material from leased access channels or not.
c. The Supreme Court overturned the section of the act that had required the operators who did carry the material to keep it on a single channel and block it to all except those who subscribed to it; it also invalidated the section that required cable to censor all sexually oriented material on public access, educational, and governmental channels.
7. *United States v. Playboy Entertainment Group,* 529 U.S. 803 (2000)
a. Supreme Court ruled in favor of Playboy, contrary to the 1996 Communications Decency Act, stating that adult programming can be run in the daytime, even if a signal bleed into regular broadcast channels cannot be completely abolished; First Amendment rights cited.

Technology: High-Definition Television (HD-TV)

HD-TV: A new technology that is still having trouble replacing analog television.
8. Broadcasters will not be required to give up the analog signals until 85 percent of their audience has the use of HD signals.
a. The biggest concerns that have held HD-TV back:
    i. People in the media production industries, such as Hollywood, are demanding that HD have a copy-protection method to stop consumers from copying anything from television with the VCR.
    ii. The cost that each broadcasting station will have to spend in buying new equipment to facilitate this conversion is enormous.
    iii. Spectrum auction—the broadcasters argue that they cannot afford to purchase their HD channels and still provide free television services.

Cable–Telephone Services

Because of the 1996 Telecommunications Act, it is now legal for cable services to provide telephone and Internet services and for telephone servers to provide cable, Internet, and long-distance services.

Direct Satellites

The Satellite Television Home Viewers Act allowed for satellites to carry local stations.

The FCC now requires that all local governments, apartments, and home-owner's associations allow the small direct broadcast satellite dishes for satellite service. This has helped expand the use of the satellite. DirecTV and EchoStar are the two largest direct satellite providers. There is also MDS (multipoint distribution service), SMATV (satellite master antenna television), LPTV (low-power television), and DARS (Digital Audio Radio Service).

Note

1. Wayne Overbeck, *Major Principles of Media Law* (Belmont, Calif.: Thomson-Wadsworth, 2004), 444.

Issues Affecting
Media Ownership

W HEN A GIVEN commodity is scarce, there seems always to be a greater perceived need to own that commodity or at least control its distribution. The mass media in the United States are such commodities, and the fact that they have been very profitable in the past makes their attractiveness even greater. A disinterested observer might think that an unregulated market of such commodities would lead to turmoil. Is that the case, or should the theory of "market forces" prevail?

Antitrust Laws

1. These antimonopoly laws began with the Sherman Antitrust Act in 1890. It outlawed many different types of contracts and so forth that would be in "restraint of trade or commerce."

   The Clayton Antitrust Act of 1914 outlawed other business practices, such as price fixing, and the Celler-Kefauver Act in 1950 made it so that business practices and business ownership could be regulated to avoid monopolistic business in the country and reduced competition.

   The practices banned by these laws include the following:
   a. price fixing and profit pooling, arrangements whereby companies enter into an agreement to share profits or to charge noncompetitive

prices (such as when all your local gas stations raise their prices at the same time);

    b. certain mergers, because when two companies combine, the merger becomes illegal if it reduces competition to the extent that it is harmful for customers;

    c. tying arrangements, such as where a large company (such as Microsoft) makes a person buy something they would not normally buy (such as certain add-on software or browsers) to get something else that they need (Windows 2000-XP); or

    d. boycotting, which is refusing to do business with someone or some company to force them to do something they would not normally be willing to do.

2. To determine whether some of these practices are illegal, the courts must look at the facts in each case:

    a. by applying "the rule of reason," where one looks at the specific facts to decide if there was a violation, which usually involves complex analysis of the facts; or

    b. by using the ***per se*** rule, where some business practices are so seriously wrong as to be unlawful in and of themselves.

3. Legal actions that might be taken in antitrust cases:

    a. criminal prosecutions by the U.S. government to punish wrongdoers;

    b. civil actions by the U.S. government to halt business practices in violation of the statutes; and

    c. civil actions for treble damages by private individuals or companies that might have been damaged by the unlawful acts.

NOTE: These are all federal actions. They pertain to businesses involved in interstate commerce and to local businesses whose actions affect interstate commerce. When only local business practices are questioned, the burden falls on the state to act.

---

4. *U.S. v. Microsoft Corporation* (2000)

    a. The U.S. Justice Department and 20 states sued the company for unlawful practices, claiming the company had a monopoly on the market with the Windows operating system.

    b. The district court ordered the company to break up into one unit to handle the Windows operating system and another to handle everything else the company did

c. Microsoft was also ordered to sell the operating system to every computer maker for the same price.

   d. The case went to the U.S. Court of Appeals, where it overturned the lower courts decision and sent the case back for rehearing. As of 2003, the case was still in progress

Antitrust Law and the First Amendment

1. *Associated Press v. National Labor Relations Board* (1937)
   a. Supreme Court ruled that the First Amendment does not exempt the media from regulations that all other industries have to deal with.
   b. Associated Press writer was fired because he was part of a union working for the American Newspaper Guild. The guild complained about the action, and the Associated Press was found guilty.
2. *Associated Press v. United States* (1945)
   a. The *Chicago Sun*'s application for membership in the Associated Press was challenged by its competitor, the *Chicago Tribune*.
   b. The *Tribune* was able to do this because under the Associated Press rules each member had "blackball" rights to keep their competitors from joining.
   c. The Supreme Court said the organization's rules violated antitrust law.

Newspapers and Antitrust Law

1. *Lorain Journal Company v. United States* (1951)
   a. The paper would not accept advertising from a business that also advertised on the local radio station.
   b. Supreme Court ruled this act illegal because the refusal to run the ads could affect many advertisers since the paper reached a large market.
2. *Time-Picayune v. United States* (1953)
   a. Case arose due to a tying arrangement stating that an advertiser had to buy space in the company's evening paper if it also wanted space in their morning paper.
   b. A competing evening paper was the suspected victim of the arrangement, but the Supreme Court ruled there was not enough evidence to show that any real damage had been done.
3. *Kansas City Star v. United States* (1957)
   a. Involved all three antitrust lawsuits allowed under the law.
   b. Employee-owned Star Corporation owned the only morning and evening papers in the city; it also owned the leading radio and television stations.

c. Several violations were alleged:
       i. one had to buy space in both papers to get space in one;
      ii. sometimes one had to buy space in the papers to get time on the radio or on the television stations; and
     iii. if one bought space in the competing paper, one was threatened with cancellation of their ads.
    d. Justice Department filed criminal and civil lawsuits against the company.
    e. The company was convicted in the criminal suit; the civil suit was settled by having the company sell the radio and television stations and by eliminating the rule forcing advertisers to buy space in both papers.
    f. There were also several private treble damage suits filed that were settled out of court.
4. *Times Mirror v. United States* (1968)
    a. The corporation that operated the *Los Angeles Times* bought out the *San Bernadino Sun-Telegram*.
    b. The Justice Department said the acquisition lessened competition in the area because the *Sun*'s only true competitor had been the *Los Angeles Times*; the federal district court agreed, ordering the paper to be resold.
    c. This case made it clear that, according to the court, it is okay to buy a paper in different markets across the United States but that it is not okay to buy one that is in an overlapping market.
    d. In 1995 the Justice Department halted the sale of the *NW Arkansas Times* to a company that was connected with its competing newspaper. This was the first time in 13 years that the department stopped a merger from forming.

An Exception to the Rule: Joint Operating Agreements

joint operating agreements—when two papers in the same town or area merge many of their business and printing operations but maintain separate editorial staffs.
1. *Citizen Publishing Company v. United States* (1969)
    a. The *Tucson Daily Citizen* and the *Arizona Daily Star* had such an arrangement since 1940.
    b. In the 1960s the *Citizen* bought out the *Star* because it was in financial difficulty, eliminating the need for two independent editorial staffs.
    c. Justice Department sued to block the acquisition.
    d. The Supreme Court agreed, stating the arrangement was illegal because neither company was having financial difficulties at the time of the purchase.
    e. This was a shock since there were 22 operating agreements involving 44 papers going on in the United States at that time.

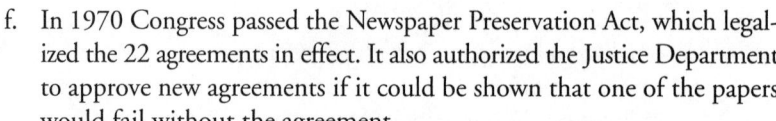

f. In 1970 Congress passed the Newspaper Preservation Act, which legal-
    ized the 22 agreements in effect. It also authorized the Justice Department
    to approve new agreements if it could be shown that one of the papers
    would fail without the agreement.

2. *Bay Guardian Company v. Chronicle Publishing Company* (1972)
    a. *Guardian* challenged the constitutionality of the 1970 act on the grounds
        that such an agreement between the *San Francisco Chronicle* and the *San
        Francisco Examiner* made it difficult for other papers to continue.
    b. The court ruled against the *Guardian*, upholding the constitutionality of
        the Newspaper Preservation Act.
        Examples of joint operating agreements:
        1974—*Anchorage Times* and *Anchorage Daily News*
        1979—*Cincinnati Examiner* and *Cincinnati Post*
        1980—*Chattanooga News-Free Press* and *Chattanooga Times*

3. *Committee for an Independent P-I v. Hearst Corporation* (1983)
    a. *Seattle Post Intelligencer* and the *Seattle Times* wanted to merge.
    b. The proposal received a lot of protest, but was approved by the attor-
        ney general.
    c. But a federal judge called a 60-day delay to hear arguments.
    d. Federal district court ruled in favor of the protestors, who argued the
        paper could have been sold to another owner, who could reorganize
        the paper and make it a competitor again.
    e. But the Ninth Circuit Court of Appeals reversed the decision, saying it
        is not necessary to put a failing company up for sale just to justify using
        such an agreement. Court said there needs to be only enough evidence
        to show the company would probably fail.

4. *Michigan Citizens for an Independent Press v. Thornburgh* (1988)
    a. The *Detroit News* and *Detroit Free Press* wanted to enter into a joint
        operating agreement.
    b. There was an ordered delay in the merger because an opposition group
        said neither company was actually in danger of failing.
    c. The federal court ruled the Justice Department was within its right to
        accept the merger.

5. *Reilly v. Hearst Corporation* (2000)
    a. The corporation that owned the *San Francisco Examiner* planned to buy the *San Francisco Chronicle* and then shut down the *Examiner.*
    b. After a legal battle, a federal judge upheld the purchase, ruling that the deal was legal.

NOTE: By 1995 only 12 of the original 22 joint operating agreements were still in existence.

The Federal Communications Commission and Broadcast Media Ownership

1. The Federal Communications Commission (FCC) has actively dealt with the business practices of the broadcast media. In the 1940s the FCC looked at how radio broadcasting was dominated by networks: 97 percent of nighttime wattage was used by the three big networks. NBC had two networks that it controlled. The FCC also looked at the restrictions these giants put on their affiliates:
   a. they could not carry any programming from other networks;
   b. they were required to stay in five-year contracts with the network;
   c. the networks controlled almost all of the affiliates' prime time; and
   d. they had limited power to reject some of the network programming.
   As a result of these abuses, the FCC set up rules called the chain broadcasting regulations in 1941, and NBC challenged this action.
2. *NBC v. United States* (1943)
   a. Supreme Court ruled against NBC, saying the First Amendment does not exempt broadcast media from regulation.
   b. Also said the FCC had the authority to issue rules to hinder monopolistic practices.
   c. NBC was required to sell one of its networks. Sold the Blue network, which later became ABC.
3. Telecommunications Act of 1996
   a. This act brought about a change in the strict philosophy of the FCC regulatory practices.
   b. It made the broadcast ownership rules more liberalized.
      Examples of the liberalization:
      i. In the beginning no company could own more than 7 television stations, 7 AM stations, and 7 FM stations (rule of sevens).
      ii. In 1984 the number changed to 12 (rule of twelves).
      iii. In 1992 the radio stations number changed to 18, then to 20 in 1994; but television stations stayed at 12.
   c. There is no limit on the number of radio and television stations one company can own nationwide.
   d. The number of television households in the country that network-owned stations could reach also increased from 25 percent to 35 percent under the act.
   e. The 35 percent limit had a UHF provision, which allowed for a greater market share if the company's stations were UHF and not VHF.
   f. The rule that one company cannot own radio *and* television stations in the same market did not change.

4. *Fox Television Stations v. FCC* (2002; federal court of appeals)
   a. Ruled that the FCC must eliminate or provide better justification for the 35 percent market cap.
   b. FCC must also do away with the rule barring a company from owning both a television station and a cable system in the same market.
5. Duopoly rule—rewritten in 1999.
   a. Placed limits on the number of television stations a company could own in one market.
   b. The 1999 rule change said a company could buy a second station in the same market if it was
      i. in financial trouble;
      ii. a startup station; or
      iii. a low-rated station in a market with at least eight independently owned stations.
   c. *Sinclair Broadcast Group v. FCC* (2002)
      i. Appellate court ruled that the television duopoly rule was unjustifiable.

NOTE: In 1999, Thomas Hicks merged his 325 radio stations with Clear Channel Communications, which placed 800 radio stations under one owner. With the continuing liberalization of the ownership rules, Clear Channel owned more than 1,200 radio stations and 37 television stations by 2004.

---

6. *local marketing agreements*—when station owners grant authority to someone outside the station the right to determine its programming.
   a. This was good for the station owner because it was cost-effective, allowing the staff of one station to program and sell advertising for others.
7. *microradio stations*—those that run on very low power and serve only a small local area or community.
   a. The FCC began toying with this new idea in 1998 in large part as a response to the "pirate" radio stations that were going on air (there were more than 100 pirate radio stations on the air in 1997).
   b. These were stations that used bootleg radio frequencies on the air for only a few hours a day.
   c. First was "Radio Free Berkeley," which was eventually forced off the air by the FCC.

d. In 2000, the FCC approved the use of microradio stations, but Congress intervened and restored the FCC's frequency interference standards, eliminating many potential on-air channels.

8. *cross-ownership*—when a company owns more than one form of media in a market.

     a. Most of these rules were liberalized or eliminated with the Telecommunications Act.

     b. One rule that was not eliminated was the newspaper–broadcast cross-ownership.

          i. It banned newspapers from buying new broadcast properties in the same market, and vice versa.

          ii. *divestiture*—required sale of media properties (FCC required this in 16 communities).

9. *FCC v. National Citizens Committee for Broadcasting* (1978)

     a. Supreme Court ruled in favor of FCC cross-ownership rules over critics for and against the rules.

     b. But in 1993 Congress authorized FCC to waive the rule so that a company can own a newspaper and a radio station in the 25 largest markets if at least 30 different companies owned radio and television stations in the affected market.

        But this rule was essentially eliminated in 2003, except in markets with fewer than four television stations.

The FCC and Other Regulatory Matters—Past and Present

The 1996 act also made it legal to have a network own and operate cable systems, whereas this practice—such as newspaper and television station cross-ownership—had been previously banned.

1. *Time-Warner Entertainment Company v. FCC* (2001)

     a. Court said that AT&T could merge with several other cable systems, contrary to the FCC's rule that prohibited cable companies from servicing more than 30 percent of cable television households in the United States.

2. Financial interest and syndication rule (1970)

     a. Limited the three major networks from producing and syndicating their own programming.

     b. They could not have a financial interest in independently produced shows they aired.

     c. Could not control or profit from the "reruns" of network shows.

     d. Rule was eliminated by the FCC in a series of moves in the early 1990s.

Development of Antitrust Cases

1. *U.S. v. Radio Corporation of America* (1959)
   a. Justice Department argued that RCA, owner of NBC, used its power to force Westinghouse Broadcasting to trade its Philadelphia station for NBC's Cleveland station, all done with FCC approval.
   b. The federal district court dismissed the suit, but the Supreme Court reversed, saying that FCC approval did not automatically mean that the Justice Department could not challenge the trade.
2. *Community Communications v. City of Boulder* (1982; municipal antitrust case)
   a. Supreme Court said cities are not free from antitrust liability when they grant exclusive cable rights.
   b. The city had allowed Community Communications to provide cable service to part of the city.
   c. Years later, Community Communications wanted to offer their services to more of the city.
   d. City banned Community Communications from expanding, then allowed other firms to come in and apply for a franchise.
3. *AT&T v. City of Portland* (2000; federal appellate court)
   a. Court ruled that cities could not order cable companies to open their lines to allow the broadcast of competing carriers with high-speed Internet access capability.
   b. Only the FCC had that power, the court said.
4. *National Cable and Telecommunications Association v. Gulf Power Company* (2002)
   a. Supreme Court ruled that the cable systems should get reduced-cost access to city utility poles, even if they are going to provide television and Internet service.

Lingering Issues

As has been shown, the policies of the FCC are often very fluid, changing significantly over the span of just a few years. The 1990s must be seen as the era of mergers and consolidations. Some of the largest communications companies in America—and the world—were involved in mergers, the size of which could not previously have been imagined. Names such as Viacom and AOL-Time-Warner have become common in the industry.

And, in 2003, the FCC's Republican majority membership (3–2) prevailed against many people and organizations who argued against lifting the restrictions on newspaper, television, and radio ownership. The controversy was long and heated. With 2004 being a presidential election year, it remains to be seen whether the policies of the 1990s and the early part of the twenty-first century will remain intact. Further, the courts have not had the full chance to review the new regulations for constitutionality. It must be noted that in June 2004, the Third Circuit Court of Appeals allowed a stay of the FCC regulations to remain in effect until certain errors have been corrected. Thus, the effective date, if any, of those regulations remains in doubt.

The Law of
Advertising

A DVERTISING MAY WELL be the fuel that drives the American economic engine, but can one say whatever one wishes to say when advertising something? Is it sufficient to bury notices of product problems
down in the fine print? Can an advertiser force a newspaper, radio station, or
magazine to accept a proposed ad? In this chapter, the place of advertising in
our society is explored in an effort to determine whether ads have special rights
or special obligations.

commercial speech doctrine—advertisers have limited power to protect themselves from the regulation of government because they do not get the full
extent of protection offered by the First Amendment.
1. *Valentine v. Chrestensen* (1942)
   a. Chrestensen had an old U.S. submarine that he wanted to dock in the
      New York City wharf.
   b. The city would not let him, so he found another dock and began adver-
      tising tours.
   c. The city officials would not let him distribute the handbills because of
      a no-littering ordinance (only political handbills were allowed).
   d. He added a statement on the back of his handbill criticizing the city for
      not allowing him to dock in the wharf.

e. Supreme Court said the note was not acceptable because the handbill was still primarily advertising.

2. *Pittsburgh Press v. Pittsburgh Commission on Human Relations* (1973)
   a. The commission had told the paper to stop classifying its job ads as gender based.
   b. The paper argued that classifying them that way was an editorial judgment.
   c. The Supreme Court said the classifieds are a part of commercial speech and were promoting discrimination, upholding the commission.

3. *Bigelow v. Virginia* (1975)
   a. Bigelow put an ad in the Virginia paper about abortion services in New York. Abortions and their advertising were illegal in Virginia but legal in New York. He was prosecuted under Virginia law.
   b. The Supreme Court said that the services were not illegal in New York, that readers had a right to receive the information, and that the message had First Amendment protection even though it was only an ad.
   c. The court also said there would have to be a compelling state interest to ban certain commercial speech. This was a major departure from existing commercial speech law.

4. *Virginia State Board of Pharmacy v. Virginia Citizens Consumer Council* (1976)
   a. Supreme Court overturned Virginia law on banning drug price advertising, emphasizing the rights of consumers to receive information.

5. *Linmark Associates v. Willingboro* (1977)
   a. New Jersey had a law that banned FOR SALE signs from being put in yards.
   b. A real estate company went to court saying New Jersey could not use the fact that there was a great deal of racial change going on ("white flight") as the reason for justifying the law.
   c. Supreme Court said that the yard signs were legal and that the city could not constitutionally deprive the public of the information offered by the FOR SALE signs.

6. *Carey v. Population Services International* (1977)
   a. Supreme Court overturned several New York laws that dealt with the advertising of contraceptives, saying there was no compelling state interest that justified them.

7. *Central Hudson Gas & Electric v. Public Service Commission of New York* (1980)
   a. The New York Public Service Commission prohibited utility companies from advertising their services over conservation of resources.
   b. The company lost in the New York Court of Appeals, but the Supreme Court reversed.

c. The court established the *Central Hudson* test to determine the legality of restrictions on advertising:
   i. whether the expression is protected by the First Amendment;
   ii. whether the claimed government interest that justifies the restriction is substantial;
   iii. whether the regulation directly advances the government interest in question; and
   iv. whether the regulation is broader than needed to fulfill the government interest.[1]

Constitutionality of Lawyer Advertising

1. *Bates v. Arizona State Bar* (1977)
   a. Two lawyers were reprimanded by the state bar for advertising their rates.
   b. The Supreme Court ruled that Arizona's ban on advertising by lawyers was not legal and that the ads could not be banned unless they were misleading or fraudulent.
2. *Ohralik v. Ohio State Bar Association* (1978)
   a. The Supreme Court ruled it permissible to discipline a lawyer who uses "ambulance chasing" to get clients because rules adopted to control lawyer conduct do not violate the constitution.
3. *Friedman v. Rogers* (1979)
   a. Supreme Court ruled that Texas's ban on trade names, instead of optometrist's personal name, was legal.
   b. It said that optometrists could not use a trade name in their practice because it could be deceiving.
4. *In re RMJ* (1982)
   a. Missouri rules said lawyers could use only certain words when advertising the types of law they practiced, but one lawyer was reprimanded for not following the rules.
   b. The Supreme Court reversed, saying the advertising by lawyers was protected by the First Amendment.
5. *Zauderer v. Office of Disciplinary Counsel* (1985)
   a. In Ohio, Zauderer placed an ad in the newspaper promoting his representation of women who were suing the maker of a contraceptive (Dalcon Shield) that was known to cause harmful side effects, and he advertised taking on more clients.
   b. The ad ran with a picture of the contraceptive.
   c. He was reprimanded for this action, but the Supreme Court overturned Ohio's ban, thereby allowing lawyers to use illustrations in their advertising.

6. *Shapero v. Kentucky Bar Association* (1988)
   a. Kentucky and other states did not allow the mailing of solicitations by lawyers to people who might be in need of a lawyer; but the Supreme Court overturned the law, saying a blanket restriction was not consistent with the First Amendment.
7. *Peel v. Attorney Registration and Disciplinary Commission* (1990)
   a. Court said that Illinois could not ban advertising that said a lawyer was a specialist in a certain field, although some circumstances could be false or misleading, the blanket prohibition could also restrict truthful advertising.
8. *Ibanez v. Florida Department of Professional and Business Regulation* (1994)
   a. Supreme Court said the board could not ban accountants from advertising that they were also lawyers.
9. *Florida Bar v. Went for It, Inc.* (1995)
   a. Supreme Court said a Florida law preventing lawyers from targeting their mailings to accident or disaster victims within 30 days of the event was legal because the state has a substantial government interest in "protecting the privacy and tranquility of personal injury victims and their loved ones against intrusive, unsolicited conduct by lawyers" (Sandra Day O'Connor).

Commercial Speech Cases in the 1980s

1. *Metromedia v. San Diego* (1981)
   a. Supreme Court ruled against a San Diego ordinance that did not allow political or commercial billboard messages, because local government did not have the power to ban all billboard signs; ordinance was overly broad.
2. *Members of the Los Angeles City Council v. Taxpayers for Vincent* (1984)
   a. Supreme Court ruled that the local government has the right to outlaw the types of signs (political) when they are on public property.
   b. The difference between this case and the one before is that this law dealt only with restricting the signs on public property, not the banning of billboards on private property.
3. *Bolger v. Young Drug Products Corporation* (1983)
   a. Supreme Court ruled the post office cannot ban the mailing of ads for contraceptives.
4. *Posadas de Puerto Rico Associates v. Tourism Company of Puerto Rico* (1986)
   a. Supreme Court upheld a Puerto Rican act that allowed casino gambling but did not allow casino advertising locally.
   b. Posadas, which owned and operated a casino and hotel on the island, protested the act, and they were fined several times for violating the advertising law.

c. The court said that advertising that is considered "harmful" has less First Amendment protection than other advertising and is therefore subject to greater regulation.

5. *State University of New York v. Fox* (1989)

a. Supreme Court upheld the university's right to restrict advertising activities on campus and said such restrictions need not be "the least intrusive."

Commercial Speech Cases in the 1990s

1. *Cincinnati v. Discovery Network* (1993)

a. The city had demanded that the free magazines remove 62 newsracks from city property.

b. But they allowed 2,000 newspaper racks to stay.

c. The Supreme Court said the city could not restrict the magazine racks while allowing the newspaper stands because the city had not provided a sufficient reason for the difference nor a "reasonable fit" between the action taken and the government purpose.

2. *United States v. Edge Broadcasting* (1993)

a. The Supreme Court ruled that a North Carolina radio station could be banned from advertising the Virginia lottery, even though a large majority of their listeners were from Virginia.

3. *Great New Orleans Broadcasting Association v. United States* (1999)

a. Supreme Court said gambling advertising cannot be prohibited in states where gambling is legal.

4. *Valley Broadcasting v. United States* (1997; court of appeals)

a. The court ruled that a Nevada rule banning gambling advertising was against the First Amendment.

EXAMPLE: In Baltimore there was a ban on the use of billboard advertising that promoted the use of beer and cigarettes. An appellate court heard the case and still upheld the ban. The Supreme Court ordered the appellate court to hear the case again in light of *44 Liquormart*. It did but still ruled the ban legal because the billboards encouraged minors to use the products. Supreme Court, certiorari denied, *Anheuser-Busch, Inc. v. Schmoke*, and *Penn Advertising v. Schmoke*.

5. *44 Liquormart v. Rhode Island* (1996)
   a. Court ruled that a state cannot prohibit the advertising of liquor prices, despite the control over alcohol given to the states under the Twenty-first Amendment.
   b. This case brought about a lot of controversy.

Commercial Speech Cases in the Twenty-first Century

1. *Lorillard Tobacco v. Reilly* (2001)
   a. Supreme Court ruled that cigarette ads were preempted by the Federal Cigarette Labeling and Advertising Act and could therefore not be regulated.
   b. The case came about from a Massachusetts regulation that would not allow a cigarette ad within 1,000 feet of a school, park, or public playground. The rule was overturned.
2. *United States v. United Foods, Inc.* (2001)
   a. The court ruled that forced advertising was against the First Amendment.
   b. There had been state and federal programs that were demanding farmers and growers to pay for common advertising campaigns of their products, even if they did not like the message the advertising presented (in this case, mushroom growers).

Corporate Speech: Noncommercial

1. *First National Bank v. Bellotti* (1978)
   a. Massachusetts law banned corporate advertising of their position on ballot measures unless the measure would "materially affect" the company's business.
   b. The Supreme Court overturned the law for a number of reasons:
      i. placed no restrictions on mass communication corporations but did on others;
      ii. no evidence to prove that corporate ads would overwhelm others;
      iii. banks and other institutions might actually add to economic discussions.[2]
2. *Consolidated Edison v. Public Service Commission of New York* (1980)
   a. The Supreme Court ruled that the commission could not prohibit utilities from sending inserts with their bills that dealt with political or controversial matters because it was an excessive restriction on the corporation's First Amendment rights.

    b. Court set up three conditions that would justify government regulation of noncommercial speech:

       i. restriction is a "precisely drawn means of serving a compelling state interest";

      ii. the restriction is required to fulfill a "significant government interest" and merely regulates time/place/manner, leaving open "ample alternate channels for communications"; and

     iii. there is a narrowly drawn restriction on speech under a few special circumstances where disruption of government activities must be avoided (i.e., military base).

3. *Pacific Gas & Electric Company v. Public Utilities Commission of California* (1986)

    a. The commission ordered the utility to insert a watchdog group's leaflet with the utility bills in place of their own newsletter four times a year.

    b. The court said this violated the company's First Amendment rights.

4. *Austin v. Michigan State Chamber of Commerce* (1990)

    a. Michigan law prevented a company from making financial contributions to candidates from a general fund but allowed the contributions to come from a special-purpose fund.

    b. The Supreme Court ruled this law legal because it still allows corporations to endorse and aid candidates by the use of special funds and political action committees.

5. *Kasky v. Nike, Inc.* (2002)

    a. Nike responded to criticism of its overseas employees' working conditions by a series of public statements; Kasky sues under California State false-advertising law.

    b. California appellate court said the statements were protected by the First Amendment; California Supreme Court disagreed and reversed.

    c. Majority of the U.S. Supreme Court agreed to hear the appeal but then decided it should go to trial before the high court got involved.

Advertising and Access to the Media

1. *Shuck v. Carroll Daily Herald* (1933)
Iowa Supreme Court ruled that newspapers are private entities and have no obligation to serve everyone.

2. *Chicago Joint Board-Amalgamated Clothing Workers of America v. Chicago Tribune* (1970)

    a. Court ruled against union that had demanded access to the paper's advertising section, saying the paper was private and did not have to serve every person's interest.

3. *Associates & Aldrich v. Times Mirror* (1971; federal appellate court)
   a. Court ruled against movie producer who claimed a newspaper censored his ads, saying the paper had no obligation to accept such ads, much less publish them exactly as sent.
4. *Miami Herald v. Tornillo* (1974)
   a. The paper attacked Tornillo, who was running for the legislature.
   b. He demanded space in the paper for a reply to the attacks.
   c. Florida had a law that was a "right of reply" for candidates who were attacked by a paper.
   d. The paper refused to print his reply, and he sued.
   e. State supreme court ruled in his favor, but the U.S. Supreme Court reversed, saying newspapers have a First Amendment right to regulate their own content.
5. *Home Placement Service v. Providence Journal* (1982)
   a. Paper refused space to a rental referral service on the grounds of trying to prevent fraud.
   b. Federal appellate court ruled that no other referral service had been cited for fraudulent claims and that the service was actually in direct competition with the paper.
   c. The point the court made was that a paper that has almost complete control in its service area runs the risk of violating antitrust law when it denies space to a business that is basically competition for the paper.

NOTE: With the case of government-sponsored media, there is a great obligation to be content neutral, which means that they often must accept advertising they may not like or agree with.

Access to Transit System Advertising

1. *Lehman v. Shaker Heights* (1974)
   a. Supreme Court ruled that a city-run bus system did not have to give space to a political candidate.
   b. The court said the space was not automatically a public forum.
   c. The case met viewpoint-neutral criteria because it did not allow any political ads.
2. *Lebron v. Washington Metropolitan Area Transit Authority* (1984)
   a. The federal appellate court said transit officials could not, after accepting other political ads, reject a photomontage that was critical of Reagan.

3. *Lebron v. National Railroad Passenger Corporation* (1995)
   a. Amtrak refused ad space to Lebron for a political ad on a large billboard in Penn Station. The court ruled that the company had not violated any law because they had never accepted political ads before.
4. *Christ's Bride Ministries v. Southeastern Pennsylvania Transportation Authority* (1998)
   a. The court said the system could not reject an antiabortion ad after it had accepted ads about sex and family planning.
5. *Children of the Rosary v. City of Phoenix* (1998)
   a. Federal appellate court said this transit system had the authority to reject antiabortion ads because it consistently ran only commercial ads.

Access to School Newspaper Advertising Space

1. *Lee v. Board of Regents* and *Zucker v. Panitz* (1960s)
   a. These cases overturned administrators' efforts to keep student newspapers from using ads with controversial ideas.
2. *Mississippi Gay Alliance v. Goudelock* (1976)
   a. The gay alliance wanted to publish an announcement about its services in the university paper but was turned down by the staff.
   b. The court said they were not violating any law, because it was the staff and not the university that opposed the ad.
3. *Yeo v. Town of Lexington* (1997; Fifth Circuit Court of Appeals)
   a. Said the editors of the Lexington High School newspaper were within their rights to reject advocacy ads because there was no state action involved.
4. *Pitt News v. Pappert* (2004)
   a. The University of Pittsburgh paper challenged a state law that banned the advertising of bars and liquor stores in student media.
   b. The paper argued that this cut into its revenue.
   c. The court of appeals agreed, saying there was a guarantee under the First Amendment that the paper could publish the liquor ads. Further, the court noted, the restriction against placing the ads was directed against the paper as a small group of newspapers, the college press. 379 F.3d 96 (2004).

Regulation of False Advertising

1. *Federal Trade Commission v. Winsted Hosiery Company* (1922)
   a. Supreme Court ruled that false advertising is unfair competition, steering customers away from honest businesses.

b. A company had claimed their clothing was "natural wool" when actually it was made of only 10 percent wool.

2. *Federal Trade Commission v. Raladam* (1931)

    a. The Supreme Court said that the Federal Trade Commission (FTC) cannot act on behalf of the customer when there is little evidence that the said advertising is unfair to the customer or to the competing businesses.

3. FTC's tools to determine deceptive advertising:

    a. identify each affirmative claim or material omission and ask the advertiser to document what the ad says;

    b. determine whether the claim could mislead a typical consumer acting reasonably; and

    c. determine whether the claim is "material," a serious enough representation that it is likely to affect the choice of whether to buy the product.[3]

4. The FTC has several ways of dealing with deceptive advertising. It will

    a. conduct a **sweep**, looking at many business of a certain kind in a certain area;

    b. make the deceptive advertising public; and

    c. use law enforcement power.

        i. First it notifies the advertiser that the ad is deceptive.

        ii. The advertiser may be provided with a proposed ***cease and desist order***.

        iii. The advertiser may choose to sign a ***consent agreement*** to discontinue ad. This does not mean that they admit any fault whatsoever.

        iv. After a 60-day waiting period, the FTC issues a ***consent order***.

        v. The advertiser then signs an ***assurance of voluntary compliance***.

5. If the advertiser refuses to halt the ad, the FTC must go through more formal measures.

    a. An ***administrative law judge*** hears the case and issues a ruling.

    b. The FTC can then review the ruling and decide what to do.

    c. In the end, the FTC can still rule the ads illegal, overturning whatever finding the judge made.

6. The FTC can publish ***guides***, which are statements about how the FTC interprets the propriety of certain advertising practices. Compliance with these by merchants is voluntary.

7. ***affirmative disclosure orders***—require that the ads show the good and the bad sides of a product.

8. *J. B. Williams v. FTC* (1967)

    a. Court ruled that an FTC order to make Geritol reveal that its products did not really help with anemia was legal.

    This is an example of **corrective advertising**.

9. *Warner-Lambert Company v. FTC* (1977)
   a. FTC had demanded that the company run advertising saying that Listerine did not cure sore throats, as previously advertised.
   b. Federal appellate court agreed but said the ads need not contain admission of prior deception.
10. *FTC v. Colgate-Palmolive Company* (1965)
    a. The ad showed Palmolive shaving cream as "shaving sand off sandpaper," even though it really wasn't. The "sandpaper" was a small, transparent plastic sheet.
    b. FTC demanded the ads be stopped.
    c. Supreme Court ruled in FTC's favor but said that **mockups** were only deceptive if they were central to the meaning of the ad.
11. *Weight Watchers International v. FTC* (1994)
    a. The federal appellate court ruled that Weight Watchers had a right to sue the FTC concerning its enforcement policies.
    b. The company claimed that the FTC was making decisions and changing its rules on a case-by-case basis instead of adhering to formal rule-making procedures.

unfairness doctrine—the FTC policy where it began looking not only at deceptive ads but also at ads they thought were unfair even if truthful.

12. FTC considered something unfair advertising if
    a. it caused or was likely to cause substantial consumer injury;
    b. it caused injury that was not avoidable by the consumers themselves; and
    c. the injury was not outweighed by countervailing benefits to consumers.[4]
13. *FTC v. Sperry Hutchinson Company* (1972)
    a. Supreme Court said the FTC can act against "business practices which have an unfair impact on consumers, regardless of whether the practice is deceptive . . . or anti-competitive in the traditional sense."
14. *Immigration and Naturalization Service v. Chadha* (1983)
    a. Supreme Court ruled that Congress does not have the power to veto actions that agencies in the executive branch make.
    b. This case came about because of new restrictions placed on the FTC under the Federal Trade Commission Improvement Act of 1980:
       i. The FTC could not take action against purely unfair ads.
       ii. It halted FTC proceedings on children's television advertising, morticians, and agricultural cooperatives.
       iii. The FTC was ordered to publish every rule it had at the start of each rule-making proceeding.

iv. FTC must give Congress advanced notice of new rules, and Congress had veto power over any new rules the FTC put into place.

15. *Mangini v. RJ Reynolds Tobacco Company* (1994)
   a. Case began with pressure by the FTC for the cigarette company to stop running the "Old Joe" camel campaign ads because it said they were targeted at minors.
   b. The company, of course, said this was not true and refused to quit running it.
   c. *Advertising Age*, a leading publication in the industry, strongly suggested to the company that it should drop the campaign, but Reynolds still refused.
   d. Finally the California Supreme Court ruled in this case that an individual could sue the company for targeting minors in campaigns because it encouraged kids to violate the law and start smoking.
   e. In 1997 the company settled the case by agreeing to stop the campaign forever. It reached a $206 billion agreement with 46 states.

16. ***Other agencies with power to regulate advertising:***
   a. Food and Drug Administration (FDA).
   b. Securities and Exchange Commission.
   c. Postal Service.
   d. Bureau of Tobacco, Alcohol, and Firearms.

17. *FDA v. Brown and Williamson Tobacco* (2000)
   a. Supreme Court ruled that the FDA did not have the power to make tobacco a "drug" and therefore regulate it as such.

18. *Beahm v. FDA* (1997; federal district court)
   a. Judge said that the FDA's rules on cigarette advertising were outside the boundaries of the statutory authority given the agency.

19. *Thompson v. Western State Medical Center* (2002)
   a. Supreme Court overturned the FDA restrictions on the advertising of compounded (prescribed) drugs based on First Amendment and the *Central Hudson* test.

20. *Western States Medical Center v. Shalala* (2001; Ninth Circuit Court of Appeals)
   a. Ruled that the FDA could not restrict advertising of compound drugs, because it violated rights of pharmacists by banning truthful messages about the drugs.

Lanham Act—has a provision that says a company may sue a competitor whose false advertising is hurting its business; statute allows for treble damages.

21. *U-Haul International v. Jartran* (1986)
    a. Jartran had an ad campaign with false and misleading information that U-Haul believed was hurting its business, so it sued.
    b. U.S. Court of Appeals agreed, upholding the largest fraud judgment ever: $40 million.
22. *Alpo Pet Foods v. Ralston Purina* (1991; federal district court)
    a. Ruled that Purina had used false ads to claim that their Puppy Chow could help with canine hip disorder; Alpo was awarded $12 million.
23. *Gillette Company v. Wilkinson Sword, Inc.* (1992; federal district court)
    a. The court awarded a $1 million judgment to Gillette from the advertising agency that came up with a false ad for Wilkinson that said their shaver got a shave six times closer than Gillette's shaver did.
24. *Pizza Hut v. Papa John's International* (2000)
    a. Pizza Hut sued Papa John's for running an ad campaign they considered fraudulent.
    b. The ad claimed "better pizza, better ingredients" and compared the stuff used in Papa John's with the competitor's.
    c. Trial jury ruled in favor of Pizza Hut, but an appellate court reversed the ruling, saying that Pizza Hut had not proved that it was hurt by the advertising.

Other Forms of Advertising Regulation

1. ***printer's ink statute***—advertising fraud law proposed in 1911; 45 states have since adopted.
   Gives state and local prosecuting attorneys the responsibility to enforce the punishment for advertising fraud, which is a crime. In some states these statutes are poorly enforced, and the states rely on individuals to bring civil actions against violators.
2. As the FTC weakened in its power to regulate advertising, the states began to join together to actively regulate.
    a. The attorneys general of the states made up national guideline for airline advertising in 1988 to try to stop fraudulent airline practices.
    b. Some states have been active in trying to enforce the law on advertising fraud.
3. *Morales v. TWA* (1992)
    a. The states had a setback when the court decided that only the Department of Transportation could set such guidelines and restrictions on the airline industry.

4. Regulation and the Internet—three problems with regulating advertising on the Internet:
   a. regulating a worldwide medium;
   b. dealing with the amount of blatant fraud;
   c. regulating the "spam," or unsolicited e-mail, which brings about a lot of questions concerning preemption of the First Amendment.

Notes

1. Wayne Overbeck, *Major Principles of Media Law* (Belmont, Calif.: Thomson-Wadsworth, 2004), 538–39.

2. Overbeck, *Major Principles of Media Law*, 549–50.

3. Overbeck, *Major Principles of Media Law*, 558.

4. Overbeck, *Major Principles of Media Law*, 564.

Glossary

absolutists   Those who believe that the First Amendment provision that "Congress shall make no law" to abridge freedom of press or speech means exactly that: no law!

actual malice   Knowledge of falsity or reckless disregard for the truth.

administrative law judge   An employee of the federal government, usually an attorney, who acts as a judge in cases brought about by the filing of a complaint by an agency against an alleged violator of the agency's regulations.

admonish the jury   An act by the judge of a trial court whereby the judge repeatedly reminds the jurors that they are not to listen to publicity surrounding a case or form any opinions concerning the guilt or innocence of the criminal defendant until all the evidence is in.

affidavit   Sworn statement in writing.

affirmative disclosure orders   Federal Trade Commission orders that require that ads show the good and bad sides of a product.

affirmed   Agreeing with judgment of trial court.

Alien and Sedition Acts (1798)   Acts passed by President John Adams and the Federalist Party members who controlled Congress in an attempt to silence opposition to Adams's possible plans for war with France.

ancillary jurisdiction   A lesser form of subject matter jurisdiction exercised by courts and some administrative agencies such as the Federal Communications Commission that allows those bodies to consider matter not normally within their jurisdiction but which are related to, or form a part of, the material normally regulated or dealt with by a court.

answer   This is the defendant's response to all of the allegations made in the plaintiff's complaint. Defendants will usually "admit" or "deny" the allegations or tell the court that they have insufficient knowledge to address the allegations. See **complaint**.

anti-SLAPP statute   Legislation brought into effect that says if a plaintiff files a meritless lawsuit to discourage the defendant, then the defendant can require the plaintiff to pay their attorney fees and/or face other sanctions.

appellant   The person who "goes up" or "takes a case up" on appeal.

appellee   The opposing party to the appellant.

balancing test, or preferred position   Will give individual words more weight when government or economic or social issues are being discussed, although the words will still involve balancing. Highest protection of words comes with those that deal with public policy.

beyond a reasonable doubt   In criminal cases, the case against the defendant must be supported by "overwhelming evidence" (Texas). Definition will vary by state. See **clear and convincing evidence** and **preponderance of the evidence**.

breach of the duty   The failure to live up to the requirements of the legal duty (question of fact, determined by jury).

buffer zone   Area around an abortion clinic worker's residence, or any other area, where time/place/manner restrictions may be legal. Supreme Court also ruled that banning the use of signs would be acceptable if it were restricted only to signs that carried threats.

bunds   Pro-German American groups that had been active in the United States in the 1930s.

burden of proof   Extent to which the plaintiffs (or prosecution in a criminal case) must prove their case in the minds of the jury.

caption   Title of the case in court.

case on point   Means the precedent directly relates to the same question of law now being faced.

cease and desist order   A directive from the Federal Trade Commission or from any number of other administrative bodies that is issued to direct an individual or business to immediately stop operating outside the boundaries of the law.

cert. den. (certiorari denied)   Appellant's petition for a writ of certiorari to issue from the Supreme Court has been denied in a particular case. Usually listed with the case's citation.

Chafee, Professor Zechariah   Spoke of the idea that speech should be limited only in cases where public safety would be impaired and only where "words will give rise to unlawful acts."

change of venue   Court action that allows a case to be moved from the place and court where it was originally filed, often done to avoid the effects of extensive prejudicial publicity.

civil contempt of court   Is not a punishment but more a form of coercion where the person who is disobeying the court order is put in jail until he or she decides to obey. This can lead to long, indefinite sentences. Reporters who refuse to reveal their sources to a court often face this type of contempt action.

class action suit   Filed by an individual as a representative for a group of people similarly situated.

clear and convincing evidence   Often needed in constitutional cases and some civil matters, such as termination of parental rights. See **beyond a reasonable doubt** and **preponderance of the evidence**.

closing arguments   Lawyers go through the evidence and the law as they see them.

commercial appropriation   The use of someone's name or likeness for commercial purposes without that someone's permission. Also called *misappropriation* or *right of publicity*.

compelling state interest   When the government has to deal with a problem that is of such overwhelming importance that it must act, even when its proposed rule hinders First Amendment rights. Consider child pornography and the need to protect children.

compensatory/actual damages   Those that are provable out-of-pocket expenses; also called **specific damages**. Term will vary by jurisdiction. See **damages**.

complaint   The statement of allegations against the defendant filed by the plaintiff in a civil suit. See **answer**.

compulsory licensing   A statutory right to use an audio recording done by an earlier artist if the second artist pays statutory royalties and performs the piece essentially as written.

concurring opinion   When a judge goes along with outcome of ruling but for different reasons.

consent agreement   A contract signed between the Federal Trade Commission and the previously offending business under the terms of which the offender agrees to voluntarily comply with the law, and the commission agrees not to pursue further legal action until a future violation occurs or the terms of a long-term agreement have been worked out.

consent order If, after a period of 60 days, the Federal Trade Commission will make arrangements for a longer-term agreement with the previously offending business. The advertiser then signs an **assurance of voluntary compliance**, designed to bring an end to the conflict by way of the advertiser's long-term agreement to follow the law.

consideration Payment for the use of the image or name; also called **quid pro quo**.

content basis Where a law seeks to outlaw specific behavior that is possibly constitutionally protected, the state must have a *compelling state interest* to justify it.

content neutrality Rules must apply to everyone, regardless of the message they are sending. When a proposed municipal ordinance is content neutral, only a rational relationship is needed between the local law and the problem it seeks to address.

contra Legal form of "contrary." Usually used to indicate a case that holds opposite the case being discussed.

copyrights Protection for books, papers, manuscripts, music, film, software, art, and so forth.

corrective advertising The result of Federal Trade Commission orders directed to advertisers to correct misstatements of fact in their ads, sometimes referring to the earlier erroneous ads.

cost of defense payment Means by which large suits are often settled. Take the probability of success (a percentage) and multiply by the largest potential judgment, then add the cost of litigating the case. Insurers will often calculate settlement values or figures based on this formula.

criminal contempt of court Is a punishment for an act of severe disrespect for a court. Often heard by a judge other than the judge who was insulted or treated disrespectfully. May result in the imposition of either a fine or jail time, or both.

cross-examination Other party talks to witness (second questioning).

cross-ownership When a company owns more than one form of media in a market.

cruel and unusual punishment Conduct forbidden by the Eighth Amendment to the U.S. Constitution, such as assault or torture by police officials, or unusually harsh or excessive sentences for crimes committed.

damages, or resulting damages The losses suffered by the plaintiff in an action at law (questions of fact as to the amount of damages and whether they are a consequence of the breach) determined by jury.

defamation Act of speaking or writing something that harms someone's reputation.

defendant One who answers to the complaint.

deliberation Jury talks over case.

depositions Face-to-face meetings under oath.

derivative work A product of the original work, such as a movie made from a book or a sequel made of a movie.

direct contempt of court When someone disrupts the courtroom or shows disrespect for the legal process in the presence of the judge, such as refusing to be seated.

direct examination Lawyer talks to his or her own witness or a neutral witness (first questioning).

dissenting opinion The statement of the judges or justices who are against the ruling.

domino theory A military theory applied to the Vietnam War, which suggested that if South Vietnam were "lost" to the Communists, then Laos, Cambodia, Thailand, Burma, and even the Philippines would follow.

duty Requirement to act in a certain fashion (judge's question of law).

en banc When all judges in a federal circuit court hear a case. Their decision becomes law for only that circuit. This course of action is not required to have a case reach the Supreme Court.

enhanced sentencing When the sentencing of a hate crime can be increased from the normal sentence and the First Amendment does not supply protection for the defendant.

entrapment The act of ensnaring or trapping; usually, in the legal sense, used in reference to police action aimed at getting, urging, or facilitating a potential defendant's commission of a crime; true entrapment shows that the defendant had no prior history of committing said offense.

establishment clause   The first clause of the First Amendment, which reads "Congress shall make no law respecting an establishment of religion, or prohibiting the free exercise thereof."

et al.   "and others."

exclusive right   Only the holder of the copyright (usually the creator) can determine how the work is used or copied. He or she can shorten, lengthen, rewrite, or rearrange the work; or perform or display the work or any derivative work he or she may choose to create. The owner can sell or give away any or all of these rights, in part or whole.

fair use   The major exception to the copyright owner's right to exclusive use. Under some circumstances, the work can be used by others. To determine fair use, the court examines the second use for
   a. the purpose of the secondary use;
   b. the nature of the original work;
   c. the percentage of total original work used in the secondary work; and
   d. the effect the use will have on the profit-making capability of the original work.

false light   One of the privacy torts; a minority rule among the states. Similar to libel and intentional infliction of emotional distress. Misrepresentation of whom an individual is.

federal question   When a case involves questions of applicable federal law or rights claimed under the U.S. Constitution.

final instructions   Judge gives information and laws concerning the case to the jury.

forum shopping   The practice of looking for the most beneficial place or venue in which to file a plaintiff's action or criminal case, such as seeking the longest statute of limitations or some other benefit in libel cases.

"gag" orders   Also called **protective orders**. These are issued by a trial court, usually against trial participants (lawyers, parties, etc.), to control out-of-court statements and limit prejudicial publicity.

groundwave   When a radio transmission signal runs along the surface of the Earth (AM stations only).

guides   Statements regarding how the Federal Trade Commission interprets the propriety of certain advertising practices. Compliance with these by merchants is voluntary.

heavy presumption   Makes it more difficult for local governments to carry the burden of proof to outlaw certain types of behavior. "There is a heavy presumption against the constitutionality of statutes that appear to limit free speech rights."

hertz   A unit of measurement within the radio spectrum. One hertz equals one electrical cycle per second and is stated as hertz, kilohertz, megahertz.

in camera ("in chambers")   A judge will often examine proposed evidence in his or her office outside the presence of the parties and the lawyers. This process is called an **in camera** (or in-chambers) examination.

indecent   Not conforming to standards of propriety, good taste, or morality.

indirect contempt of court   When someone does a disrespectful act away from the courtroom, as in refusing to answer a subpoena.

intellectual property   The law governing copyright, TM, and patent.

interrogatories   Written questions to be answered under oath.

intestate   Person dies without a will in force.

intrusion   One of the privacy torts; legal action to compensate a person when a journalist unduly enters into their physical seclusion of private affairs.

intrusive   Behavior that "invades" the zone of privacy expected by many people. When an audience cannot get away from a speech, for example, the speakers are intruding.

joint operating agreements   When two papers in the same town or area merge their business and printing operations but maintain separate editorial staffs.

judgments/decisions/orders   Courts enter the result.

jurisdiction   In courts, this means that the court in question has the power, under law, to hear the case, either because of where the case arose or because of the subject matter at issue. In administrative government, it generally means that an administrative agency has the authority, by law or constitution, to regulate an area of law, such as where the federal government regulates commerce between the states because of the "commerce clause" of the Constitution.

Lanham Act   Federal legislation that contains a provision that allows a company to sue a competitor who has issued false advertising that is hurting the first company's business; statute allows for treble damages.

legitimate public interest   A factor examined by courts to weigh the validity of the purpose of the secondary use.

libel   Written defamation.

libel by implication   When you do not directly state the connection between the plaintiff and some action or situation but a jury can see the connection in context.

libel per quod   Adding other facts or circumstances to the situation allows one to be able to prove or define libel.

libel per se   The very words themselves constitute defamation, as in calling someone a Nazi, or a politician corrupt, or a religious figure immoral.

majority opinion   The ruling of appeals court that finds for the winner.

marketplace of ideas   The idea according to John Milton that freedom of expression should be open to everyone except those who wished to express ideas that he believed to be false.

Meiklejohn, Alexander   Responsible for the "weighting of words" philosophy.

microradio stations   Those that run on very low power and serve only a small local area or community.

moot   When a case is dead or pointless because circumstances have changed.

moral copyrights   Rights retained by the creator of a copyrighted piece under the Berne Convention regarding the future use of the piece so that the creator's permission is required before the piece may be altered.

motion for new trial   Filed if either party disagrees with verdict; also called **motion to correct errors**. Motion for new trial is first step for appeal. Lawyers must cite particular argument or error.

motion to dismiss   Based on the argument that even if everything the plaintiff says is true, he or she is still not entitled to money damages under the law.

motion to quash   Motion to keep out a case, subpoena, or evidence ("motion to kill").

must-carry rules   Federal Communications Commission regulations that require cable television systems to carry local television stations. The stations receive no payment from the cable networks for the carriage.

negligence   Common law term for a common tort.

obscenity Under *Miller v. California*, material is obscene if
   a. an average person, applying contemporary community standards, would find that the work, as a whole, appeals to the prurient interest;
   b. the work depicts or describes, in a patently offensive way, sexual conduct, and the applicable state law specifically defines what depictions or descriptions are prohibited; and
   c. the work, as a whole, lacks serious literary, artistic, political, or scientific value.

opening statements Unimpassioned statements by lawyers about what they expect the evidence to be during the trial.

overbreadth (overbroad) Law is written so that it outlaws protected behavior with behavior that a government could legitimately control.

pandering Catering to or exploiting the sexual desires or weaknesses of others.

parody A humorous imitation of a serious piece of literature, music or other writing that makes fun of the particular work itself.

patently offensive Openly or obviously obnoxious or outrageous.

patents Protection for inventions and scientific processes.

Pentagon Papers This was the nickname for the *New York Times v. United States* (1971) case and to the material itself, which was copied from the Pentagon, ostensibly by Daniel Ellsberg.

peremptory challenges Those challenges of jury pool members (and potential jurors) that may be exercised for any reason, or no reason at all, to remove a potential juror from further consideration.

per se Clearly; on its face; of its own nature.

persona The essence of whom a person is; their traits and characteristics.

personal right A right to sue or make a legal claim that dies with the injured individual.

plaintiff Party that filed complaint for damages.

pornography Literature, films, or other media that depicts or describes erotic behavior with an intention to cause sexual excitement.

preemptive jurisdiction When the power of the federal government allows it to act in an area, this doctrine preempts state action in the same area.

prejudicial publicity   One-sided publicity, usually extensive, surrounding what is usually a controversial trial, leading to a condition within the local community that serves to deny a criminal defendant his or her right to a fair trial by an unbiased jury.

preliminary jury instructions   Usually instructions given about behavior during the trial and a brief statement of what the trial is about.

preponderance of the evidence   In civil cases, "tips the scale of justice just a little bit" or sometimes argued to be 50.1 percent of the case. Many courts use the definition of "more likely true than not true." See **beyond a reasonable doubt** and **clear and convincing evidence**.

presumptions   The practice of looking at a case or fact situation with a pre-existing thought that the case or fact situation should be handled in a particular manner. For example, consider the idea that we would change a presumption from "when a (state) statute is enacted, it is considered valid until a challenger proves otherwise." Now, after the 1948 Congress of Industrial Organizations case, where the act appeared on its face to be a restriction on First Amendment freedoms, we will presume it to be invalid until the state can prove otherwise.

primary service area   The central area where a radio station's signal is the clearest, usually seen as a circle around the station's broadcasting base. A lesser service area exists—the Grade B contour—where the signal can be heard but is weaker.

prior restraint   Censorship.

privilege   Immunity from legal liability by reason of some constitution, statutory of common law protection.

product disparagement   When the product of a business is libeled.

promissory estoppel   Legal doctrine used as a remedy when a person is harmed because he or she agreed to do something for someone else, relying on that second person's promise and the promise was broken. Under this doctrine, the second party may be barred from denying the existence of the agreement.

property right   This type of right stays with whatever property is being fought over or may pass to the survivors of a deceased person.

prurient interest   Appealing to lustful, lewd, or salacious thoughts or desires.

public disclosure of embarrassing private facts   One of the privacy torts; arises out of the publication of the nonnewsworthy private matters of an individual in such a manner as would outrage the community's notion of decency.

public forum Sidewalks are traditionally public forums where speech may be freely expressed, but there may be other types of forums.

qualified privilege Libel defense that allows media to report on government proceedings and records without fear of suit, provided they give fair and accurate account. Sometimes called **conditional privilege** or **fair reports privilege**.

quasi-public Private land used for public purposes and treated as public under the law.

radio spectrum The range of radio frequencies used for radio, television, and other electromagnetic communications, between 1 kilohertz and 300 megahertz.

rational relationship There must be a rational relationship between a proposed law and the government's stated reason for its goal (what it wants to do versus the means by which it wants to do it).

re-cross-examination Other party asks questions again, if necessary.

redacted Removed or edited. Usually, documents produced under a freedom of information request will have information redacted, particularly if the document contains criminal or national security references or matters of a highly personal nature.

redirect examination First lawyer talks to witness again, if necessary.

remand the case Sends it back to the court.

request for production Request for documents or things to be examined in relation to the lawsuit. May be addressed to parties or nonparties.

retransmission An option for local stations that would bar cable networks from carrying local station programming without their permission or some form of payment.

reversed Disagreeing with trial judgment and issuing order for a new trial.

rhetorical hyperbole A great exaggeration used to describe someone—such as a public official or public figure—often in such terms as to be totally unbelievable.

scarcity rationale Because only a limited number of frequencies exist, only a limited number of stations can broadcast, thereby justifying government regulations.

seditious libel Term applied to any expression of opinion or fact that tends to damage the reputation of government or government officials or to arguably promote dissension, disorder, or treason. Also called **criminal sedition**, **criminal syndicalism**, **sedition**, **seditious anarchy**, and a number of other names.

self-censorship When publishers or writers "censor themselves" by calming down their words advocating some issue so as not to offend the government or someone else.

self-righting process The theory that true ideas would succeed over false ones in a free-speech society, making censorship unnecessary.

sequester the jury The act of removing a jury panel from the regular community for the duration of a trial; generally an effort to isolate jurors from extensive publicity surrounding the case with which they are involved.

shield laws Statutes passed by the states that serve to protect journalists from being forced to identify their sources of information. These laws generally keep a reporter from being jailed for contempt of court for refusing to identify those sources.

sky wave A means of travel for AM radio signals at night, when they travel out into space and are reflected back to Earth by the ionosphere. This can become a problem because the use of the sky wave increases the AM signal, causing interference for other night broadcasters.

slander Verbal defamation.

SLAPP lawsuits Strategic lawsuits against public participation.

Smith Act Also called the Alien Registration Act of 1940, which made it a crime to advocate the violent overthrow of the government or to belong to a group that advocated same.

social contract theory Basically express the belief that the government is to serve the people, which is directly contrary to the idea of the divine right of kings. The power to govern is given to the government by the people with the understanding that the government will protect the natural rights of the people. Included in these natural rights are the right to life, liberty, and property ownership.

stare decisis Literally, let the decision stand, the basis of the doctrine of precedent which relies on earlier cases as the reference for deciding new ones.

statutory damages Sum of money a court may award based on the copyright statute when actual damages are either hard to prove or very nominal.

strict judicial scrutiny The standard applied by a court to any administrative practices, such as affirmative action, where key elements are based strictly—or to a large extent—on matters of race or gender.

student forum of expression   Any area of a college campus or a high school campus that has become recognized as a place for the statement of divergent opinions; including any publication, such as a student newspaper that traditionally prints letters to the editor and other statements of student opinion.

subpoenas   Order to appear for questioning or something.

subpoenas duces tecum   Order to show up "and bring documents with you."

subsequent punishment   This doctrine or belief allows you to publish without being censored in advance, but the consequences afterward are yours alone to bear, as in libel cases.

substantial similarity   An element required for proof of a copyright infringement; that is, the secondary work must be substantially similar to the original copyrighted piece before an infringement can be found.

symbolic speech   Actions that deliver messages and can be interpreted as "speech," such as flag burning or the giving of the Nazi salute.

testate   Person dies with a will in force.

time/place/manner restrictions   Usually placed by local governments on such things as picketing and demonstrations.

tort actions   Civil wrongs from the common law tried in state courts, the trials of which usually include money damages and a jury trial. It is generally not a constitutional question but one of common law.

trademarks   Protection for words, phrases, symbols identifying products, services, or companies.

transparency   The degree to which the operations of government are open to examination by the press and the citizenry.

treble damages   An amount of damages set by a court that reflects three times the actual amount of damages, such as those in violation of the Trademark Law Revision Act.

unfair competition or news piracy   Repeatedly taking the news production from another source and claiming it and using it as your own.

Unfairness Doctrine   The Federal Trade Commission policy of looking not only at deceptive ads but also at ads it thought were unfair even if truthful. The commission considered something unfair advertising if

   a. it caused or was likely to cause substantial consumer injury;
   b. it caused injury that was not avoidable by the consumers themselves; and
   c. the injury was not outweighed by countervailing benefits to consumers.

verdicts   Jury renders verdicts; the decision by the jury.

voir dire ("to see, to say")   Ask questions to potential jurors to see what they say and their reactions to the questions.

work product   A term applied to notes, tapes, writings, photographs, charts, or diagrams used by a journalist in constructing a story from its earliest stages.

works made for hire   When a person creates a work for their employer, the copyright is the employer's, not the creator's, if the facts determine that an employer–employee relationship exists.

writ   An old-fashioned word for an order from the court.

Constitution of
the United States
of America

Preamble

WE THE PEOPLE of the United States, in Order to form a more perfect Union, establish Justice, insure domestic Tranquility, provide for the common defence, promote the general Welfare, and secure the Blessings of Liberty to ourselves and our Posterity, do ordain and establish this Constitution for the United States of America.

Article I: The Legislative Branch

Section 1: The Legislature

All legislative Powers herein granted shall be vested in a Congress of the United States, which shall consist of a Senate and House of Representatives.

Section 2: The House

The House of Representatives shall be composed of Members chosen every second Year by the People of the several States, and the Electors in each State shall have the Qualifications requisite for Electors of the most numerous Branch of the State Legislature.

No Person shall be a Representative who shall not have attained to the Age of twenty-five Years, and been seven Years a Citizen of the United States, and who shall not, when elected, be an Inhabitant of that State in which he shall be chosen.

(Representatives and direct Taxes shall be apportioned among the several States which may be included within this Union, according to their respective Numbers, which shall be determined by adding to the whole Number of free Persons, including those bound to Service for a Term of Years, and excluding Indians not taxed, three fifths of all other Persons.) [The sentence in parentheses was superseded by Amendment XIV, section 2.] The actual Enumeration shall be made within three Years after the first Meeting of the Congress of the United States, and within every subsequent Term of ten Years, in such Manner as they shall by Law direct. The Number of Representatives shall not exceed one for every thirty Thousand, but each State shall have at Least one Representative; and until such enumeration shall be made, the State of New Hampshire shall be entitled to chuse [*sic*] three, Massachusetts eight, Rhode Island and Providence Plantations one, Connecticut five, New York six, New Jersey four, Pennsylvania eight, Delaware one, Maryland six, Virginia ten, North Carolina five, South Carolina five and Georgia three.

When vacancies happen in the Representation from any State, the Executive Authority thereof shall issue Writs of Election to fill such Vacancies.

The House of Representatives shall chuse [*sic*] their Speaker and other Officers; and shall have the sole Power of Impeachment.

Section 3: The Senate

The Senate of the United States shall be composed of two Senators from each State *(chosen by the Legislature thereof)* [The words in parentheses were superseded by Amendment XVII, section 1] for six Years; and each Senator shall have one Vote.

Immediately after they shall be assembled in Consequence of the first Election, they shall be divided as equally as may be into three Classes. The Seats of the Senators of the first Class shall be vacated at the Expiration of the second Year, of the second Class at the Expiration of the fourth Year, and of the third Class at the Expiration of the sixth Year, so that one third may be chosen every second Year *(and if Vacancies happen by Resignation, or otherwise, during the Recess of the Legislature of any State, the Executive thereof may make temporary Appointments until the next Meeting of the Legislature, which shall then fill such Vacancies).* [The words in parentheses were superseded by Amendment XVII, section 2.]

No person shall be a Senator who shall not have attained to the Age of thirty Years, and been nine Years a Citizen of the United States, and who shall not, when elected, be an Inhabitant of that State for which he shall be chosen.

The Vice President of the United States shall be President of the Senate, but shall have no Vote, unless they be equally divided.

The Senate shall chuse [*sic*] their other Officers, and also a President pro tempore, in the absence of the Vice President, or when he shall exercise the Office of President of the United States.

The Senate shall have the sole Power to try all Impeachments. When sitting for that Purpose, they shall be on Oath or Affirmation. When the President of the United States is tried, the Chief Justice shall preside: And no Person shall be convicted without the Concurrence of two thirds of the Members present.

Judgment in Cases of Impeachment shall not extend further than to removal from Office, and disqualification to hold and enjoy any Office of honor, Trust or Profit under the United States: but the Party convicted shall nevertheless be liable and subject to Indictment, Trial, Judgment and Punishment, according to Law.

Section 4: Elections, Meetings

The Times, Places and Manner of holding Elections for Senators and Representatives, shall be prescribed in each State by the Legislature thereof; but the Congress may at any time by Law make or alter such Regulations, except as to the Place of Chusing [*sic*] Senators.

The Congress shall assemble at least once in every Year, and such Meeting shall *(be on the first Monday in December)* (The preceding words in parentheses were superseded by Amendment XX, section 2) unless they shall by Law appoint a different Day.

Section 5: Membership, Rules, Journals, Adjournment

Each House shall be the Judge of the Elections, Returns and Qualifications of its own Members, and a Majority of each shall constitute a Quorum to do Business; but a smaller number may adjourn from day to day, and may be authorized to compel the Attendance of absent Members, in such Manner, and under such Penalties as each House may provide.

Each House may determine the Rules of its Proceedings, punish its Members for disorderly Behavior, and, with the Concurrence of two-thirds, expel a Member.

Each House shall keep a Journal of its Proceedings, and from time to time publish the same, excepting such Parts as may in their Judgment require Secrecy; and the Yeas and Nays of the Members of either House on any question shall, at the Desire of one fifth of those Present, be entered on the Journal.

Neither House, during the Session of Congress, shall, without the Consent of the other, adjourn for more than three days, nor to any other Place than that in which the two Houses shall be sitting.

Section 6: Compensation

(The Senators and Representatives shall receive a Compensation for their Services, to be ascertained by Law, and paid out of the Treasury of the United States.) [The words in parentheses were modified by Amendment XXVII.] They shall in all Cases, except Treason, Felony and Breach of the Peace, be privileged from Arrest during their Attendance at the Session of their respective Houses, and in going to and returning from the same; and for any Speech or Debate in either House, they shall not be questioned in any other Place.

No Senator or Representative shall, during the Time for which he was elected, be appointed to any civil Office under the Authority of the United States which shall have been created, or the Emoluments whereof shall have been increased during such time; and no Person holding any Office under the United States, shall be a Member of either House during his Continuance in Office.

Section 7: Revenue Bills, Legislative Process, Presidential Veto

All bills for raising Revenue shall originate in the House of Representatives; but the Senate may propose or concur with Amendments as on other Bills.

Every Bill which shall have passed the House of Representatives and the Senate, shall, before it become a Law, be presented to the President of the United States; If he approve he shall sign it, but if not he shall return it, with his Objections to that House in which it shall have originated, who shall enter the Objections at large on their Journal, and proceed to reconsider it. If after such Reconsideration two thirds of that House shall agree to pass the Bill, it shall be sent, together with the Objections, to the other House, by which it shall likewise be reconsidered, and if approved by two thirds of that House, it shall become a Law. But in all such Cases the Votes of both Houses shall be determined by Yeas and Nays, and the Names of the Persons voting for and against the Bill shall be entered on the Journal of each House respectively. If any Bill shall not be returned by the President within ten Days (Sundays excepted) after it shall have been presented to him, the Same shall be a Law, in like Manner as if he had signed it, unless the Congress by their Adjournment prevent its Return, in which Case it shall not be a Law.

Every Order, Resolution, or Vote to which the Concurrence of the Senate and House of Representatives may be necessary (except on a question of Adjournment) shall be presented to the President of the United States; and before the Same shall take Effect, shall be approved by him, or being disapproved by him, shall be repassed [*sic*] by two thirds of the Senate and House of Representatives, according to the Rules and Limitations prescribed in the Case of a Bill.

Section 8: Powers of Congress

The Congress shall have Power

To lay and collect Taxes, Duties, Imposts and Excises, to pay the Debts and provide for the common Defence [*sic*] and general Welfare of the United States; but all Duties, Imposts and Excises shall be uniform throughout the United States;

To borrow money on the credit of the United States;

To regulate Commerce with foreign Nations, and among the several States, and with the Indian Tribes;

To establish an uniform Rule of Naturalization, and uniform Laws on the subject of Bankruptcies throughout the United States;

To coin Money, regulate the Value thereof, and of foreign Coin, and fix the Standard of Weights and Measures;

To provide for the Punishment of counterfeiting the Securities and current Coin of the United States;

To establish Post Offices and Post Roads;

To promote the Progress of Science and useful Arts, by securing for limited Times to Authors and Inventors the exclusive Right to their respective Writings and Discoveries;

To constitute Tribunals inferior to the supreme Court;

To define and punish Piracies and Felonies committed on the high Seas, and Offenses against the Law of Nations;

To declare War, grant Letters of Marque and Reprisal, and make Rules concerning Captures on Land and Water;

To raise and support Armies, but no Appropriation of Money to that Use shall be for a longer Term than two Years;

To provide and maintain a Navy;

To make Rules for the Government and Regulation of the land and naval Forces;

To provide for calling forth the Militia to execute the Laws of the Union, suppress Insurrections and repel Invasions;

To provide for organizing, arming, and disciplining the Militia, and for governing such Part of them as may be employed in the Service of the United States, reserving to the States respectively, the Appointment of the Officers, and the Authority of training the Militia according to the discipline prescribed by Congress;

To exercise exclusive Legislation in all Cases whatsoever, over such District (not exceeding ten Miles square) as may, by Cession of particular States, and the acceptance of Congress, become the Seat of the Government of the United States, and to exercise like Authority over all Places purchased by the Consent of the Legislature of the State in which the Same shall be, for the Erection of Forts, Magazines, Arsenals, dock-Yards, and other needful Buildings; And

To make all Laws which shall be necessary and proper for carrying into Execution the foregoing Powers, and all other Powers vested by this Constitution in the Government of the United States, or in any Department or Officer thereof.

Section 9: Limits on Congress

The Migration or Importation of such Persons as any of the States now existing shall think proper to admit, shall not be prohibited by the Congress prior to the Year one thousand eight hundred and eight, but a tax or duty may be imposed on such Importation, not exceeding ten dollars for each Person.

The privilege of the Writ of Habeas Corpus shall not be suspended, unless when in Cases of Rebellion or Invasion the public Safety may require it.

No Bill of Attainder or ex post facto Law shall be passed.

(No capitation, or other direct, Tax shall be laid, unless in Proportion to the Census or Enumeration herein before directed to be taken.) [Section in parentheses modified by Amendment XVI.]

No Tax or Duty shall be laid on Articles exported from any State.

No Preference shall be given by any Regulation of Commerce or Revenue to the Ports of one State over those of another: nor shall Vessels bound to, or from, one State, be obliged to enter, clear, or pay Duties in another.

No Money shall be drawn from the Treasury, but in Consequence of Appropriations made by Law; and a regular Statement and Account of the Receipts and Expenditures of all public Money shall be published from time to time.

No Title of Nobility shall be granted by the United States: And no Person holding any Office of Profit or Trust under them, shall, without the Consent of the Congress, accept of any present, Emolument, Office, or Title, of any kind whatever, from any King, Prince or foreign State.

Section 10: Powers Prohibited of States

No State shall enter into any Treaty, Alliance, or Confederation; grant Letters of Marque [*sic*] and Reprisal; coin Money; emit Bills of Credit; make any Thing but gold and silver Coin a Tender in Payment of Debts; pass any Bill of Attainder, ex post facto Law, or Law impairing the Obligation of Contracts, or grant any Title of Nobility.

No State shall, without the Consent of the Congress, lay any Imposts or Duties on Imports or Exports, except what may be absolutely necessary for executing its inspection Laws: and the net Produce of all Duties and Imposts, laid by any State on Imports or Exports, shall be for the Use of the Treasury of the United States; and all such Laws shall be subject to the Revision and Controul [*sic*] of the Congress.

No State shall, without the Consent of Congress, lay any duty of Tonnage, keep Troops, or Ships of War in time of Peace, enter into any Agreement or Compact with another State, or with a foreign Power, or engage in War, unless actually invaded, or in such imminent Danger as will not admit of delay.

Article II: The Executive Branch

Section 1: The President

The executive Power shall be vested in a President of the United States of America. He shall hold his Office during the Term of four Years, and, together with the Vice-President chosen for the same Term, be elected, as follows:

Each State shall appoint, in such Manner as the Legislature thereof may direct, a Number of Electors, equal to the whole Number of Senators and Representatives to which the State may be entitled in the Congress: but no Senator or Representative, or Person holding an Office of Trust or Profit under the United States, shall be appointed an Elector.

(The Electors shall meet in their respective States, and vote by Ballot for two persons, of whom one at least shall not lie an Inhabitant of the same State with themselves. And they shall make a List of all the Persons voted for, and of the Number of Votes for each; which List they shall sign and certify, and transmit sealed to the Seat of the Government of the United States, directed to the President of the Senate. The President of the Senate shall, in the Presence of the Senate and House of Representatives, open all the Certificates, and the Votes shall then be counted. The Person having the greatest Number of Votes shall be the President, if such Number be a Majority of the whole Number of Electors appointed; and if there be more than one who have such Majority, and have an equal Number of Votes, then the House of Representatives shall immediately chuse [sic] by Ballot one of them for President; and if no Person have a Majority, then from the five highest on the List the said House shall in like Manner chuse [sic] the President. But in chusing [sic] the President, the Votes shall be taken by States, the Representation from each State having one Vote; a quorum for this Purpose shall consist of a Member or Members from two-thirds of the States, and a Majority of all the States shall be necessary to a Choice. In every Case, after the Choice of the President, the Person having the greatest Number of Votes of the Electors shall be the Vice President. But if there should remain two or more who have equal Votes, the Senate shall chuse [sic] from them by Ballot the Vice-President.) [This clause in parentheses was superseded by Amendment XII.]

The Congress may determine the Time of chusing [*sic*] the Electors, and the Day on which they shall give their Votes; which Day shall be the same throughout the United States.

No person except a natural born Citizen, or a Citizen of the United States, at the time of the Adoption of this Constitution, shall be eligible to the Office of President; neither shall any Person be eligible to that Office who shall not have attained to the Age of thirty-five Years, and been fourteen Years a Resident within the United States.

(In Case of the Removal of the President from Office, or of his Death, Resignation, or Inability to discharge the Powers and Duties of the said Office, the same shall devolve on the Vice President, and the Congress may by Law provide for the Case of Removal, Death, Resignation or Inability, both of the President and Vice President, declaring what Officer shall then act as President, and such Officer shall act accordingly, until the Disability be removed, or a President shall be elected.) [This clause in parentheses has been modified by Amendments XX and XXV.]

The President shall, at stated Times, receive for his Services, a Compensation, which shall neither be increased nor diminished during the Period for which he shall have been elected, and he shall not receive within that Period any other Emolument from the United States, or any of them.

Before he enter on the Execution of his Office, he shall take the following Oath or Affirmation:

"I do solemnly swear (or affirm) that I will faithfully execute the Office of President of the United States, and will to the best of my Ability, preserve, protect and defend the Constitution of the United States."

Section 2: Civilian Power over Military, Cabinet, Pardon Power, Appointments

The President shall be Commander in Chief of the Army and Navy of the United States, and of the Militia of the several States, when called into the actual Service of the United States; he may require the Opinion, in writing, of the principal Officer in each of the executive Departments, upon any subject relating to the Duties of their respective Offices, and he shall have Power to Grant Reprieves and Pardons for Offenses against the United States, except in Cases of Impeachment.

He shall have Power, by and with the Advice and Consent of the Senate, to make Treaties, provided two thirds of the Senators present concur; and he shall nominate, and by and with the Advice and Consent of the Senate, shall appoint Ambassadors, other public Ministers and Consuls, Judges of the supreme Court, and all other Officers of the United States, whose Appointments are not herein otherwise provided for, and which shall be established by Law: but the Congress may by Law vest the Appointment of such inferior Officers, as they think proper, in the President alone, in the Courts of Law, or in the Heads of Departments.

The President shall have Power to fill up all Vacancies that may happen during the Recess of the Senate, by granting Commissions which shall expire at the End of their next Session.

Section 3: State of the Union, Convening Congress

He shall from time to time give to the Congress Information of the State of the Union, and recommend to their Consideration such Measures as he shall judge necessary and expedient; he may, on extraordinary Occasions, convene both Houses, or either of them, and in Case of Disagreement between them, with Respect to the Time of Adjournment, he may adjourn them to such Time as he shall think proper; he shall receive Ambassadors and other public Ministers; he shall take Care that the Laws be faithfully executed, and shall Commission all the Officers of the United States.

Section 4: Disqualification

The President, Vice President and all civil Officers of the United States, shall be removed from Office on Impeachment for, and Conviction of, Treason, Bribery, or other high Crimes and Misdemeanors.

Article III: The Judicial Branch

Section 1: Judicial Powers

The judicial Power of the United States, shall be vested in one supreme Court, and in such inferior Courts as the Congress may from time to time ordain and establish. The

Judges, both of the supreme and inferior Courts, shall hold their Offices during good Behavior, and shall, at stated Times, receive for their Services a Compensation which shall not be diminished during their Continuance in Office.

Section 2: Trial by Jury, Original Jurisdiction, Jury Trials

(The judicial Power shall extend to all Cases, in Law and Equity, arising under this Constitution, the Laws of the United States, and Treaties made, or which shall be made, under their Authority; to all Cases affecting Ambassadors, other public Ministers and Consuls; to all Cases of admiralty and maritime Jurisdiction; to Controversies to which the United States shall be a Party; to Controversies between two or more States; between a State and Citizens of another State; between Citizens of different States; between Citizens of the same State claiming Lands under Grants of different States, and between a State, or the Citizens thereof, and foreign States, Citizens or Subjects.) [This section in parentheses is modified by Amendment XI.]

In all Cases affecting Ambassadors, other public Ministers and Consuls, and those in which a State shall be Party, the supreme Court shall have original Jurisdiction. In all the other Cases before mentioned, the supreme Court shall have appellate Jurisdiction, both as to Law and Fact, with such Exceptions, and under such Regulations as the Congress shall make.

The Trial of all Crimes, except in Cases of Impeachment, shall be by Jury; and such Trial shall be held in the State where the said Crimes shall have been committed; but when not committed within any State, the Trial shall be at such Place or Places as the Congress may by Law have directed.

Section 3: Treason

Treason against the United States, shall consist only in levying War against them, or in adhering to their Enemies, giving them Aid and Comfort. No Person shall be convicted of Treason unless on the Testimony of two Witnesses to the same overt Act, or on Confession in open Court.

The Congress shall have power to declare the Punishment of Treason, but no Attainder of Treason shall work Corruption of Blood, or Forfeiture except during the Life of the Person attainted.

Article IV: The States
Section 1: Each State to Honor All Others

Full Faith and Credit shall be given in each State to the public Acts, Records, and judicial Proceedings of every other State. And the Congress may by general Laws prescribe the Manner in which such Acts, Records and Proceedings shall be proved, and the Effect thereof.

Section 2: State Citizens, Extradition

The Citizens of each State shall be entitled to all Privileges and Immunities of Citizens in the several States.

A Person charged in any State with Treason, Felony, or other Crime, who shall flee from Justice, and be found in another State, shall on demand of the executive Authority of the State from which he fled, be delivered up, to be removed to the State having Jurisdiction of the Crime.

(No Person held to Service or Labour in one State, under the Laws thereof, escaping into another, shall, in Consequence of any Law or Regulation therein, be discharged from such Service or Labour, But shall be delivered up on Claim of the Party to whom such Service or Labour may be due.) [This clause in parentheses is superseded by Amendment XIII.]

Section 3: New States

New States may be admitted by the Congress into this Union; but no new States shall be formed or erected within the Jurisdiction of any other State; nor any State be formed by the Junction of two or more States, or parts of States, without the Consent of the Legislatures of the States concerned as well as of the Congress.

The Congress shall have Power to dispose of and make all needful Rules and Regulations respecting the Territory or other Property belonging to the United States; and nothing in this Constitution shall be so construed as to Prejudice any Claims of the United States, or of any particular State.

Section 4: Republican Government

The United States shall guarantee to every State in this Union a Republican Form of Government, and shall protect each of them against Invasion; and on Application of the Legislature, or of the Executive (when the Legislature cannot be convened) against domestic Violence.

Article V: Amendment

The Congress, whenever two thirds of both Houses shall deem it necessary, shall propose Amendments to this Constitution, or, on the Application of the Legislatures of two thirds of the several States, shall call a Convention for proposing Amendments, which, in either Case, shall be valid to all Intents and Purposes, as part of this Constitution, when ratified by the Legislatures of three fourths of the several States, or by Conventions in three fourths thereof, as the one or the other Mode of Ratification may be proposed by the Congress; Provided that no Amendment which may be made prior to the Year One thousand eight hundred and eight shall in any Manner affect the first and fourth Clauses in the Ninth Section of the first Article; and that no State, without its Consent, shall be deprived of its equal Suffrage in the Senate.

Article VI: The United States

All Debts contracted and Engagements entered into, before the Adoption of this Constitution, shall be as valid against the United States under this Constitution, as under the Confederation.

This Constitution, and the Laws of the United States which shall be made in Pursuance thereof; and all Treaties made, or which shall be made, under the Authority of the United States, shall be the supreme Law of the Land; and the Judges in every State shall be bound thereby, any Thing in the Constitution or Laws of any State to the Contrary notwithstanding.

The Senators and Representatives before mentioned, and the Members of the several State Legislatures, and all executive and judicial Officers, both of the United States and of the several States, shall be bound by Oath or Affirmation, to support this Constitution; but no religious Test shall ever be required as a Qualification to any Office or public Trust under the United States.

Article VII: Ratification

The Ratification of the Conventions of nine States, shall be sufficient for the Establishment of this Constitution between the States so ratifying the Same.

Done in Convention by the Unanimous Consent of the States present the Seventeenth Day of September in the Year of our Lord one thousand seven hundred and Eighty seven and of the Independence of the United States of America the Twelfth. In Witness whereof We have hereunto subscribed our Names.

The Amendments

The following are the Amendments to the Constitution. The first ten Amendments collectively are commonly known as the Bill of Rights.

Amendment I: Freedom of Religion, Press, Expression (ratified December 15, 1791)

Congress shall make no law respecting an establishment of religion, or prohibiting the free exercise thereof; or abridging the freedom of speech, or of the press; or the right of the people peaceably to assemble, and to petition the Government for a redress of grievances.

Amendment II: Right to Bear Arms (ratified December 15, 1791)

A well regulated Militia, being necessary to the security of a free State, the right of the people to keep and bear Arms, shall not be infringed.

Amendment III: Quartering of Soldiers (ratified December 15, 1791)

No Soldier shall, in time of peace be quartered in any house, without the consent of the Owner, nor in time of war, but in a manner to be prescribed by law.

Amendment IV: Search and Seizure (ratified December 15, 1791)

The right of the people to be secure in their persons, houses, papers, and effects, against unreasonable searches and seizures, shall not be violated, and no Warrants shall issue, but upon probable cause, supported by Oath or affirmation, and particularly describing the place to be searched, and the persons or things to be seized.

Amendment V: Trial and Punishment, Compensation for Takings (ratified December 15, 1791)

No person shall be held to answer for a capital, or otherwise infamous crime, unless on a presentment or indictment of a Grand Jury, except in cases arising in the land or naval forces, or in the Militia, when in actual service in time of War or public danger; nor shall any person be subject for the same offense to be twice put in jeopardy of life or limb; nor shall be compelled in any criminal case to be a witness against himself, nor be deprived of life, liberty, or property, without due process of law; nor shall private property be taken for public use, without just compensation.

Amendment VI: Right to Speedy Trial, Confrontation of Witnesses (ratified December 15, 1791)

In all criminal prosecutions, the accused shall enjoy the right to a speedy and public trial, by an impartial jury of the State and district wherein the crime shall have been committed, which district shall have been previously ascertained by law, and to be informed of the nature and cause of the accusation; to be confronted with the witnesses against him; to have compulsory process for obtaining witnesses in his favor, and to have the Assistance of Counsel for his defence.

Amendment VII: Trial by Jury in Civil Cases (ratified December 15, 1791)

In Suits at common law, where the value in controversy shall exceed twenty dollars, the right of trial by jury shall be preserved, and no fact tried by a jury, shall be otherwise re-examined in any Court of the United States, than according to the rules of the common law.

Amendment VIII: Cruel and Unusual Punishment
(ratified December 15, 1791)

Excessive bail shall not be required, nor excessive fines imposed, nor cruel and unusual punishments inflicted.

Amendment IX: Construction of Constitution
(ratified December 15, 1791)

The enumeration in the Constitution, of certain rights, shall not be construed to deny or disparage others retained by the people.

Amendment X: Powers of the States and People
(ratified December 15, 1791)

The powers not delegated to the United States by the Constitution, nor prohibited by it to the States, are reserved to the States respectively, or to the people.

Amendment XI: Judicial Limits
(ratified February 7, 1795)

The Judicial power of the United States shall not be construed to extend to any suit in law or equity, commenced or prosecuted against one of the United States by Citizens of another State, or by Citizens or Subjects of any Foreign State.

Amendment XII: Choosing the President, Vice-President
(ratified June 15, 1804)

The Electors shall meet in their respective states, and vote by ballot for President and Vice-President, one of whom, at least, shall not be an inhabitant of the same state with themselves; they shall name in their ballots the person voted for as President, and in distinct ballots the person voted for as Vice-President, and they shall make distinct lists of all persons voted for as President, and of all persons voted for as Vice-President and of the number of votes for each, which lists they shall sign and certify, and transmit sealed to the seat of the government of the United States, directed to the President of the Senate;

The President of the Senate shall, in the presence of the Senate and House of Representatives, open all the certificates and the votes shall then be counted;

The person having the greatest Number of votes for President, shall be the President, if such number be a majority of the whole number of Electors appointed; and if no person have such majority, then from the persons having the highest numbers not exceeding three on the list of those voted for as President, the House of

Representatives shall choose immediately, by ballot, the President. But in choosing the President, the votes shall be taken by states, the representation from each state having one vote; a quorum for this purpose shall consist of a member or members from two-thirds of the states, and a majority of all the states shall be necessary to a choice. And if the House of Representatives shall not choose a President whenever the right of choice shall devolve upon them, before the fourth day of March next following, then the Vice-President shall act as President, as in the case of the death or other constitutional disability of the President.

The person having the greatest number of votes as Vice-President, shall be the Vice-President, if such number be a majority of the whole number of Electors appointed, and if no person have a majority, then from the two highest numbers on the list, the Senate shall choose the Vice-President; a quorum for the purpose shall consist of two-thirds of the whole number of Senators, and a majority of the whole number shall be necessary to a choice. But no person constitutionally ineligible to the office of President shall be eligible to that of Vice-President of the United States.

Amendment XIII: Slavery Abolished
(ratified December 6, 1865)

1. Neither slavery nor involuntary servitude, except as a punishment for crime whereof the party shall have been duly convicted, shall exist within the United States, or any place subject to their jurisdiction.
2. Congress shall have power to enforce this article by appropriate legislation.

Amendment XIV: Citizenship Rights
(ratified July 9, 1868)

1. All persons born or naturalized in the United States, and subject to the jurisdiction thereof, are citizens of the United States and of the State wherein they reside. No State shall make or enforce any law which shall abridge the privileges or immunities of citizens of the United States; nor shall any State deprive any person of life, liberty, or property, without due process of law; nor deny to any person within its jurisdiction the equal protection of the laws.
2. Representatives shall be apportioned among the several States according to their respective numbers, counting the whole number of persons in each State, excluding Indians not taxed. But when the right to vote at any election for the choice of electors for President and Vice-President of the United States, Representatives in Congress, the Executive and Judicial officers of a State, or the members of the Legislature thereof, is denied to any of the male inhabitants of such State, being twenty-one years of age, and citizens of the United States, or in any way abridged, except for participation in rebellion, or other crime, the basis of representation therein shall be reduced in the proportion which the number of such male citizens shall bear to the whole number of male citizens twenty-one years of age in such State.

3. No person shall be a Senator or Representative in Congress, or elector of President and Vice-President, or hold any office, civil or military, under the United States, or under any State, who, having previously taken an oath, as a member of Congress, or as an officer of the United States, or as a member of any State legislature, or as an executive or judicial officer of any State, to support the Constitution of the United States, shall have engaged in insurrection or rebellion against the same, or given aid or comfort to the enemies thereof. But Congress may by a vote of two-thirds of each House, remove such disability.
4. The validity of the public debt of the United States, authorized by law, including debts incurred for payment of pensions and bounties for services in suppressing insurrection or rebellion, shall not be questioned. But neither the United States nor any State shall assume or pay any debt or obligation incurred in aid of insurrection or rebellion against the United States, or any claim for the loss or emancipation of any slave; but all such debts, obligations and claims shall be held illegal and void.
5. The Congress shall have power to enforce, by appropriate legislation, the provisions of this article.

Amendment XV: Race No Bar to Vote (ratified February 3, 1870)

1. The right of citizens of the United States to vote shall not be denied or abridged by the United States or by any State on account of race, color, or previous condition of servitude.
2. The Congress shall have power to enforce this article by appropriate legislation.

Amendment XVI: Income Taxes Authorized (ratified February 3, 1913)

The Congress shall have power to lay and collect taxes on incomes, from whatever source derived, without apportionment among the several States, and without regard to any census or enumeration.

Amendment XVII: Senators Elected by Popular Vote (ratified April 8, 1913)

The Senate of the United States shall be composed of two Senators from each State, elected by the people thereof, for six years; and each Senator shall have one vote. The electors in each State shall have the qualifications requisite for electors of the most numerous branch of the State legislatures.

When vacancies happen in the representation of any State in the Senate, the executive authority of such State shall issue writs of election to fill such vacancies: Provided, That the legislature of any State may empower the executive thereof to make temporary appointments until the people fill the vacancies by election as the legislature may direct.

This amendment shall not be so construed as to affect the election or term of any Senator chosen before it becomes valid as part of the Constitution.

Amendment XVIII: Liquor Abolished
(ratified January 16, 1919;
repealed by Amendment XXI, December 5, 1933)

1. After one year from the ratification of this article the manufacture, sale, or transportation of intoxicating liquors within, the importation thereof into, or the exportation thereof from the United States and all territory subject to the jurisdiction thereof for beverage purposes is hereby prohibited.
2. The Congress and the several States shall have concurrent power to enforce this article by appropriate legislation.
3. This article shall be inoperative unless it shall have been ratified as an amendment to the Constitution by the legislatures of the several States, as provided in the Constitution, within seven years from the date of the submission to the States by the Congress.

Amendment XIX: Women's Suffrage
(ratified August 18, 1920)

The right of citizens of the United States to vote shall not be denied or abridged by the United States or by any State on account of sex.

Congress shall have power to enforce this article by appropriate legislation.

Amendment XX: Presidential, Congressional Terms
(ratified January 23, 1933)

1. The terms of the President and Vice President shall end at noon on the 20th day of January, and the terms of Senators and Representatives at noon on the 3d day of January, of the years in which such terms would have ended if this article had not been ratified; and the terms of their successors shall then begin.
2. The Congress shall assemble at least once in every year, and such meeting shall begin at noon on the 3d day of January, unless they shall by law appoint a different day.
3. If, at the time fixed for the beginning of the term of the President, the President elect shall have died, the Vice President elect shall become President. If a President shall not have been chosen before the time fixed for the beginning of his term, or if the President elect shall have failed to qualify, then the Vice President elect shall act as President until a President shall have qualified; and the Congress may by law provide for the case wherein neither a President elect nor a Vice President elect shall

have qualified, declaring who shall then act as President, or the manner in which one who is to act shall be selected, and such person shall act accordingly until a President or Vice President shall have qualified.

4. The Congress may by law provide for the case of the death of any of the persons from whom the House of Representatives may choose a President whenever the right of choice shall have devolved upon them, and for the case of the death of any of the persons from whom the Senate may choose a Vice President whenever the right of choice shall have devolved upon them.

5. Sections 1 and 2 shall take effect on the 15th day of October following the ratification of this article.

6. This article shall be inoperative unless it shall have been ratified as an amendment to the Constitution by the legislatures of three-fourths of the several States within seven years from the date of its submission.

Amendment XXI: Amendment XVIII Repealed (ratified December 5, 1933)

1. The eighteenth article of amendment to the Constitution of the United States is hereby repealed.

2. The transportation or importation into any State, Territory, or possession of the United States for delivery or use therein of intoxicating liquors, in violation of the laws thereof, is hereby prohibited.

3. The article shall be inoperative unless it shall have been ratified as an amendment to the Constitution by conventions in the several States, as provided in the Constitution, within seven years from the date of the submission hereof to the States by the Congress.

Amendment XXII: Presidential Term Limits (ratified February 27, 1951)

1. No person shall be elected to the office of the President more than twice, and no person who has held the office of President, or acted as President, for more than two years of a term to which some other person was elected President shall be elected to the office of the President more than once. But this Article shall not apply to any person holding the office of President, when this Article was proposed by the Congress, and shall not prevent any person who may be holding the office of President, or acting as President, during the term within which this Article becomes operative from holding the office of President or acting as President during the remainder of such term.

2. This article shall be inoperative unless it shall have been ratified as an amendment to the Constitution by the legislatures of three-fourths of the several States within seven years from the date of its submission to the States by the Congress.

Amendment XXIII: Presidential Vote for District of Columbia (ratified March 29, 1961)

1. The District constituting the seat of Government of the United States shall appoint in such manner as the Congress may direct: A number of electors of President and Vice President equal to the whole number of Senators and Representatives in Congress to which the District would be entitled if it were a State, but in no event more than the least populous State; they shall be in addition to those appointed by the States, but they shall be considered, for the purposes of the election of President and Vice President, to be electors appointed by a State; and they shall meet in the District and perform such duties as provided by the twelfth article of amendment.
2. The Congress shall have power to enforce this article by appropriate legislation.

Amendment XXIV: Poll Tax Barred (ratified January 23, 1964)

1. The right of citizens of the United States to vote in any primary or other election for President or Vice President, for electors for President or Vice President, or for Senator or Representative in Congress, shall not be denied or abridged by the United States or any State by reason of failure to pay any poll tax or other tax.
2. The Congress shall have power to enforce this article by appropriate legislation.

Amendment XXV: Presidential Disability and Succession (ratified February 10, 1967)

1. In case of the removal of the President from office or of his death or resignation, the Vice President shall become President.
2. Whenever there is a vacancy in the office of the Vice President, the President shall nominate a Vice President who shall take office upon confirmation by a majority vote of both Houses of Congress.
3. Whenever the President transmits to the President pro tempore of the Senate and the Speaker of the House of Representatives his written declaration that he is unable to discharge the powers and duties of his office, and until he transmits to them a written declaration to the contrary, such powers and duties shall be discharged by the Vice President as Acting President.
4. Whenever the Vice President and a majority of either the principal officers of the executive departments or of such other body as Congress may by law provide, transmit to the President pro tempore of the Senate and the Speaker of the House of Representatives their written declaration that the President is unable to discharge the powers and duties of his office, the Vice President shall immediately assume the powers and duties of the office as Acting President.

Thereafter, when the President transmits to the President pro tempore of the Senate and the Speaker of the House of Representatives his written declaration that no inability exists, he shall resume the powers and duties of his office unless the Vice President and a majority of either the principal officers of the executive department or of such other body as Congress may by law provide, transmit within four days to the President pro tempore of the Senate and the Speaker of the House of Representatives their written declaration that the President is unable to discharge the powers and duties of his office. Thereupon Congress shall decide the issue, assembling within forty eight hours for that purpose if not in session. If the Congress, within twenty one days after receipt of the latter written declaration, or, if Congress is not in session, within twenty one days after Congress is required to assemble, determines by two thirds vote of both Houses that the President is unable to discharge the powers and duties of his office, the Vice President shall continue to discharge the same as Acting President; otherwise, the President shall resume the powers and duties of his office.

Amendment XXVI: Voting Age Set to 18 Years (ratified July 1, 1971)

1. The right of citizens of the United States, who are eighteen years of age or older, to vote shall not be denied or abridged by the United States or by any State on account of age.
2. The Congress shall have power to enforce this article by appropriate legislation.

Amendment XXVII: Congressional Pay Increases (ratified May 7, 1992)

No law, varying the compensation for the services of the Senators and Representatives, shall take effect, until an election of Representatives shall have intervened.

About the Authors

AMBER NIETO is a 2003 graduate of Texas State University–San Marcos. She received her bachelor of arts degree in English and print journalism. When she is not searching for her next book topic, Amber enjoys writing for the *Moulton Eagle*.

JOHN F. SCHMITT is assistant professor of mass communication at Texas State University–San Marcos. He practiced law in Indiana for twelve years before returning to his first love, journalism. He holds degrees in political science, journalism, and law from Indiana University. He has been acknowledged for his First Amendment–related activities by the College Media Advisers, Inc., the Oxford Round Table, and the Playboy Foundation.